Directory of think tank publications

Matt Innis
and Justin Johnson

First published in Great Britain 2001
Politico's Publishing
8 Artillery Row
London
SW1P 1RZ
Tel: 0207 931 0090
Fax: 0207 828 8111
Email: publishing@politicos.co.uk
www.politicospublishing.co.uk

Coypright © Politico's Publishing 2001

Printed and bound in Great Britain by CPD(Wales)

Contents

Introduction

This book is the first ever directory to list the publications of all major British policy think tanks. We have decided to list all those publications published between 1990 and 2000 – to have gone back beyond 1990 would have made the book too unwieldy. The compilation process has taken far longer than anticipated and we are grateful for the patience of those who have been awaiting the book's publication with baited breath. We hope the wait has been worthwhile.

We are grateful to all the think tanks who have co-operated with this book. The formats for each think tank vary according to the amount of information provided. A standardised format would have been preferable but we decided that it was more important to get the book out than rekey each entry.

One major problem we faced was what constituted a think tank. In the end our decision was made on the criteria of policy input in key policy areas. We have not included economic think tanks such as the Institute for Fiscal Studies or the Henley Centre but instead have concentrated on think tanks whose policy papers work is fed directly into the policy formation process of the three main political parties.

Lastly our thanks to everyone at Politico's, particularly to Iain Dale and John Berry, whose advice and patience have made this book possible.

Matt Innis
and Justin Johnson

March 2001

Action Centre for Europe

Address	29 Tufton Street
	London
	SW1P 3QL
Tel	020 7976 7706 or 01257 276992
Fax	020 7979 8331 or 01257 231254
Website	None
President	Lord Howe of Aberavon
Chairman	Sir Michael Jenkins
Chief Executive	Michael Welsh
Number of Employees	0
Cost of Subscription	Corporate £500, Individual £25

Publications

Publications 2000

- **Is the Sovereign Nation-State Obsolete?**
  By J M Veranneman de Watervliet
  A4 booklet – 32 pages, £5

- **Enlargement: Poland and the EU**
  By Andrew Cave
  A5 booklet – 32 pages, £5

- **The Road to Nice: Flexibility and Enlargement**
  By Lord Hurd of Westwell
  A4 booklet – 24 pages, £5

- **Partridge Revisited:**
  A Follow-Up to the Partridge Enquiry: Social Europe – Risk or Opportunity?
  A4 booklet – 32 pages – £5

- **Fog Over the Atlantic: Britain and the NAFTA Option**
  By Desmond Butler
  A4 booklet – 38 pages, £5

- **The Role of the Commission and the European Parliament**
  By Dr. John Temple Lang
  A4 booklet – 24 pages, £5

Impact of EMU Series

- **The Challenge for the Electricity and Gas Industries**
  By Mark Braithwaite
  A5 booklet – £5

- **EMU and the European Pharmaceutical Industry**
  By Michael Owen
  A5 booklet – £5

- **A General Review of the Series**
  By Sir David Hancock
  A5 booklet – £5

Previous Publications

- **The Kingsdown Enquiry**
  Report by the ACE Working Group on the Implications of Monetary Union for Britain
  A4 booklet – 36 pages, £10

- **The Templeman Enquiry**
  Report by the ACE Working Group on Open Frontiers and European Union
  A4 booklet – 44 pages, £10

- **Europe and the World – Britain's Trading Patterns Today and Tomorrow**
  ACE Occasional Paper by David Goodchild
  A4 leaflet – 44 pages, £10

- **Majority Voting and the European Union – What is Britain's Interest?**
  Pamphlet by Dick Taverne, Foreword by Sir David Hannay
  A5 booklet – 29 pages, £5

- **Gilding the Lily – An examination of the Application of the EU Meat Directives in the UK**
  Pamphlet by Ben Woodhams, Foreword by Lord Plumb
  A5 booklet – 34 pages, £5

- **CFSP – The European Union's Common Foreign and Security Policy: A menu for reform**
  Pamphlet by Sir David Hannay, Foreword by the Rt Hon Douglas Hurd
  A5 booklet – 29 pages, £5

- **Fiction Prize for Booker**
  ACE Occasional Paper by Adam Fergusson
  A4 pamphlet – 15 pages, £10

- **The Constant Partner – France, the French and Europe**
  Pamphlet by Bertrand Benoit, Foreword by Sir Ewen Fergusson
  A5 booklet – 44 pages, £5

- **Europe – In the National Interest**
  Speeches by the Rt Hon Kenneth Clarke QC MP and Ian Taylor MBE MP
  A5 booklet – 32 pages, £5

- **Britain's Trading Patterns in Europe and with the Rest of the World**
  ACE Occasional Paper by Bella Thomas
  A4 pamphlet – 17 pages, £10

- **No Panic on Pensions**
  ACE Occasional Paper by Andrew Griffin
  A4 pamphlet – 7 pages, £5

- **The Sheppard Enquiry**
  Report by the ACE Working Group on Competitiveness and the Single Market
  A4 booklet – 58 pages, £10

- **Inward Investment in the UK**
  ACE Occasional Paper by Jill Leyland
  A4 pamphlet – 29 pages, £10

- **What's Right with the Amsterdam Treaty?**
  Pamphlet by Brendan Donnelly MEP and Anthony Teasdale, Foreword by Lord Howe of Aberavon
  A5 booklet – 41 pages, £5

- **Promises to Keep. The Reality of Turkey – EU Relations**
  Pamphlet by Ebru Loewendahl
  A5 booklet – 56 pages, £5

- **Kingsdown Revisited – A Follow-Up to the 1995 Kingsdown Enquiry on the Implications for Britain of Economic and Monetary Union**
  A4 pamphlet – 17 pages, £5

- **Democracy in the European Union**
  by Derek Prag, Foreword by Lord Kingsdown
  A4 booklet – 36 pages, £10

- **The Partridge Enquiry**
  Report by the ACE Working Group on Social Europe: Risk or Opportunity?
  A4 booklet – 76 pages, £10

- **Cohesion & Enlargement – Perspectives for the Structural Funds**
  Simon Kirby
  A5 pamphlet, Foreword by Leon Brittan, 21 pages, £5

- **Sheppard Revisited – A Follow-Up to the 1997 Sheppard Enquiry on Competitiveness and the Single Market**
  A4 booklet – 14 pages, £5

- **The Impact of EMU – The Challenge for UK Agribusiness**
  Richard Guerterbock, Foreword by Lord Plumb
  A5 booklet – 30 pages, £5

- **The Impact of EMU – EMU & the British Retailer**
  Glyn Thomas
  A5 booklet – 32 pages, £5

- **The Impact of EMU – The Euro & the UK Automotive Industry**
  Vaughan Freeman
  A5 booklet – 30 pages, £5

- **The Impact of EMU – Opportunities for Financial Services**
  Graham Bishop
  A5 booklet – 32 pages, £5

- **The Impact of EMU – EMU & the Construction Industry**
  Peter Cooper
  A5 booklet – 22 pages, £5

- **The Impact of EMU – The European Property Market**
  Anna Minton
  A5 booklet – 41 pages, £5

- **The Impact of EMU – Aerospace & the Defence Industries**
  Professor Keith Hayward
  A5 booklet – 26 pages, £5

- **The Impact of EMU – The Challenge for the Electricity & Gas Industries**
  Mark Braithwaite
  A5 booklet – 20 pages, £5

- **The Euro & the Power of Britain's Parliament**
  Rupert Blum
  A4 pamphlet – 28 pages, £5

- **Is the Sovereign Nation State Obsolete?**
  Sir Leslie Fielding
  A5 pamphlet – 28 pages, £5

Adam Smith Institute

Address	23 Great Smith Street Westminster London SW1P 3BL
Tel	020 7222 4995
Fax	020 7222 7544
Email	info@adamsmith.org.uk
Website	www.adamsmith.org.uk
President	Dr Madsen Pirie
Director	Dr Eamonn Butler
Director, International Division	Peter Young
Director, International Division	Paul Reynolds
Director, Conference Division	Jane Adams and Louise Pacha
Number of Employees	3
Cost of Annual Subscription	£50 for copies of all reports, policy briefings, quaterly bulletins, advance details on conferences and other events. Corporate/institutional subscription £250 a year for 5 people at the same address to receive the same package as the individual subscription.
Donations	Individuals who donate a minimum of £100 a year and corporations which donate a minimum of £500 become associates for the year and are able to attend our key policy-maker events.

History

The Institute takes its name from the eighteenth century Scottish author of The Wealth of Nations, who virtually created modern economics. It was founded in 1977, and has been active since then in developing new policy ideas.

The ASI was a pioneer in privatisation in the 1970s. It developed the use of private contrcators to perform public services at local and national level. It played a key role in the introduction of freeports in the UK. The ASI developed internal market reforms in both education and health policy and influenced the emergence of private-public partnerships. It actively promoted deregulatory policies, and has introduced several initiatives to reduce the burden imposed upon individuals and business by both regulation and taxation.More recently, the ASI has spearheaded a drive to replace tax-funded pensions and welfare by a system of fully funded Fortune Accounts, owned by individual savers and ivested on their behalf.

Its Omega Report (1983–85) was designed to provide a range of worked-out policy options to the government elected in 1983, and was used by several government departments as the basis for a reform programme. The ASI published The First Hundred to mark the adoption of the first hundred of the Omega proposals.

The ASI is not a registered charity, though it has always maintained an independent status, strictly separate from any political party or lobby group.

Objectives

The Adam Smith Institute develops policy initiatives designed to solve economic and social problems. Starting from a philosophical preference for liberty, freedom of choice and free markets, it introduces innovative and often radical policy proposals designed to to increase the range of options available to legislators. The Institute prefers to work in the public domain, publishing its ideas and inviting public discussion of them. Its International Division undertakes market reform overseas, and its Conference Division helps to train people in the formerly Socialist countries to adjust to market realities.

Publications

Published 1990

- **Privatisation Now!**
  From the Third London Conference on Privatization: political objectives, popular capitalism, sales without stockmarkets, reviving lossmakers, contracting-out local services, and private finance of infrastructure.
  ISBN: 1870109759
  UK Price: £50 (£52 elsewhere)

- **A Moving Experience**
  Edward Brooks
  Brooks shows how to simplify the English system of selling houses. He proposes a hybrid of the Scottish system, but with open bidding, and legally binding house log-books.
  ISBN: 1870109872
  UK Price: £10 (£12 elsewhere)

- **Vision, Identity, and Environment**
  Sir James Goldsmith
  "Goldsmith is calling for a radical plan to save tropical forests: pay Latin American countries not to chop them down." *Washington Times.*
  ISBN: 1870109805
  UK Price: £5 (£6 elsewhere)

- **The Tender Traps**
  David Hunt, Steve Evans, et al
  The process of local council tendering needs to be tightened up to prevent abuse.
  ISBN: 1870109821
  UK Price: £30 (£32 elsewhere)

- **Take-Off for Business**
  Kenneth Warren, Ian Mcgrath, et al
  "The ASI has reinforced calls for a military airfield near London to be opened up for development as Britain's premier business airport" *Flight International*
  ISBN: 1870109902
  UK Price: £25 (£27 elsewhere)

- **Fast Track Forward**
  Kenneth Irvine
  Calls for the creation of a system of high-speed tilting trains using existing track network.
  ISBN: 1870109864
  UK Price: £10 (£12 elsewhere)

- **Schools Out!**
  Andrew Wallace
  Schools should be obliged to hold ballots at regular, fixed intervals.
  ISBN: 1870109856
  UK Price: £10 (£12 elsewhere)

- **The Wayward Elite: A Critique of British Teacher-Education**
  Dennis O'Keefe
  Teacher training colleges are creating a *Blue Peter* curriculum, leaving children ignorant of basic skills.
  ISBN: 1870109767

- **A Duty to Repeal: The Ending of Stamp Duty**
  Nicholas Gibb
  A tax specialist makes a compelling case against stamp duty on houses, shares and other capital.
  ISBN: 1870109716
  UK Price: £8 (£10 elsewhere)

- **A Social Charter for Ownership**
  Peter Young
  Not a corporatist social charter for worker representation on company boards, but real worker ownership through company ESOP schemes.
  ISBN: 1870109732
  UK Price: £20 (£22 elsewhere)

- **Wider Still and Wider**
  How far can EC enlargement go? Is it a way of halting centralism?
  ISBN: 1870109775
  UK Price: £14 (£16 elsewhere)

- **EurOmega Project: A Constitution for Europe**
  Frederick de Lisle and William Forrest
  The EC bureaucracy must be restrained by a constitution which gives member states a clear right to withdraw if they choose.
  ISBN: 1870109929
  UK Price: £10 (£12 elsewhere)

- **Does Socialism Mean Never Having to say You're Sorry?**
  Prof. Kenneth Minogue
  European Socialists should abjectly apologise, says Prof. Minogue. They blew it, and the ruin they caused is now clear. We should all admit our past mistakes.
  ISBN: 1870109813
  UK Price: £8 (£9 elsewhere)

- **Green Machines**
  Dr. Madsen Pirie
  Using tax concessions to promote low-pollution electric cars.
  ISBN: 1870109890
  UK Price: £10 (£12 elsewhere)

- **European Pharmaceutical Policies**
  Peter Young
  A Catalogue of the different European countries' regulations on research, manufacturing, testing and marketing. Can Europe still compete?
  ISBN: 1870109791
  UK Price: £28 (£30 elsewhere)

- **Competition for the Phone**
  Mark Call
  The cosy duopoly must be broken as a matter of urgency if consumers and industry are to benefit from the rapid advances in technology.
  ISBN: 1870109910
  UK Price: £12 (£14 elsewhere)

- **Adam Smith's Legacy: His Thought in our Time**
  Norman Barry, William Letwin et al
  Prominent academics, journalists and politicians highlight the historical contribution of Adam Smith and the role of his ideas in the shaping of modern economic thinking.
  ISBN: 1870109848
  UK Price: £15 (£17 elsewhere)

Published 1991

- **The Manual on Privatization**
  Dr Eamonn Butler and Dr Madsen Pirie
  The complete guide to privatization, drawn from past papers as well as specially comissioned new material.
  ISBN: 1870109740
  UK Price: £75 (£79 elsewhere)

- **Privatization and Economic Revival**
  Strategies for developing and post-communist countries, icluding the fund and voucher concepts and contract management of state industries: from the Fourth London Conference.
  ISBN: 1870109937
  UK Price: £60 (£62 elsewhere)

- **The Last Post: Monopoly vs Competition in Delivery Services**
  Francis Migone, Robert Cohen, Prof David Meza et al
  Increased competition in postal services would reduce business costs and provide a model for mail competition across Europe,
  ISBN: 1870109945
  UK Price: £30 (£32 elsewhere)

- **Long Term Commitment: The Potential for LTC Insurance**
Prof Nick Bosanquet, Jim Webber, Dr Lothar Butz, et al
Experts look at the potential for insurance plans to provide care services for elderly and disabled people. Tax incentives could take some of the growing pressure off public-sector care providers.
ISBN: 1873712081
UK Price: £28 (£30 elsewhere)

- **Empowerment: The Theme for the 1990s**
Dr Madsen Pirie, John Willman, Christopher Monckton, et al
"The institute claimes credit for developing the idea of empowerment, which is the concept behind the Citizen's charter" *Financial Times.*
ISBN: 1870109961
UK Price: £12 (£14 elsewhere)

- **The Citizen's Charter**
Dr Madsen Pirie
How a Citizen's Charter must work to guarantee good public services – including performance targets, monitoring, and complaints.
ISBN: 1870109988
UK Price: £12 (£14 elsewhere)

- **Working Capital: The Future of British Coal**
Malcolm Edwards, Roy Lynk, Richard Budge, et al
Experts discuss the marketing, legal, policy, and organizational issues in coal privatization and suggest a two-dimensional structure that might save industry under private ownership.
ISBN: 1873712073
UK Price: £30 (£32 elsewhere)

- **Why Not Work? A Radical Solution to Unemployment**
Sir Ralph Howell
Instead of giving people benefit when they do not work, we should be giving them more money if they do. Ralph Howell builds on the workfare principle and shows how to apply it in the UK.
ISBN: 1873712006
UK Price: £15 (£17 elsewhere)

- **Taming the Trade Unions**
Charles Hanson
Mrs Thatcher's Trade Union reforms – and their effect.
ISBN: 0333559029
UK Price: £15 (£17 elsewhere)

- **An Arresting Idea: The Management of Police Services in Britain**
Timothy Evans, Nicholas Elliott and Simon McIlwaine
Police services are too centralized, costly, bureaucratic and resistant to change.
ISBN: 1870109996
UK Price: £25 (£27 elsewhere)

- **Mobilizing the Markets**
  John Redwood
  London must pioneer private infrastructure projects and innovate if it is to remain a leading centre for insurance, investment, equities and currency dealing.
  ISBN: 1873712049
  UK Price: £16 (£18 elsewhere)

- **The Power of the State: Economic Questions over Nuclear Generation**
  Prof Colin Robinson
  Decisions on building new nuclear plant should be made by private generators, not by governments.
  ISBN: 1870109953
  UK Price: £40 (£42 elsewhere)

- **EuroOmega: Agriculture**
  Linda Whatstone, et al
  All price subsidies for EC farmers should be phased out, as they are expensive and ineffective.
  ISBN: 187010997X
  UK Price: £18 (£20 elsewhere)

Published 1992

- **Privatization in the Nineties**
  Dr Eamonn Butler
  Privatization can spread wealth and reduce budget deficits in post-communist and developing countries.
  ISBN: 1873712219
  UK Price: £24 (£26 elsewhere)

- **Eastern Promise**
  Paul Reynolds and Peter Young
  The international privatization experts show how the West can best help the former communist countries-in clarifying the objectives of economic transformation, pushing for price liberalization and organising the rapid transfer of state assets to owners who really care about how they are used.
  ISBN: 1873712200
  UK Price: £65 (£68 elsewhere

- **Privatisation East and West**
  From the Fifth London Conference on Privatization. Contributors include Peter Lilley, Brian Pomeroy and Guy de Selliers
  ISBN: 1873712146
  UK Price: £60 (£62 elsewhere)

- **Rethinking the Environment**
  Russell Lewis, et al
  The comprehensive reader on market environmentalism. Leading experts show how to tackle our most urgent problems using market forces instead of bureaucratic interventionism.
  ISBN: 1873712227
  UK Price: £25 (£28 elsewhere)

- **Wood for the Trees**
  Doug Mason
  The future of forestry lies in the private sector.
  ISBN: 187371212X
  UK Price: £5 (£6 elsewhere)

- **The Market in Environment**
  By Robert Taylor
  Taylor shows that environmental goods not only can be provided by the market, but are being provided by private entrepreneurs and conservation groups. He catalogues how to tackle other environmental problems – from water shotages to ivory poaching – using market principles.
  ISBN: 187371209X

- **Retail Rents: Fair and Free Market?**
  Prof John Burton
  Britain's high streets will be blighted by more empty shops for as long as we have a system that can produce rent increases of 1000% and more. Do we need to restore transparency to the market that is no longer free?
  ISBN: 1873712162
  UK Price: £10 (£12 elsewhere)

- **Tomorrow's Way: The Management of Roads in a Free Society**
  By John Hibbs and Gabriel Roth
  New roads built with private capital and paid for by tolls; prices rising on congested roads; people leaving their cars at home instead of adding to the jam: two of the world's leading transport economists look at the global experience of road pricing and show how the idea could work in the UK.
  ISBN: 1873712065
  UK Price: £24 (£26 elsewhere)

- **The Student's Charter**
  Peter Yorke
  Simpler applications, prompt payment of cash, better incentives on colleges, and the right to opt out of student unions.
  ISBN: 1873712189
  UK Price: £12 (£14 elsewhere)

- **Opening up the Medical Monopoly**
  David Gladstone
  The restrictive practices of senior doctors mean that qualified specialists are unable to practice independently, while patients must wait longer than necessary for appointments and treatment. Gladstone shows how to open up the medical monopoly, while still maintaining high standards of care.
  ISBN: 1873712324
  UK Price: £14 (£16 elsewhere)

- **The Radical Edge**
  Madsen Pirie
  Parents should be able to set up state schools with grant maintained status; local police could become autonomous budget holders; colleges could reject central funding and be paid by the students they attract.
  ISBN: 1873712170
  UK Price: £12 (£14 elsewhere)

- **999 Emergency**

  John G Jackson

  The UK's emergency services are out of date, reactive, inefficient and in desperate need of reform, says a London fire officer. The key is the amalgamation of all three emergency services.

  ISBN: 1873712243

  UK Price: £15 (£17 elsewhere)

- **An ACT Against Trade**

  Dr Barry Bracewell-Milnes

  Surplus ACT lays a burden of £8bn on industry making UK companies less able to complete. The reform of this 27-year-old anomaly would mean a significant boost to trade.

  ISBN: 1873712235

  UK Price: £25 (£28 elsewhere)

- **Judgement Day: The Case for ADR**

  Adam Thierer

  This pathbreaking report calls for the reform of our inefficient, costly and overcrowded court system, proposing the adoption of alternative dispute resolution (ADR) as an effective back-up to the courts.

  ISBN: 1873712138

  UK Price: £17 (£19 elsewhere)

- **What Price Public Service?**

  Will Bracken and Scott Fowler

  Revolutionizing the BBC through a public share offer, advertising and sponsorship.

  ISBN: 18737122226X

  UK Price: £10 (£21 elsewhere)

- **False Economy**

  Dr Barry Bracewell-Milnes

  UK Capital Gains Taxes are too punitive. Revenue would be maximised at 15%, or preferably lower.

  ISBN: 1873712251

  UK Price: £25 (£27 elsewhere)

Published 1993

- **But Who Will Regulate the Regulators?**

  Colin Robinson, John Kay, Cento Veljanovski, et al

  Privatization spawned the new regulators: but how much power should these officials have, and would more competition make them redundant anyway?

  ISBN: 1873712332

  UK Price: £18 (£20 elsewhere)

- **Europe at Risk**

  Tim Evans and Russell Lewis

  The ideal of Europe as a free and open single market is sinking beneath a tide of paternalist regulation. They chart the rising regulatory burdens on European industry.

  ISBN: 1873712308

  UK Price: £15 (£18 elsewhere)

- **The Issues in Sunday Trading**
  Terry Burke and JR Shackleton
  Drawing upon the practical experience of Sunday trading in Scotland, Sweden, and the United States, the authors argue that it will be nothing like as disruptive in England and Wales as critics claim.
  ISBN: 187371243X
  UK Price: £10 (£12 elsewhere)

- **The Environment Alphabet**
  Russel Lewis
  The complete glossary on enviro-nonsense, from acid rain to zoos.
  ISBN: 1873712383
  UK Price: £18 (£20 elsewhere)

- **Into the Voids: A Partial Solution to Homelessness**
  Hartley Booth
  All over the country there are empty or underused properties- the result of bad management by public authorities or perverse tax incentives on private owners. Booth outlines an innovative paint to rent scheme to bring void property back into use to house the homeless.
  ISBN: 1873712359
  UK Price: £12 (£14 elsewhere)

- **Unhealthy Competition? The Public-Private Mix in Health**
  Dr David Gladstone, Dr Clive Froggatt, et al
  Prominent health experts ask what can be done to bring real market principles to bear on the entire health-care service.
  ISBN: 1873712367
  UK Price: £24 (£26 elsewhere)

- **Blueprint for a Revolution**
  Dr Madsen Pirie
  A complete guide through the theory, strategy and record of rolling back the state in the UK- privatization, internal markets in health and education, making executive agencies more independent, and the Citizen's Charter.
  ISBN: 1873712375
  UK Price: £15 (£17 elsewhere)

- **The Radical Agenda**
  Dr Madsen Pirie
  The fourth phase of policy initiatives following privatization, internal markets and the Citizen's Charter- the Choice initiative- is explained as a series of major policy proposals, including private alternatives to state benefits.
  ISBN: 1873712278
  UK Price: £10 (£12 elsewhere)

- **The Hunting of the Quango**
  Sir Phillip Holland
  Britain's ace quango-hunter stalks his quarry again. He reviews the history and growth of quangos and the departments with the worst record in harbouring them. Then he proposes sunset legislation by which Quangos would face automatic extinction after a few years, and new disclosure rules for the quangurus.
  ISBN: 1873712537
  UK Price: £20 (£22 elsewhere)

- **The Consultant's Report on the Church of England**
  Brian Pepper
  The Church of England is losing its market share. Is this because it has lost customer loyalty and neglected its core, historic, function of welfare provision?
  ISBN: 1873712340
  UK Price: £17 (£19 elsewhere)

- **Banking on the Future**
  Iain Smedley
  Privatizing the Bank of England will remove political interference and provide a better way to fight inflation. A new regulator would extend competition by licensing competitors to the Bank.
  ISBN: 1873712421
  UK Price: £24 (£26 elsewhere)

- **Exorcising Inflation**
  Charles Hanson
  Governments should aim for zero inflation, since even moderate inflation leads to higher interest rates, business failures and ultimately higher unemployment.
  ISBN: 1873712316
  UK Price: £15 (£18 elsewhere)

- **EurOmega Project: A Bill of Rights for Europe**
  Sean Gabb
  Could the US Constitution provide pointers for the future of Europe?
  ISBN: 1873712057
  UK Price: £20 (£22 elsewhere)

- **Moldova: Privatization Plan**
  Review of the Moldovan reform experience, the legal framework for reform, voucher, auction and sales plan and future strategy.
  ISBN: 1873712405
  UK Price: £65 (£67 elsewhere)

- **A Disorderly House**
  Barry Bracewell-Milnes
  UK excise duties are too high. If cut by 60%, an extra £1,220 million would be collected.
  ISBN: 1873712286
  UK Price: £28 (£30 elsewhere)

Published 1994

- **The Amnesia of Reform: A Review of Post-Communist Privatization**

  Peter Young and Paul Reynolds

  The purpose of economic reform and privatization has been forgotten or even deliberately ignored in Post-Communist countries. Firms are privatized in an unreconstructed and shoddy state, shareholders have no power, monopolies are protected, conflicts between ministries continue. UK policy must change to ensure that reform is effective. The authors outline new ways to overcome the problems and make privatization popular and beneficial.

  ISBN: 1873712529

  UK Price: £20 (£22 elsewhere)

- **There Goes the Neighbourhood**

  Hartley Booth

  Neighbourhood watch shows how local spirit can be tapped. So extend the idea to new schools, elderly care, helping fledgling enterprises, and environmental clean-ups.

  ISBN: 1873712499

  UK Price: £16 (£18 elsewhere)

- **Plane Commonsense: The Case for Feeder-Reliever Airports**

  Keith Boyfield

  London's airports could process an extra 30m passengers each year by the development of two satellite airports at Northolt and Redhill which could be used by smaller aircraft. The privatization of RAF Northolt and of air traffic control would help the scheme.

  ISBN: 1873712553

  UK Price: £18 (£20 elsewhere)

- **Shephard's Warning: Setting Schools Back on Course**

  Prof Anthony Flew

  A stripped-down curriculum, no-nonsense testing, compulsory leaving exams, stiffer GCSEs- and all are needed if educational standards are to be improved.

  ISBN: 1873712472

  UK Price: £12 (£14 elsewhere)

- **The End of the Welfare State**

  Michael Bell, Dr Eamonn Butler, et al

  A viable and coherent alternative to state welfare, much reported for its practical proposals on how to replace the pay-as-you-go state pension system with a funded and personal alternative. Private lifetime savings accounts and the separation of the insurance and savings functions are all explored as the authors trace the social pathology of the state welfare and explore practical solutions.

  ISBN: 1873712456

  UK Price: £25 (£27 elsewhere)

- **Operation Underclass**

  Dr Madsen Pirie and Iain Smedley

  Three radical new schemes to create work for the urban unemployed.

- **20–20 Vision: Targets for Britain**

  Dr Madsen Pirie

  This well reported series of ambitious yet practicable targets for the year 2020 offers a vision for every field from housing to health, education to the economy. ASI experts set out a radical agenda for improving the quality of life and the standards of public and private services into the next century.

  ISBN: 1873712464

  UK Price: £18 (£20 elsewhere)

- **A Space for Enterprise**

  BR Stott and Mark Watson

  Space research could be a growing and productive business if governments would let it happen.

  ISBN: 1873712480

- **A House Divided**

  Barry Bracewell-Milnes

  Updated and non-technical edition of *A Disorderly House*. The booze cruises and the welfare drain to the UK economy continue unabated.

  ISBN: 1873712510

  UK Price: £16 (£18 elsewhere)

- **Mongolia: Privatization Plan**

  Current situation, key issues, objectives, priorities, plans for bankrupt firms, regulatory reform and skills development.

  ISBN: 1873712561

  UK Price: £65 (£67 elsewhere)

- **Will to Succeed: Inheritance Without Taxation**

  Barry Bracewell-Milnes

  Inheritance Tax hits ordinary people proportionately more than the rich. It is a powerful disincentive to save and costly to collect.

  ISBN: 1873712510

  UK Price: £24 (£26 elsewhere)

Published 1995

- **All the Right Places**

  Prof Antony Flew

  Increase parental choice for low income families by expanding the assisted places scheme.

  ISBN: 1873712650

  UK Price: £10 (£12 elsewhere)

- **Pre-Schools for All**

  David Soskin

  There is a commitment to high quality pre-school education, but how is it to be paid for? Soskin draws on personal experience to show how a voucher system could bring private money into providing this public good.

  ISBN: 187371252X

  UK Price: £15 (£17 elsewhere)

- **The Fortune Account**

  Dr Eamonn Butler and Dr Madsen Pirie

  Individuals should be able to opt out of the state welfare system into an individual, funded and privately managed 'Fortune Account' which will provide lifetime insurance and basic pension benefits. This will allow people to accumulate savings when young, fit, and in work, in order to fund their needs in retirement or when unemployed, sick or disabled.

  ISBN: 1873712693

  UK Price: £5 (£7 elsewhere)

- **Letter to Lisbon**

  Keith Boyfield

  Cut European duties on tobacco and alcohol is the message to the European Commission. Boyfield argues for tax harmonisation through cross-border competition rather than imposing minimum duty rates on everyone.

  ISBN: 1873712685

  UK Price: £14 (£16 elsewhere)

- **Too Much to Swallow**

  Keith Boyfield

  Equivalency – taxing alcohol by unit – is the solution proposed by Boyfield. Excessively high duties have already cost 10,000 jobs. Action must be taken to stop more being lost.

  ISBN: 1873712669

  UK Price: £16 (£18 elsewhere)

- **Captive Capital**

  Barry Bracewell-Milnes

  UK capital taxes are the world's most complex, putting us at a disadvantage against EC Partners. On UK and US figures, the author shows that the revenue-maximising level for CGT is only 15% and argues for a cut to below 10%.

  ISBN: 1873712634

  UK Price: £5 (£6 elsewhere)

- **Free Wills: Inheritance Without Taxation**

  Dr Barry Bracewell-Milnes

  Ordinary people pay more IHT than the rich. The UK rate is far above the EU avaerage, hitting much smaller estates. The tax is a powerful disincentive on saving, kills family businesses, is costly to collect, and destroys far more youth than it yields.

  ISBN: 1873712642

  UK Price: £10 (£12 elsewhere)

- **Minimum Wage Costs Jobs**

  Prof Richard Vedder and Prof Lowell Gallaway

  The report dispels the myth that a minimum wage increases living standards for unskilled workers. Research reveals how each minimum wage increase has destroyed jobs and increased unemployment, especially among teenagers and non-whites – the groups it was supposed to help!

  ISBN: 1873712626

- **Transmission to the Private Sector: The Future of the BBC Transmission Network**
Keith Boyfield
The BBC has been granted leave to carry on for another decade; but should it continue in exactly its present form? Boyfield asks whether the Corporation's physical network of land transmitters might best be restructured as a joint venture or a privatized company, and explores the potential benefits of the change.
ISBN: 1873712596
Uk Price: £18 (£20 elsewhere)

- **Readings in Liberalism**
Dr Detmar Doering
Classic and essential texts from Locke, Smith, Bastiat, Burke, Mill, Hume, Hayek, Mises and others.
ISBN: 1873712391
Uk Price: £15 (£16 elsewhere)

Published 1996

- **Seize the Initiative!**
Allan Stewart MP and Dr Eamonn Butler
The government has fallen short of its target of letting out £14 Billion ot the PFI contracts. Instead of being encouraged to come up with new and better ways of providing public services, contractors are asked to bid for schemes they know will be expensive to run. The initiative can be resecued if there is clear leadership and direction from the top.
UK Price: £18 (£20 elsewhere)

- **A Power of Good: The Verdict on Electricity Privatization**
Peter Young, Andrew Kuhn and Andrew Shutler
The first comprehensive analysis of the impact of Britain's electricity reforms. Although the report considers the balance of benefits to tilt too much infavour of the shareholder, the fact that 26 countries are implementing at least some of the British reforms is proof enough that they have been a 'very necessary and very welcome advance'
ISBN: 1873712758
UK Price: £39 (£41 elsewhere)

- **Post Office Reform**
Ian Senior
The Post Office is not a natural monopoly whose market is difficult to contest. There is no interdependence between the three services: letters, parcels and counters thus they should be separated and privatized within a framework of 3–5 years.
ISBN: 1873712774
UK Price: £18 (£20 elsewhere)

- **Forests for the People**
Allan Stewart MP and Miles Saltiel
Forestry Commission lands currently represent 15% of mainland Scotland– all outside local control. Under this new scheme they would be placed under the regulatory ambit of the local authorities concerned, similar to the 'voucher' privatizations of Eastern and central Europe. Such a transfer would place ownership and control into local communities who are far more sympathetic to the environment.
ISBN: 1873712766
UK Price: £12 (£14 elsewhere)

- **The Why and How of Welfare State Reform**

  Dr Eamonn Butler

  The present welfare state is an outdated scatter-gun system with perverse incentives and poverty traps.

  It is an inefficient savings mechanism for pensions, which at present are not backed by investment but only by the promises of politicians. This inadequate system is in need of overhaul.

  Copies are complimentary

- **What's Wrong with the Welfare State**

  Dr Eamonn Butler and Matthew Young

  The numbers eligible for welfare benefits have doubled since 1979 despite a 40% rise in average pay. The future cost of state benefits amounts to government liabilities of £2 trillion on health and pension schemes alone. It is not surprising that the current pay-as-you-go system is unsustainable. The solution is individual saving and insurance.

  ISBN: 187371274X

  UK Price: £10 (£12 elsewhere)

- **Singapore vs. Chile: Competing models for Welfare reform**

  Dr Eamonn Butler, Mukal Asher and Dr Karl Borden

  The authors argue that UK welfare reform should combine the best features of successful reforms in other countries, rather than copying any single model. Contrasting the system in Singapore with the Chilean model, they maintain that important lessons can be learnt. Where Chile highlights the significance of private management, Singapore shows the possible flexibility of new welfare provision. Both show the importance of moving to personalized, funded welfare accounts.

  ISBN: 1873712723

  UK Price: £18 (£20 elsewhere)

- **Over to You**

  John Willman, Stephen Pollard, Bernard Jenkin MP et al

  Policy experts from both left and right agree that the welfare state cannot survive without a radical programme of reforms. The new Fortune Account would provide for retirement savings and lifetime insurance against unemployment and other risks. Positive incentives would reduce fraud while the extra investment could produce an additional 3% rise in economic growth as experienced in Chile.

  ISBN: 1873712782

  Uk Price: £10 (£12 elsewhere)

- **A Fund for Life**

  Dr Eamonn Butler and Matthew Young

  The UK State pension should be remodelled on Chile's privatized system which replaced its state pension with compulsory personal savings accounts which have become actuarially sound and secure and offer flexible retirement ages, higher rates of return and stimulates economic growth.

  ISBN: 1873712790

  Uk Price: £10 (£12 elsewhere)

- **Health to the People**

  Dr Michael Goldsmith and Prof David Gladstone

  The NHS should be more explicit about rationing and should develop a 'core curriculum' of essential services always available to all. New methods of funding should be introduced which would allow the use of private top-up insurance to cover extra amenities

  ISBN: 1873712820

  UK Price: £12 (£14 elsewhere)

- **The Kiwi Effect**

  Robert O'Quinn and Nigel Ashford

  New Zealand has been rated the world's most free economy by *The Economist* due to reforms initiated by the Labour government. The old Crown departments have been split into their policy, regulatory, service-delivery and commercial functions. The government has also become the first to adopt the same kind of rigorous accounting standards that are demanded of commercial firms. Having seen New Zealand as the world's laboratory for public sector reform, there is much we could learn from the Kiwi effect.

  ISBN: 1873712731

  Uk Price: £18 (£20 elsewhere)

- **The Eastern Market**

  Michael Bell

  Eastern European countries should create their own free trade, free market area – not aim to join the EC

  ISBN: 1873712715

  UK Price: £14 (£16 elsewhere)

- **Technology, the Workplace and the Future**

  Prof James Bennett

  Nations should realise the challenges presented by a world of technological change, and prepare for the further 'down-sizing' of businesses to minimal labour intensity: the 'vitual firm'. Such an approach is necessary to prevent the threat of economic stagnation in a world of advanced information technology, and should be welcomed for the previously unimagined opportunities the future promises to those willing to seize them.

  ISBN: 1873712855

  UK Price:£5 (£7 elsewhere)

Published 1997

- **The Great Escape: Financing the Transition to Funded Welfare**

  Dr Eamonn Butler

  The argument against scrapping the state's chain-letter pensions and benefits system is that 'one generation has to pay twice' – to pay off the state's obligations to today's pensioners and to lay down savings for itself. This report says the opposite is true. Moving to a funded system would bring enormous benefit both to individuals and the economy. The extra growth would easily allow the transition within a generation-while leaving everyone better off.

  ISBN: 187371288X

  UK Price: £16 (£18 elsewhere)

- **Beyond Pensions Plus**

  Dr Eamonn Butler, Dr Madsen Pirie and Matthew Young

  Starting from the Institute's 1995 report on The Fortune Account, the authors go deeper into the details of how an individually-based personal insurance and retirement savings system would work. The contribution requirements, tax rules, provider profiles, and regulation of the new system are all outlined, as are the options for what benefits should be in account and how withdrawals can be made.

  ISBN: 1873712871

  Uk Price: £18 (£20 elsewhere)

- **Who Owns the Past?**

  Andrew Selkirk

  Archeology has suffered from an increase in state intervention and subsidies since 1973. Moves away from the traditional Treasure Trove solution to wipe out looting will only serve to promote it. The answer is to 'amateurize' archeology and resist all temptations to nationalize Britain's heritage

  ISBN: 187371291X

  UK Price: £5 (£7 elsewhere)

Published 1998

- **The Millenial Generation**

  Madsen Pirie & Robert Worcester

  The ASI and MORI have teamed up to produce this comprehensive survey of the attitudes and aspirations of the 16-21 year olds who come of age at the turn of the millennium

  ISBN: 1902737008

  UK Price: £10 (£12 elsewhere)

- **In Defence of the Dome**

  Penny Lewis, Vicky Richardson & James Woudhuysen

  A vigorous defence of the dome by three experts in design and architecture.

  ISBN: 1873712987

  UK Price: £12 (£14 elsewhere)

- **Hayek: A Commemorative Album**

  John Raybould

  Illustrates the life and work of Friedrich Hayek.

  ISBN: 1873712952

  UK Price: £12 (£14 elsewhere)

- **Simply Secure**

  Dr Eamonn Butler, Adrian Boulding & Mathew Young

  Personal saving, insurance and pensions plans should be made simple and afforsable by a radical reformation of the sale and regulation of financial packages.

  ISBN: 1873712960

  UK Price: £12 (£14 elsewhere)

- **Trouble with Authorities**

  Professor John Hibbs

  Passenger Transport Authorities and Passenger Transport Eexecutives have ceased to perform their original function and should be abolished.

  ISBN: 1873712839

  UK Price £12 (£14 elsewhere)

Published 1999

- **A Successful National Health Service**
  Professor Nick Bosenquet
  Those who suggest there is no role for the private sector in the future of the NHS are wrong.
  ISBN: 1902437040
  UK price £14 (£16 elsewhere)

- **Medical Savings Account**
  Cynthia Ramsay
  A radical plan for curtailing overdemand on the NHS: focus the service on the big ticket items and give everyone medical savings accounts to cover their other needs.
  ISBN: 1902373121
  UK Price £18 (elsewhere £20)

- **Don't Stop the Bus**
  Professor John Hibbs
  Bus services would be more efficient if local transport officials just got out of the way and let private bus companies manage things more freely.
  ISBN: 1902737032
  UK Price £16 (£18 elsewhere)

- **Raping the Land**
  Alastair McFarquhar
  Britain's planning system is now wildly out of date, but vested interests in the profession and in local government resist change.
  ISBN: 1902373083
  UK Price £14 (£16 elsewhere)

- **Risky Business**
  John Adams
  Governments have completely mishandled risk issues such as BSE, GM Food and mobile telephones. People's reaction to risk depends on their own view of it, not on anything they hear from government. Trying to make people avoid risk – by wearing seatbelts, for example – can easily backfire as people seek new ways to get back up to normal risk levels
  ISBN: 1902373067
  UK Price: £12 (£14 elsewhere)

- **The Next Leaders?**
  Madsen Pirie & Robert Worcester
  University students spend more on drink and entertainment than on tuition fees, and twice as much on clothes as on books, according to the MORI survey. But they do not tolerate intolerance in their friends, and think that their investment in education will help them far more than any UK or EU government initiatives.
  ISBN: 19023736091
  UK Price £10 (£12 elsewhere)

- **Tax Freedom Day**
  ISBN: 19027370204
  Price £16 (£18 elsewhere)

- **Freedom an' Whisky Gang Thegither**
  Dr Paul Haines
  Dr Haines' rigorous economic analysis concludes that the duty on spirits should be halved and alcoholic excises frozen until they match EU levels – which would produce big employment gains in Scotland
  ISBN: 1902737113
  UK Price £14 (£16 elsewhere)

- **Respectable Trade**
  Professor Norman Barry
  A critique of the 'dangerous delusions of the corporate social responsibility and business ethics'. Should we ask more of our business people than that they conduct their affairs as openly and honestly as anyone else?
  ISBN: 1902373105
  Price £14 (£16 elsewhere)

- **Inflexible Friend**
  Professor John Burton
  Examines the likely impact of the government's IR35 proposals to force many self-employed contractors into the tax net of full time employment.
  ISBN: 190273713X
  UK Price: £14 (£16 elsewhere)

Published 2000

- **Respectable Trade**
  Norman Barry
  £10.00

- **Simpler Taxes**
  Jacob Braestrup
  £10.00

- **The Big Turn Off**
  Madsen Pirie and Robert Worcester
  £15.00

- **Facing the Future**
  Madsen Pirie and Robert Worcester
  £15.00

- **Housing Benefit**
  Dr. Peter King
  £10.00

Bow Group

Address	1a Heath Hurst Road Hampstead London NW3 2RU
Tel	020 7431 6400
Fax	020 7431 6668
Website	www.bowgroup.org.uk
Key Staff	Bow Group Council Members are elected annually. The key posts are: Chairman, Research Secretary, Political Officer, Treasurer, Secretary, Editor of Crossbow, Commercial Director. Details of the incumbents of each position are available from the Bow Group office (0207 431 6400)
Cost of Membership	Varies according to age and geographical location of member, ranging between £15 and £50 per annum
Cost of Annual Subscription	All Bow Group literature and research material is sent without charge to members. In addition, a publication subscription service is available whereby subscribers receive all Bow Group publications and Crossbow for £90 per annum within the UK, or for £150 overseas (by air mail).

Objectives

According to the Group's constitution, the Group shall consist of persons of Conservative views. The objects shall be:

a. To provide opportunity for constructive thought about, and research into, political and social problems of interest to the Conservative Party and the general public.

b To contribute to the formation of Conservative Party policy and the development of Conservative views among the general public.

c. To publish members' works. To arrange or carry on such meetings, debates, conferences, publications and other functions and activities as may be desirable and in the interest of the Group.

The Group shall have no collective policy.

Conditions of Joining

Anyone holding Conservative views is welcome to apply for membership. However, members do not need to be members of the Conservative Party to join The Bow Group. Applicants may be asked to attend an interview panel, although this is unlikely. Prospective members should preferably demonstrate some interest in, or experience of, politics prior to applying for membership.

History

The inaugural meeting of The Bow Group took place at 149 Bow Road, in the buildings of the Bow and Bromley Constitutional Club, on February 7th 1951. The names of 38 founders are inscribed in the minute book, including those of Peter Emery, Geoffrey Howe, William Rees-Mogg and Norman St John Stevas.

The Group wanted, in Peter Emery's words, to "focus and centre Graduate and Undergraduate thought, acting as a stimulus to the Conservative Party and providing an effective counter to 'Intellectual' Socialism and the Fabian Society".

The Group's links to Bow and the East End were the result mainly of Peter Emery's selection as the Prospective Conservative Candidate for Poplar and his association with the Chairman of the local Conservative Association, Colonel HC Joel, who suggested the local Constitutional Club as a suitable venue for a new Group.

Independence from the Conservative Party was enshrined in the first constitution, which clarified the Group's approach of 'no corporate view' and thus allowed writers from all sides of the Conservative Party the freedom to publish and discuss ideas.

The Group quickly found favour and attracted the patronage of the Party Chairman of the time, Lord Woolton. Early papers were particularly directed at social and colonial issues and also at encouraging free-enterprise and, as its reputation grew on the strength of these early papers, the Group was able to persuade the Prime Minister, Harold Macmillan, to officiate at the launch of the new journal, Crossbow, in 1957.

Crossbow gave the Group new profile and impetus. A membership of just over 200 in that year grew steadily to around 1000 by 1962, which has remained the approximate size of the Group since then. In 1961, it was able to afford offices in central London and a small staff. The pattern of standing committees, regional branches and Council, meetings with senior politicians and public figures and the publishing of research papers and Crossbow was developed by this stage and these patterns still characterise the Group's activities. Three Bow Group members were returned as MPs in 1959, fifteen in 1963, rising to 95 in the landslide Parliament of 1983. Over time many graduated to the Cabinet, and to Shadow Cabinets, and the importance of the Group as a fertile source of politicians as well as political ideas became increasingly evident.

Relaunched to face the demands of Opposition in 1997, a roster of Past Chairmen shows a Group with a great Conservative history behind it.

Publications

Published 1990

- **M673**
  Hong Kong
  N Waterson

- **M674**
  Aids: A Darkness over Africa
  C Butler

- **P675**
  Reunited Kingdom
  C Villers

- **P676**
  To No Man Will We Deny
  J Exten Wright

- **P678**
Single Market in Insurance
Lisle, Rossi & Hawkins

- **M679**
London's Transport Problem
Wellesley

- **M680**
Less People Less Pollution
R Ottaway

- **P682**
Widening Share Ownership
Shaw & Marsella

- **M683**
The Savings Trap
J Brazier

- **M684**
Finding the Right Way
C Grayling

- **M685**
Marriage of Convenience
C Tannock

Published 1991

- **P686**
Conservatism in Danger
R Atkinson

- **P692**
The National Parliament & Europe.
Teasdale et al

- **P688**
A Green and Pleasant Land
C Spelman

- **P690**
Sharpening the Sword
J Brazier

- **P691**
Energy: The New Priorities
P Rost & N Essex

- **P693**
  Five Themes for a 4th Term
  J Smith

- **P694**
  Defence Industry after IGCs
  Inglewood & Huxham

Published 1992

- **Financing Public Transport**
  D C Bannerman et al

- **M695**
  Comm. Of Employee Shareholders
  I Taylor MP

- **M696**
  What is to be Done
  Exten–Wright et al

- **M698**
  Reduce Small Business Tax
  Simon Blunt

- **M699**
  A Students Charter
  Richard Patient

- **M701**
  Bow Green
  Chris Grayling

- **P702**
  To Heal the Wounds
  Julian Braizier

Published 1993

- **Nuclear Electric & the Energy Review**
  Dr Robert Hawley

- **P700**
  Levelling the Tracks
  D C Bannerman

- **P701**
  Charing Cross Hospital
  S & R Greenhaigh

- **P704**
  The EEC – A Case for Democracy
  Michael Welsh MEP

- **P705**
  Audio Visual Conferencing
  Julian Roche

- **P706**
  Yugoslavia – Intervention Case
  Brendan Simms

- **P707**
  The 'Get to Work' Scheme
  Julian Roche

- **M708**
  The State of the C. of E.
  Rev Eric Shegog

- **M709**
  Public Expenditure Options
  Christopher Prior

- **M710**
  Bosnia: The Last Chance
  Brendan Simms

- **P703**
  Fresh Start in Europe
  Daniel Hannan

- **P711**
  On-Line Government
  Julian Roche

- **M712**
  Reform of the Civil Service
  Jonathan Smith

- **P713**
  The State, The Party & People
  Virginia Bottomley

Published 1994

- **P714**
  Red Tape – Scourge of the 90s
  Bryan Cassidy MEP

- **P715**
Reform of Capital Gains Tax
Anthony Coombs MP

- **P716**
Choice and Empowerment
J Exten-Wright

- **P717**
Political Nationalism in Eastern Europe
Robert Thomas

- **P719**
Educating the Whole Child
Nancy Morgan

- **P718**
Competitive Sport in Education
Nick Hawkins MP

- **P720**
Action on Youth
Snell & J Brazier MP

- **P721**
No Referenda Please We're British
Julian Roche

- **P722**
Enriching Childhood
Andrew Newton

- **P723**
Achieving Caring Society
Nicholas Brittain

- **P724**
Revolution, Market and Democracy
Robert Thomas

- **P725**
Bosnia: The American Approach
Dr Brendan Simms

- **P726**
Armed Forces in 2010
Julian Brazier

- **P727**
  Nicholas Ridley Memorial Lecture
  Rt Hon J Aitken

- **P728**
  The Third Culture: Education
  Max Taylor

- **P729**
  Restoring the Feel Good Factor
  Nicholas Brittain

- **P731**
  Housing Cooperatives
  K McKenna and J M Smith

Published 1995

- **P733**
  A Response to the Disability Consultation Paper
  Jonathan Kaye

- **P734**
  USA Disability Legislation
  Jonathan Kaye

- **P732**
  R&D: Bridging Exploitation Gap
  Maurice Button

- **P743**
  Examination of American Disability Legislation
  Jonathan Kaye

- **M735**
  A Blueprint to Unite the Accounting Profession
  Nicholas Brittain

- **P736**
  Supporting Excellence – dance and drama training
  P Luff MP & Dr S Berry

- **P737**
  Survival of the Fattest – competition policy reform
  Roger Bird

- **P738**
  Schools: The Way Forward
  Dr Dennis Singh

- **M739**
  Bosnia: The National Interest
  Dr Simms & Cllr Nichol

- **P740**
  Executive Pay: Put Shareholders Back in Control
  Maurice Button

- **P741**
  The Conservative Party for the 21st Century
  John E Strafford

- **P742**
  'Saviour of 'his Country'
  Julian Brazier MP

- **P743**
  Politics and the Internet
  Julian Roche

- **P744**
  Urgency of Europe's Enlargement: Poland's Case
  J Hesketh & W Stephens

Published 1996

- **P745**
  Loan Trusts for Small and Medium Enterprises
  Stephen Kershaw

- **P746**
  Rethinking Regulation
  Roger Bird

- **P747**
  Devolution or Evolution?
  Alexandra Robson

- **P747a**
  Representing Wales: Evolution in Government
  R Edwards & E Price

- **P748**
  Institutional Reform and the 1996 IGC
  Jeremy Bradshaw

- **P750**
  Napoleon or Ross Perot? Sir James Goldsmith
  Michael Welsh

- **P147**
  Privatising the State Pension
  G Clifton Brown

Published 1997

- **P752**
  Bringing Order to the Law
  B Binge & N Hawkins MP

- **P753**
  Labour's Multiplying Mandarins
  J Smith & D Smith

- **P754**
  Members' Rights
  Phil Gott & John Penrose

- **P755**
  Japan: No More to Learn?
  Jeremy Hunt

Published 1998

- **Japan: No more to learn?**

  J Hunt

- **What Gets Measured Gets Done**

  G Strafford

- **Looking Over Your Opponent's Shoulder**

  Lord Saatchi

- **Putting Our House In Order**

  D Sinclair

- **Lifting the Shadow: Why Conservatives Must Reclaim Human Rights**

  A Rankin

Published 1999

- **An English Parliament**

  J Ormond

- **Equal Balance: Electing More Women MPs for the Conservative Party**

  F Buxton

- **Power to the People: Putting Us Back in Control**

  G Strafford and D Hinds

- **Education Education Education**

  M Portillo

- **A Conservative Ethical Foreign Policy**

  M Grenfell

Published 2000

- **The Worst Parent in Britain: Proposals for Reforms in Institutionalised Childcare**

  R Bolland and M Nicholson

- **Making the NHS Better**

  C Philp

- **Access to Government: Genuine Freedom of Information**

  M Marsh

- **The Bow Group Ideas Book 2000**

  D Hinds, C Philp, A Bogdanor, F Ingham et al

In addition, three issues of the Bow Group magazine, *Crossbow*, are published each year.

Catalyst

Address	The Catalyst Trust
	PO Box 274
	London
	SW9 8WT
Tel	020 7733 2111
Fax	020 7733 2111
Email	catalyst@catalyst-trust.co.uk
Website	www.catalyst-trust.co.uk
Director	John Underwood
Chair	Roy Hattersley
Research Editor	Martin McIvor
Number of Employees	1
Year of Formation	1998
Cost of Subscription	Individuals: £25.00 (Overseas Rates, For OECD countries add £20, For non OECD countries add £7), Not for Profit/Supporting Subscriber Rate: £40.00, Corporate/Supporting Institution Rate: £100.00

History and Objectives

Catalyst in an independent organisation which has been established to promote economic and social policies which are radical and modern, but rooted in practical experience.

Catalyst's values are long-standing and are firmly established in the labour movement. As democratic socialists Catalyst believes in the redistribution of power, wealth and opportunity – so that everyone has the chance to share fully in the civic, economic and cultural life of society. People should have as much power over their own lives as possible – which means extending democracy, encouraging particiaption and protecting individual liberty.

Catalyst was formed in the first year of the new government. Its aim is to provide some of the intellectual energy and commitment that the Labour Government will need if it is to achieve its ambitious objectives. To be both radical and durable, policies must be based on the insights of the academic community and the practical experience of those who use and deliver services. Catalyst will publish original ideas which are innovative yet grounded in experience. Catalyst believes strongly on the value of public debate, and that proposals which are well-scrutinised will prove more effective in implementation. The organisation's regular pamphlets will therefore provide commentary on existing policies, while offering new proposals in a form which can be readily implemented. Catalyst's challenge is to open a dialogue between decision makers and the public at large, and to convince both of the need for the truly radical agenda it intends to promote.

Publications

- **Creating a Railtrack in the Sky: The Privatisation of the National Air Traffic Control Services**
  Peter Read
  Online Paper: http://www.catalyst-trust.co.uk/nats.htm

- **After Seattle: Globalisation and its Discontents**
  Editors: Barbara Gunnell and David Timms
  Contributors: Bernard Crick, Meghnad Desai, John Edmonds, Larry Elliot, William Keegan, Doreen Massey, George Monbiot, Hilary Wainwright
  Book – 58 pages, £5.99
  ISBN: 0953322459, April 2000

Previous Publications

- **Labour's First Year**
  A departmental assessment.
  Roland Wales
  ISBN: 0953322408

- **Government by Task Force**
  A Review of the reviews.
  Steve Platt
  ISBN: 0953322416

- **Tough on Soundbites, Tough on the Causes of Soundbites**
  New Labour and news management.
  Bob Franklin
  ISBN: 0953322424

- **The British Union State**
  Imperial hangover or flexible citizens' home?
  Simon Partridge
  ISBN: 0953322432

- **Equity and the environment**
  Social Justice Guidelines for a Green Government.
  Dr Brenda Boardman
  ISBN: 0953322440

All Pamphlets priced £5

Centre for Economic Policy Research

Address	90–98 Goswell Road
	London
	EC1V 7RR
Tel	020 7878 2900
Fax	020 7878 2999
Email	cepr@cepr.org
Website	www.cepr.org
President	Richard Portes
Chief Executive Officer	Stephen Yeo
Chief Operating Officer	Tessa Ogden
External Relations Manager	Rita Gilbert
Programme Officer	Kate Millward
Meetings Manager	Monique Muldoon
Office Manager	Martin Davies
Publications Manager	Sue Chapman
Number of Employees	26
Cost of Subscription	N/A

History

The Centre for Economic Policy Research (CEPR) is a network of more than 350 Research Fellows and Affiliates, based primarily in European universities. The Centre coordinates the research activities of its Fellows and Affiliates and communicates their results to the public and private sectors. CEPR is an entrepreneur developing research initiatives with the producers, consumers and sponsors of research. Established in 1983, CEPR is a European economics research organisation with uniquely wide-ranging scope and activities.

CEPR is a registered educational charity. Institutional (core) finance for the Centre is provided by major grants from the Economic and Social Research Council, under which an ESRC Resource Centre operates within the CEPR; the Esmee Fairbairn Charitable Trust and the Bank of England; the Bank for International Settlements; 22 national central banks and 45 companies. The Centre is also supported by the European Central Bank.

None of these organisations gives prior review to the Centre's publications, nor do they necessarily endorse the views expressed therein.

The Centre is pluralist and non-partisan, bringing economic research to bear in the analysis of medium and long-run policy questions. CEPR research may include views on policy, but the Executive Committee of the Centre does not give prior review to its publications, and the Centre takes no institutional policy positions.

Objectives

The CEPR aims to improve the quality of 'policy relevant' research done in Europe, by selecting the best researchers, providing them with the resources and services necessary to do good research and encouraging them to apply their skills to policy relevant research issues. It tries to build a strong and cohesive economics research community within Europe, by fostering collaborations between researchers on a pan-European basis. It disseminates this research in a clear and comprehensible manner to the users of the research in the private and public sectors.

Publications

Books

- **Trawling for Minnows: European Competition Policy and Agreements Between Firms**
  Damien Neven, Penelope Papandropoulos, Paul Seabright
  April 1998, ISBN:1898128340, 228pp
  This book considers what the literature in industrial economics has to say about the effects of agreements between firms and looks at the procedures of the Commission and the way it undertakes investigations and reaches decisions.

- **Regional Partners in Global Markets: Limits and Possibilities of the Euro–Med Agreements**
  Ahmed Galal & Bernard Hoekman
  February 1997, ISBN: 1898128286, 317pp
  After emphasizing new developments in thinking on regional integration, this book provides evidence of the actual and possible effects of recent trade agreements: NAFTA, AFTA, and the agreements that the EU negotiated with Tunisia and with Morocco.

- **Competition Policy and the Transformation of Central and Eastern Europe**
  John Fingleton, Eleanor Fox, Damien Neven, Paul Seabright
  September 1996, ISBN: 1898128251, 253pp
  This book examines the implementation of competition policy during the 1990s in Hungary, Poland and the Czech and Slovak Republics and looks at the economic predicament of countries in transition, considering how far this has required the state actively to police the competitive process.

- **Inflation Targets**
  Leonard Leiderman & Lars E O Svensson
  August 1995, ISBN: 1898128197, 214pp
  This wide-ranging theoretical and empirical analysis of the role, announcement and achievement of targets, and of the institutional reforms that might be necessary to support price stability, provides the first comprehensive evaluation of the impact of inflation targets on monetary policy and inflation performance.

- **Tax and Benefit Reform in Central and Eastern Europe**
  David M G Newbery
  August 1995, ISBN: 1898128197, 217pp
  The contributions in this book teach important lessons about the design, sequencing and impact of tax and benefit reforms, not only for further reforms in the Visegrád nations, but also for countries further east.

- **European Union Trade with Eastern Europe: Adjustment and Opportunities**
  Riccardo Faini & Richard Portes
  May 1995, ISBN: 1898128170, 278pp
  This book breaks new ground in analysing the actual impact of the changes in Central and Eastern Europe on trade and investment flows in Europe.

- **Foundations of an Open Economy: Trade Laws and Institutions for Eastern Europe**
  L Alan Winters
  December 1994, ISBN: 189812816 2, 223pp
  This book focuses closely on the European experience both in terms of the EAs, and in terms of the discussions of the actual institutions that have emerged so far. Its relevance is not restricted to the CEECs, however, for the other emerging market economies face the same challenges.

- **Exchange Rate Policies in the Nordic Countries**
  Johnny Åkerholm & Alberto Giovannini
  October 1994, ISBN: 1898128111, 286pp
  The papers in this volume contribute to developing an understanding of the motivations behind the drive to peg currencies in the Nordic countries to the Deutsche mark, and of the problems these countries encountered in that process.

- **Towards an Integrated Europe**
  Richard Baldwin
  April 1994, ISBN: 1898128138, 234pp + xxiv
  In this volume, Richard Baldwin has marshalled the best available empirical evidence and analytic techniques to establish a framework for organizing our thinking on why the structure and pattern of trade arrangements matters.

- **Merger in Daylight: The Economics and Politics of European Merger Control**
  Damien Neven, Robin Nuttall and Paul Seabright
  June 1993, ISBN: 1898128014, 296pp
  This is the first independent review of the EC Merger Regulation and has wide implications for other issues such as regulatory capture and transparency.

- **Economic Transformation in Central Europe: A Progress Report**
  Richard Portes
  May 1993, ISBN: 1898128006, No. of pages: 294 + xiii
  This book provides an up-to-date assessment of Central Europe's difficult, but ultimately positive and rewarding, process of economic transformation, in which the European Community has so great a stake.

Reports

B1. Monitoring European Integration Series

- **Social Europe: One for All?**
  Charles Bean, Samuel Bentolila, Giuseppe Bertola, Juan Juse Dolado
  September 1998, ISBN: 1898128332, 110pp
  The eighth Monitoring European Integration Report provides a detailed analysis of European labour markets, and sets out specific recommendations for the design and implementation of social policies within the EU. The report addresses many of the issues raised in the debate surrounding the Social Chapter of the Maastricht Treaty.

- **EMU: Getting the Endgame Right**
  David Begg, Francesco Giavazzi, Jürgen von Hagen, Charles Wyplosz
  March 1997, ISBN: 189812826X, 75pp + xiv
  Written by a team of distinguished European academics, CEPR's 7th Monitoring European Integration Report argues that the final stage of transition to EMU remains poorly understood, that many extant proposals (whether from academics or policy-makers) have fatal flaws, and that finding a safer transition strategy is a matter of urgent priority.

- **Flexible Integration: Towards a More Effective and Democratic Europe**
Mathias Dewatripont, Francesco Giavazzi et al
October 1995, ISBN: 1898128 227, 190pp + xviii
Written by a distinguished team of academics from six countries to inform public opinion before the 1996 Intergovernmental Conference, CEPR's sixth Monitoring European Integration Report argues for significant economic, political and legal reforms of the Union to meet the challenges faced by the European Union.

- **Unemployment: Choices for Europe**
George Alogoskoufis, Charles Bean et al
October 1995, ISBN: 1898128 227, 147pp + xi
CEPR's fifth annual Monitoring European Integration Report brings together a distinguished team of European economists to analyse unemployment and review the many policy choices that have been proposed.

- **Making Sense of Subsidiarity: How Much Centralization for Europe?**
David Begg, Jacques Crémer et al
November 1993, ISBN: 1898128030, 165pp + xvii
This report argues that until detailed arguments for and against centralization are made, the principle of subsidiarity remains an incomplete guide to decisions as to where power should reside.

- **Is Bigger Better? The Economics of EC Enlargement**
Richard Baldwin, David Begg et al
October 1992, ISBN: 1898128065, 115pp + xv
This Report examines the enlargement of the European Community to include the EFTA members and the Central and East European Countries (CEECs).

- **The Making of Monetary Union**
David Begg, Pierre-André Chiappori et al
October 1991, ISBN: 1898128057, 120pp + xiv
This Report examines the monetary unification of Europe and the creation of a European Central Bank. It deals first with the macroeconomics of monetary union and highlights the major four issues.

- **The Impact of Eastern Europe**
David Begg, Jean-Pierre Danthine
November 1990, ISBN: 898128049, 76pp + viii
The first title in CEPRs Monitoring European Integration series, this reports offers the first major study of how developments in Eastern Europe would affect the economies of Western Europe and the process of economic integration among them.

B2. Monitoring European Central Bank (MECB) Series

- **The ECB: Safe at Any Speed?**
David Begg, Francesco Giavazzi, Charlie Wyplosz, Paul de Grauwe, Harald Uhlig
October 1998, ISBN 1898128391
Assessment of the issues facing the new European Central Bank including targeting; open market operations; cyclical factors; and decentralisation of operations. The authors then review the economic conditions throughout the area of monetary union and discuss the options for monetary policy.

- **Monitoring European Central Bank Update**

  David Begg, Francesco Giavazzi, Charlie Wyplosz, Paul de Grauwe, Harald Uhlig

  June 1999

  Published after the ECB's first annual report, the authors assess how well the ECB has coped with the challenges it has faced. They conclude that the ECB has avoided many of the dogmatic positions into which it may have fallen and has proved open to ideas and suggestions.

- **One Money, Many Countries and MECB Update: June** 2000

  Carlo A Favero, Xavier Freixas, Torsten Persson, Charles Wyplosz

  February 2000, ISBN: 189812843X, £30.00

  Concludes that the ECB had had a successful first year and displayed more flexibility than expected regarding asymmetries within the euro-zone.

B3. Monitoring European Deregulation (MED) Series

- **Integration and the Regions of Europe: how the Right Policies Can Prevent Polarization**

  Various

  April 2000, ISBN 1898128464, £25.00

  Further European integration will increase the incentives for regional specialisation of economic activity. People and firms will increasingly cluster together with those that share their particular know-how and skilly. Will this lead to a polaraised Europe, in which some regions buzz with activity while others decline? Polarization is not inevitable: growth and cohesion are not necessarily enemies. Unless misguided policies determine otherwise, they are allies.

- **A European Market for Electricity?**

  Various

  December 1999, ISBN: 1898128421, 294pp

  Can Europe achieve a single market for electricity? If it is to become a reality it must be as easy to trade electrical power between countries as between different parts of the same country and that access charges are the key to an integrated electricity market.

- **Europe's Network Industries: Conflicting Priorities (Telecommunications)**

  Various

  October 1998, ISBN: 1898128375, 258pp

  Explores the ten conflicting priorities that European policymakers face in defining an appropriate competition and regulatory policy framework for the network industires. The authors examine the risk that new national or Europe-wide regulation will tilt the playing field in favour of some competitors with potentially detrimental consequences both for consumers and for the long-term development of the industry.

B4. Geneva Reports on the World Economy

- **Can the Moral Hazard Caused by IMF Bailouts be Reduced?**

  Barry Eichengreen

  September 2000, ISBN: 1898128537, £10.00

  It is argued that institutional reforms that address present dilemmas are needed if the international policy community is to succeed in containing moral hazard. Two new approaches to containing and resolving financial crises are IMF-sanctioned payments standstills and the addition of renegotiation-friendly collective action clauses to loan contracts.

- **Asset Prices and Central Bank Policy**
  Stephen G Cecchetti, Hans Genberg, John Lipsky, and Sushil B Wadhwani
  July 2000, ISBN: 1898128537, £25.00
  Addresses a number of questions such as how central banks should view movements in equity, housing and foreign exchange markets, whether policy makers can improve economic performance by paying attention to asset prices and do asset prices contain information about future consumer price inflation.

- **An Independent and Accountable IMF**
  Barry Eichengreen, Jose De Gregorio, Takatoshi Ito and Charles Wyplosz
  September 1999, ISBN: 1898128456, 134pp
  Presents a detailed proposal for a new IMF, insisting on accountability and governance. Contends that many of the IMF's practices have to be rethought and its role redefined since its traditional views of exchange rate regimes and the desirability of unfettered capital mobility no longer correspond to the situations of many developing countries.

B5. Economic Policy Initiative Series

- **EMU and Portfolio Adjustment**
  Various
  November 2000, ISBN: 1898128588, £10.00
  Examination of the principal factors influencing the portfolio reallocation process following the introduction of the euro. Three broad categories of possible portfolio allocation are considered: domestic versus non-domestic investment, debt versus equity investment, and public debt versus private debt investment.

- **Putting 'Humpty' Together Again: Including Developing Countries in a Consensus for the WTO**
  Zhen Kun Wang and L Alan Winters
  April 2000, ISBN: 1898128485, £10.00
  Discussion of the failure of the WTO Ministerial meeting to initiate a new round of world trade talks in Seattle in December 1999. The authors propose an eight-point plan to balance the needs of the developing and developed worlds and conclude that the best strategy for developing countries is not to resist a round and liberalisation, but to embrace them, and focus on their development needs.

- **EMU and Public Debt Management: One Money, One Debt?**
  Carlo A Favero, Alessandro Missale, Gustavo Piga
  January 2000, ISBN: 1898128502, £10.00
  Disscusses changes in public debt management under EMU and its implications for monetary policy. With the advent of EMU, government securities have been redenominated in euros. The speculative demand and the demand for portfolio diversification related to exchange rate variation have disappeared. Common euro denomination has made liquidity and default-risk the distinguishing dimensions of government securities issued by EMU member states.

- **Monetary and Exchange Rate Policies, EMU, Central & Eastern Europe.**
  David Begg, Laszlo Halpern, Charles Wyplosz
  October 1999, ISBN: 1898128413, 108pp
  The continuing global crisis reinforces the need for Europe's transition economies to find a robust strategy for macroeconomic policy in the period leading up to accession and in preparation for joining EMU.

- **Mediating the Transition: Labour Markets in Central and Eastern Europe**
Tito Boeri and Janos Köll
March 1998, ISBN: 1898128324, 135pp + xvi
Economic transformation has sent employment rates plummeting in Central and Eastern Europe and placed an unbearable social security burden on the active population. This Report discusses the policies that should be implemented to enhance labour supply in the region and prepare these countries for meeting the standards for social security.
Fiscal Policy in Transition

- **Coming to Terms with Accession**
Fabrizio Coricelli, Marek Dabrowski and Urszula Kosterna
June 1997, ISBN: 1898128308, 83pp + xiii
This is a succinct yet comprehensive account of the fiscal situation in Central and Eastern Europe, of interest to anyone concerned with the economics and politics of the region.

- **Elzbieta Kawecka-Wyrzykowska, Andrej Kumar and Jürgen von Hagen**
November 1996, ISBN:1898128 278, 113pp + xiv
This issue of the EPI Forum Report presents three different perspectives on the contentious issue of how the EU and the Central and East European (CEE) countries, should come to terms with accession.

- **Banking Sector Development in Central and Eastern Europe**
Ronald W Anderson, Erik Berglögf and Kálmán Mizsei
May 1996, ISBN: 1898128243, 109pp + xiv
This report was produced in advance of the EPI Forum Report of the same name to inform policy-makers in Western and Eastern Europe of the arguments contained within the Report.

B6. Conference Reports

- **Asset Prices & Monetary Policy**
Mark Gertler, Marvin Goodfriend, Otmar Issing and Luigi Speventa
August 1998, ISBN: 1898128405, 27pp
This report collects the views of several prominent scholars and central bankers on whether and how asset price developments can be incorporated in the design of monetary policy.

- **Financial Crises and Asia**
Robert Chote
March 1998. ISBN: 1898128367, 62pp + xvi
Asset price volatility on world financial markets and foreign exchange markets has increased significantly since the Mexican peso crisis of December 1994. The Asian financial crisis is still underway, and there are clear signs that it too will leave significant costs in its wake. This is a report of a February 1998 CEPR conference that addressed this issue with particular emphasis on the important lessons that can be learnt from the recent events in Asia.

- **International Stock Returns and Business Cycles**
Robert Chote
July 1994, ISBN: 1898128154, 72pp + xii
This is a report of a conference held in June 1994, convened to promote interaction between two groups of research, stimulate the cross-fertilization of ideas, and tease out some possible explanations for the puzzling behaviour of stock markets and real economies.

- **New Trade Theories: A Look at the Empirical Evidence**
Paul Krugman
March 1994, ISBN: 1898128103, 64pp + xiii
This is a report of a conference on the new trade theories, held in May 1993. It constitutes an overview of the most recent empirical research in this field, containing a review essay by David Dodwell, World Trade Editor of the *Financial Times*, a survey paper by Paul Krugman, and non-technical summaries of the remaining papers presented.

- **A Single Currency for Europe: Monetary and Real Impacts**
Clive Crook
March 1992, ISBN: 189812809X, 76pp + xii
This is a report of a conference organized by the Banco de Portugal and CEPR in Estoril on 16-18 January 1992. It contains summaries of each paper presented, plus an overview written by Clive Crook of *The Economist*.

- **The Road to EMU: Managing the Transition to a Single European Currency**
Edward Balls
December 1991, ISBN: 1898128081, 10pp + x
This Report from CEPR and the Paolo Baffi Centre for Monetary and Financial Economics focuses on the key issues involved in Stage II of Europe's transition to economic and monetary union.

- **The European Monetary System in Transition**
Clive Crook
September 1989, ISBN: 1898128073, 61pp + xiv
This is a report of a conference organized by CEPR and the Secretaría General de Comercio of the Ministerio de Economía y Hacienda in Madrid on 11/12 May 1989.

B7. General Reports

- **Stuck in Transit: Rethinking Russian Economic Reform**
Erik Berglof, Romesh Vaitilingam
December 1999, ISBN: 1898128448, 50pp
This report discusses the policy options for rebuilding the Russian economy in the light of traumatic events of the late 1990s and explores their underying causes and the deep flaws they exposed in the process of reform. Also examined are the long term policy changes in key areas of the Russian economy, including fiscal and monetary policy, the labour market, the financial sector, industrial restructuring and the barter economy.

- **Sustainability of Public Finances**
Roberto Perotti, Rolf Strauch and Jürgen Von Hagen
April 1998, ISBN: 1898128359, 67pp + xiii
After reviewing the theoretical and empirical arguments for a disaggregate and institutions-oriented approach to correcting non-sustainable deficits, the authors of this report propose a practical procedure to assess the sustainability of a country's public finances.

- **The Ostrich and The EMU**
  Charles Bean, David Begg, Peter Gregson KCB, Jeremy Hardie et al
  May 1997, ISBN: 1898128316, 51pp + xiv
  This is the first thorough assessment of the practical implications, rather than the desirability of EMU. This report is a vital tool for those concerned with, or participating in, the economic and political debate; policy-makers, practitioners and academics alike.

- **Crisis? What Crisis? Orderly Workouts for Sovereign Debtors**
  Francesca Cornelli, Barry Eichengreen et al
  September 1995, ISBN: 1898128235, 134pp + xviii
  This report analyses various approaches to coping better with Mexico-style crises. One particularly prominent proposal is for a bankruptcy procedure for developing countries analogous to Chapter 11 of the US bankruptcy code.

- **Spanish Unemployment: Is there a Solution?**
  Javier Andrés and Charles Bean et al
  May 1995, ISBN: 1898128189, 146pp + xiii
  Is there a solution to Spanish unemployment? Standing at an extraordinary rate of 25% of the workforce (in 1995), its reduction to 5% within 10 years requires the annual creation of 400,000 jobs, and economic growth of at least 5% a year. This report contends that such a goal is not only possible, but that it should be the primary focus of Spain's economic policy.

- **The Future of the European Economy**
  Leon Brittan
  February 1994, ISBN: 189812812X, 21pp + xiv
  This is a report of Sir Leon's speech, in which he lists three main tasks for European policy-makers: the preservation and extension of the open world economy, the reconstruction of Europe's industry, and the creation of a stable long-run macroeconomic policy framework.

- **Independent and Accountable: A New Mandate for the Bank of England**
  David Begg, Brian Corby et al
  November 1993, ISBN: 1898128022, 76pp + xii
  This report is of a panel of experts, chaired by Eric Roll, which examined proposals for changing the Bank of England's mandate and its relationship with the Treasury. It comes out strongly in favour of a central bank free to set monetary policy; pursuing only price stability without Treasury control.

C. Conference Volumes

- **Asian Financial Crises: Causes, Consequences and Contagion**
  Pierre-Richard Agenor, Marcus Miller, David Vines and Axel Wber
  November 1999 ISBN (hardback): 0521770807, ISBN (paperback): 0521000000
  Presents the first analysis, both theoretical and empirical, of the Asian Financial Crisis drawing out general lessons from an event whose potential long-term effects have been likened to the crash of 1929.

- **Dynamic Issues in Applied Commercial Policy Analysis**
  Richard Baldwin, Joseph Francois
  May 1999, ISBN: 0521641713
  Looks at the implications of dynamic processes for the applied modelling of commercial policy. Examines dynamic aspects of international trade and investment policy.

- **Hungary: Towards a Market Economy**
  Charles Wyplosz, Laszlo Halpern
  September 1998, ISBN: 0521630681
  Follows the evolution of the Hungarian economy once the dust of the initial shock which swept Central and Eastern Europe had begun to settle.

- **Migration: the Controversies and the Evidence**
  Riccardo Faini, Jaime de Melo, Klaus Zimmerman
  November 1999, ISBN: 0521662338
  Takes a critical look at the current divide over immigration polciies.

- **Market Integration: Regionalism and the Global Economy**
  Richard Baldwin, Daniel Cohen, Andre Sapir and Anthony Venables
  September 1999, ISBN (hardback): 0521641810, ISBN (paperback): 0521645891
  Looks at new techniques of economic analysis to study changed in the global economy in relationship to the process of regional integration and to draw out policy implications of such changes.

- **Enterprise and Social Benefits After Commumism**
  Martin Rein, Barry L Friedman and Andreas Wörgötter
  June 1997, ISBN: 0521584035

- **Unemployment Policy: Government Options for the Labour Market**
  Dennis Snower and Guillermo de la Dehesa
  May 1997, ISBN (hardback): 0521571391, ISBN (paperback): 0521599210

- **Quantitative Aspects of Post-War European Economic Growth**
  Bart van Ark and Nicholas Crafts
  January 1997, ISBN: 0521496284

- **The New Transatlantic Economy**
  Matthew B Canzoneri, Wilfred J Ethier and Vittorio Grilli
  November 1996, ISBN: 0521562058

- **Acquiring Skills: Market Failures, Their Symptoms and Policy Responses**
  Alison L Booth and Dennis J Snower
  April 1996, ISBN (hardback): 0521472059, ISBN (paperback): 0521479576

- **Economic Growth in Europe Since 1945**
  Nicholas Crafts and Gianni Toniolo
  April 1996, ISBN (hardback): 0521496276, ISBN (paperback): 052149964X

- **The Economics of Organized Crime**
  Gianluca Fiorentini and Sam Peltzman
  March 1996, ISBN (hardback): 0521472482, ISBN (paperback): 0521629551

- **Expanding Membership of the European Union**
  Richard E Baldwin, Pertti Haaparanta and Jaakko Kiander
  November 1995, ISBN: 0521481341

- **North-South Linkages and International Macroeconomic Policy**
  David Vines and David Currie
  September 1995, ISBN: 0521462347

- **The Economics of Sustainable Development**
  Ian Goldin and L Alan Winters
  March 1995, ISBN (hardback): 0521465559, ISBN (paperback): 0521469570

- **Capital Mobility: The Impact on Consumption, Investment and Growth**
  Leonardo Leiderman and Assaf Razin
  July 1994, ISBN: 0521454387

- **Banks, Finance and Investment in Germany**
  Jeremy Edwards and Klaus Fischer
  February 1994, ISBN (hardback): 0521453488, ISBN (paperback): 0521566088

- **Adjustment and Growth in the European Monetary Union**
  Francisco Torres and Francesco Giavazzi
  October 1993, ISBN: 052144019X

- **New Dimensions in Regional Integration**
  Jaime de Melo and Arvind Panagariya
  July 1993, ISBN (hardback): 0521444314, ISBN (paperback): 0521556686

- **Capital Markets and Financial Intermediation**
  Colin Mayer and Xavier Vives
  May 1993, ISBN (hardback): 0521443970, ISBN (paperback): 0521558530

- **Labour Markets in an Ageing Europe**
  Paul Johnson and Klaus F Zimmermann
  May 1993, ISBN: 0521443989

- **Finance and Development: Issues and Experience**
  Alberto Giovannini
  March 1993, ISBN: 0521440173

- **Hungary: An Economy in Transition**
  István P Székely and David M G Newbery
  February 1993, ISBN: 0521440181

- **Trade Flows and Trade Policy After '1992'**
  L Alan Winters
  January 1993, ISBN (hardback): 0521440203

- **Establishing a Central Bank: Issues in Europe and Lessons from the US**
  Paul Masson
  July 1992, ISBN: 0521420899

- **Open Economies: Structural Adjustment and Agriculture**
  Ian Goldin and L Alan Winters
  May 1992, ISBN: 0521420563

- **Exchange Rate Targets and Currency Bands**
  Paul Krugman and Marcus Miller
  October 1991, ISBN (hardback): 0521415330, ISBN (paperback): 0521435269

- **External Constraints on Macroeconomic Policy: The European Experience**
  George Alogoskoufis, Lucas Papademos and Richard Portes
  August 1991, ISBN: 0521405270

- **European Integration: Trade and Industry**
  L Alan Winters and Anthony J Venables
  May 1991, ISBN (hardback): 0521405289, ISBN (paperback): 0521435277

- **European Financial Integration**
  Colin Mayer
  April 1991, ISBN (hardback): 0521402441, ISBN (paperback): 0521428904

- **Mismatch and Labour Mobility**
  Fiorella Padoa Schioppa
  March 1991, ISBN: 0521402434

- **Public Debt Management: Theory and History**
  Rudiger Dornbusch and Mario Draghi
  January 1991, ISBN: 0521392667

- **Unity with Diversity in the European Economy: The Community's Southern Frontier**
  Christopher Bliss and Jorge Braga de Macedo
  July 1990, ISBN: 0521395208

- **Primary Commodity Prices: Economic Models and Policy**
  L Alan Winters and David Sapsford
  March 1990, ISBN: 0521385504

OTHER CEPR PUBLICATIONS

A. Economic Policy

Since 1985, the Centre has collaborated with the Maison des Sciences de l'Homme, Paris, and the Centre for Economic Studies, Munich, in producing the bi-annual journal Economic Policy, in association with the European Economic Association. Articles for the review are submitted to rigorous scrutiny at the bi-annual Economic Policy meetings by a panel of distinguished economists from Europe and around the world. The results are authoritative and accessible articles, each followed by the comments of panel members, which have influenced both policy discussions and the profession's research agenda. Each issue of the journal contains a collection of papers (usually 5) commissioned by a team of editors: Richard Portes, Georges de Menil, Hans-Werner Sinn (Senior Editors), David Begg, Charles Wyplosz and Kai Konrad (Managing Editors). Unlike most academic journals, this is targeted at the busy policy-maker or private-sector economist, as well as academic economists.

Sales: Sold only by Blackwell Publishers.

B. Discussion Papers

CEPR publishes more than 300 Discussion Papers each year and all current papers are now available to download as pdf. files from www.cepr.org. The CEPR distributes these to a wide audience of academics, policy-makers and private- and public-sector economists. Established in 1984, CEPR's Discussion Paper series is the core of the publications programme. A unique feature of the series are the non-technical summaries, which communicate the essential findings of each paper to those who are not specialists in the field, or who may be unfamiliar with some of the arguments, methods or terminology used in the papers.

Centre for European Reform

Address	29 Tufton Street
	London
	SW1P 3QL
Tel	020 7233 1199
Fax	020 7233 1117
Email	info@cer.org.uk
Website	www.cer.org.uk
Director	Charles Grant
Research Director	Heather Grabbe
Website/Publications Manager	Clare Booth
Research Fellow (Defence)	Daniel Keohane
Research Fellow (Transatlantic Rel.)	Steven Everts
Economist	Alastair Murray
Number of Staff	7
Cost of Membership	Individual £50, Library/Academic £150, Corporate £250.

History

The Centre for European Reform is a think tank devoted to improving the quality of the debate on the future of the European Union. It is a forum for people with ideas from Britain and across the continent to discuss the many social, political and economic challenges facing Europe. It seeks to work with similar bodies in other EU countries, in North America and elsewhere in the world.

In the two years since it began, the CER has won a world-wide reputation for its stimulating, readable and informative pamphlets, essays and working papers on a diverse range of European issues. It also publishes a regular policy bulletin keeping its readers up to date with European events and information.

Objectives

The CER seeks to publish pamphlets, essays and working papers alongside the CER bulletin. It organises seminars, conferences and speaker meetings as well as carrying out research on EU issues. Its main areas of activity are on the euro and economic governance, the enlargement of the the EU and institutional reform, entrepreneurship and competitiveness, Europe and the wider world and European defence policy.

Publications

- **Opening the US defence market**
  Alex Ashbourne
  November 2000, Free

- **How Flexible should Europe be?**
  Ben Hall
  October 2000, Free

- **EU 2010: An optimistic sketch of the future**
  Charles Grant
  19012219X
  September 2000, £10

- **Two essays on the EU and the WTO Millenium Round**
  Julie Wolf, Richard Cunningham and Paeter Lichtenbaum
  1901229181
  September 2000, £10

- **Doing less to do more: a new focus for the EU**
  Nick Clegg
  1901229173
  September 2000, Out of Print

- **Tackling Fraud in the European Union**
  Stephen Grey
  No ISBN
  June 2000, £5

- **Intimate Relations: Can Britain play a leading role in European defence – and keep its special links to US intelligence?**
  Charles Grant
  May 2000, Free

- **European Governance and the Future of the Commission**
  Ben Hall
  May 2000, Free

- **The Spectre of Tax Harmonisation**
  Kitty Ussher
  1901229165
  February 2000, £10

- **The Impact of the Euro on Transatlantic Relations**
  Steven Everts
  1901229157
  January 2000, £10

- **Europe's New Economy**
  Charles Leadbeater
  1901229149
  November 1999, £10.00

- **Policing Europe: EU Justice & Home Affairs Cooperation**
  Ben Hall
  1901229130
  November 1999, £10.00

- **Europe's Defence Industry: A Transatlantic Future?**
  Adams et al
  1901229122
  July 1999, £10.00

- **Will EMU lead to European Economic Government?**
  D Currie, A Donnelly, H Flassbeck, B Hall, J Lemierre, T Padoa-Schioppa and N Wicks
  1901229114
  April 1999, £10.00

- **Name the Day: the business case for joining the Euro.**
  Colin Sharman
  No ISBN
  April 1999, £5.00

- **Scotland Europa: independence in Europe?**
  Matthew Happold
  No ISBN
  April 1999, Free

- **Europe's Uncertain Identity**
  Giles Andreani
  No ISBN
  March 1999, £5.00

- **Russia in Europe**
  Roderic Braithwaite
  February 1999, £10.00

- **The EU budget: an agenda for reform?**
  John Peet and Kitty Ussher
  No ISBN
  February 1999, Free

- **Can Britain lead in Europe?**
  Charles Grant
  1902229092
  October 1998, £10.00

- **Turkey and the European Union**
  David Barchard
  July 1998, £10.00

- **Weak Dollar, Strong Euro? The international impact of EMU**
  C Fred Bergsten
  1901229076
  May 1998, £10.00

Other Pamphlets

- **Britain and the New European Agenda**
  Lionel Barber
  1901229076
  January 1998, £5.00

- **Bridging the Atlantic**
  Mark Nelson
  1901229068
  January 1998, £5.00

- **Britain and EMU: the case for joining**
  C Bishop, C Boyd, A Cottrell, D Coyle, A Donnelly et al
  190122905X
  March 1997, £5.00

- **Opening the Door: the enlargement of NATO and the European Union**
  1901229041
  William Wallace
  October 1996, £5.00

- **Reshaping Europe – Visions for the Future**
  Nick Butler, Philip Dodd, Stephanie Flanders, Timothy Garton Ash, et al
  ISBN: 1901229016
  1996, £5.00, 42pp

- **Strength in Numbers: Europe's foreign and defence policy**
  Charles Grant
  1901229025
  September 1996, £5.00

Centre for Policy Studies

Address	57 Tufton Street
	London
	SW1P 3QL
Tel	020 7222 4488
Fax	020 7222 4388
Email	mail@cps.org.uk
Website	www.cps.org.uk
Director	Tessa Keswick
Secretary	Jennifer Nicholson
Editor	Tim Knox
Number of Staff	6 Full-time, 2 Part-time
Cost of Membership	£50 p.a. by Standing order or £55 p.a. by Cheque Membership includes all Pamphlets plus invitations to CPS Seminars and Lectures.

History and Objectives

The Centre for Policy Studies (CPS) is an independent centre-right think tank which develops and publishes public policy proposals and arranges seminars and lectures on topical policy issues, as part of its mission to influence policy around the world. It also maintains a range of informal contacts with politicians, policymakers, civil servants and the press, in Britain and abroad.

The CPS was founded in 1974 by Margaret Thatcher and Keith Joseph, and can claim a large share of the credit for initiating policies such as privatisation, trade union reform, council house sales, pensions deregulation, education reform, free trade, health service reform and the recent restructuring of the tax system to favour traditional families.

The Centre bases all its policy proposals on a set of core principals, including the value of free markets, the importance of individual choice and responsibility, and the concepts of duty, family, respect for the law, national independence, individualism and liberty.

Publications

1. Political Philosophy

- **Conservative Women**
  Tessa Keswick et al
  ISBN 1903219035, 62pp, A4
  Women, once among the Conservative Party's strongest supporters, are deserting the Party. The authors show that the culture and public face of the Party is predominantly male. This culture must change, so too must the profile of candidates and senior party managers.
  £7.50, 1999

- **Happiness Can't Buy Money**

  Lord Saatchi

  ISBN 189796997X, 17pp, A5

  Conservatives seem unsure of their identity, of their raison d'etre following the 1997 defeat. They fear that economics has lost its potency at the ballot box. But they should concentrate on economic perceptions. This is what changed in 1997. The Party must return to its historic mission to 'elevate the condition of the people'.

  £5.00, 1999

- **After the Landslide: Learning the Lessons from 1906 and 1945**

  David Willetts & Richard Fosdyke

  ISBN 1897969996, 112pp, A5

  Analysis of previous landslide defeats this century suggests that the Conservative Party needs to recognise the need for change – not just in terms of party organisation, but also in terms of policy. Ideas and principles matter. And they must be grounded in the needs and aspirations of the voters.

  £7.50, 1999

- **Moral Evasion**

  David Selbourne

  ISBN 1897969864, 55pp, A5

  Many protagonists and participants in the ongoing moral debates in Britain seek, through the media, to mis-interpret the issues before us or evade the real questions. Some of the evasions are intended to paralyse the debate altogether. David Selbourne examines how language is used and misused by the protagonists in the debate.

  £7.50, 1998

- **Conservatism, Democracy & National Identity**

  John O'Sullivan

  ISBN 1897969899, 34pp, A4

  The full text of the third Keith Joseph Memorial Lecture. Conservatism flourishes when existing institutions and beliefs are under threat. Although it appears that no such threat exists at the moment, the Tory Party can find fertile ground in the defence of democracy and our parliamentary institutions.

  £5.00, 1999

- **Who do we think we are?**

  David Willetts

  ISBN 1897969813, 14pp, A5

  Conservatism is the embodiment of instincts and emotions which have characterised our nation. Conservatives would be right to appeal to the intrinsically British disposition, founded in history, in favour of enterprise, in favour of a mobile and open society, and in favour of local, not regional communities.

  £5.00, 1998

- **One Year On**

  David Selbourne

  ISBN: 1897969724, 57pp, A5

  What is new Labour? What has it done during its first twelve months in office? What has it failed to do? And what are the implications of its enduring popularity for the Conservative party? David Selbourne shows that Labour is a party of contradictory principles (and too often of no principles at all). And while it has done as much right as wrong, many of its actions have been ambiguous and confused. Selbourne concludes that the

Conservative Party is now faced with a historic opportunity. Having seen so many of its own policies adopted and even extended by Labour, the Tories must recapture their faith in civic traditions and institutions.
£7.50, 1997

- **The Ghost of Toryism Past; the Spirit of Conservatism Future**
  Michael Portillo
  ISBN: 1897969694, 21pp, A5
  The full text of Michael Portillo's historic speech to the Centre for Policy Studies Lecture at the Conservative Party Conference at Blackpool, 1997
  £6.00, 1997

- **Blue Skies Ahead**
  James Bethall, Simon Brocklebank Fowler, Andrew Honnor and Andrew Reid
  ISBN: 1897969688, 33pp, A4
  By the time of the next General Election, the Conservative Party will, on current trends, have ceased to exist. Its membership is declining, ageing and is out of touch with the sympathies of the great majority of the British population. The authors call for practical steps to be taken so that the Party can be elected to government again.
  £7.50, 1997

- **The Corruption of Liberalism**
  Melanie Phillips
  ISBN: 1897969643, 25pp, A5
  The author demonstrates the dangers of the new permissiveness and shows how our definition of 'liberal' has become corrupted. It has fallen victim to a mindset which says that the individual is paramount, that 'values' are subjective and that there is no such thing as objective right and wrong. This ignores the great paradox: that personal freedom can only be protected within a structure of constraints.
  £5.00, 1997

- **Class on the Brain**
  Peter Bauer
  ISBN: 1897969635, 25pp, A5
  It remains part of contemporary political folklore that a restrictive and divisive class system is the bane of this country. The system is supposed to be a major barrier to economic progress and a significant source of justified discontent. This, writes Professor Bauer, is not true. Class distinctions may exist, but class barriers are illusory and preoccupation with class disguises the fact that British society is open and mobile. Furthermore, as Lord Bauer shows, the misleading stereotype of the British class system obstructs achievement and causes social resentment.
  £7.50, 1997

- **Liberty and Limited Government**
  The Rt Hon The Baroness Thatcher LG OM FRS
  ISBN: 1897969406, 16pp, A5
  This pamphlet contains the complete text of the historic speech given by Baroness Thatcher at the Keith Joseph Memorial Lecture in January 1996.
  £5.00, 1996

- **A Conservative Agenda**
Tessa Keswick & Edward Heathcoat Amory
ISBN: 189796952X, 37pp, A4
The Conservative Party should sail into the 1997 election with high hope by striking a note of imagination and daring. The authors put forward policy proposals which meet these demanding criteria. They undoubtedly have a major influence on the 1997 Conservative Manifesto.
£7.50, 1996

- **Conservative Realism**
Edited by Kenneth Minogue, with a foreword by Baroness Thatcher.
180pp , 234 x 152mm
In the 1980s, Conservatism experienced a historic intellectual revival. Today, however, the problems which Conservatives now face are more subtle and complex than before. This collection of essays, published in association with HarperCollins, explores the Conservative response to the most problematic political questions facing us today.
£14.99, 1996

- **Conservatism in the Twentieth Century**
Malcolm Rifkind MP QC
ISBN: 1897969538, 26pp, A5
The full text of the historic speech given to the Centre for Policy Studies Lecture at the 1996 Conservative Party Conference..
£5.00, 1996

- **Blair's Gurus**
David Willetts MP
ISBN: 1897969473, 73pp, A5
David Willetts undertakes the first systematic analysis of the ideas behind Blairism and finds that while they may be becoming the conventional wisdom, they are certainly not wise.
£7.50, 1996

- **What is a Conservative?**
Paul Johnson
ISBN: 1897969465, 13pp, A5
In this pamphlet, Paul Johnson surveys the beliefs of the great figures of the Conservative Party – and finds a central paradox: many of them were themselves not Conservatives. Indeed the very indefinability of the term 'Conservative' is one of the greatest strengths of the Party.
£5.00, 1996

- **How to be British**
Charles Moore
ISBN: 1897969384, 19pp, A5
This pamphlet contains the text of the CPS lecture at the Conservative Party Conference in October. Charles Moore elegantly and forcefully argues that British institutions and laws reflect the character of the British people, and offer the best hope for their future.
£5.00, 1995

- **A Conservative Disposition**
  John Gray
  ISBN: 1897969187, 35pp, A5
  This lecture criticises the Utopianism of so much neo-liberalism that masquerades as conservative thought. Conservatives must remember the imperfectibility of all institutions – including the market itself; and try to palliate, rather than cure, their shortcomings
  £4.95, 1990

- **HUBRIS – the tempting of modern Conservatives**
  ed. Digby Anderson & Gerald Frost
  ISBN: 1897969186, 127pp, A5
  In this collection of essays, the authors warn against promising things which it is beyond the power of government to perform. Politicians cannot override the judgement of the market. Nor can they straitjacket the country into a tightly integrated Europe. Nor engineer 'the nation's health'. Traditional wisdom is worth more than that of lobbies and ideologues
  £10.00, 1992

- **The Blue Horizon**
  Michael Portillo
  ISBN: 1897969139, 14pp, A5
  What carried the day in the restoration of sound finances in the 80s was fixity of purpose. Steady, sensible policies backed by sound arguments of principle are what people want from their leaders. This paper gives the text of Michael Portillo's acclaimed CPS lecture.
  £5.00, 1993

2. Education

- **The End of Illiteracy: The Holy Grail of Clackmannanshire**
  Tom Burkard
  ISBN 1897969872
  39pp, A5
  Evidence from a remarkable series of recent trials shows that literacy levels in schools can be greatly increased by the use of synthetic phonics. The architects of the National Literacy Strategy have failed to keep up with developments.
  £7.50, 1999

- **Fair Funding or Fiscal Fudge: Continued Chaos in School Funding**
  Nick Seaton
  ISBN 1897969937
  12pp, A4
  The Government's coversion to the publication of LEA spending tables is to be welcomed, but the figures published obscure as much as they reveal. The main point to be drawn from them is that LEAs continue to cream off far too much of the money destined for schools.
  £5.00, 1999

- **Plans, Plans, Plans**
  Andrew Povey
  ISBN 1897969945
  17pp, A4
  Despite manifesto promises not to intervene in successful schools, the government's approach to raising educational standard has had the opposite effect. LEAs and schools are now burdened with the production of vast numbers of centrally-dictated plans. The result is an increase in red tape, resources diverted from the classroom and a lessening of choice and diversity.
  £5.00, 1999

- **Value for Money in LEA Schools**
  John Marks
  ISBN 1897969856
  17pp, A4
  Research by Dr Marks shows that higher standards in primary and secondary schools are associated with lower spending per pupil and higher class sizes. His counter-intuitive results are a thought-provoking contribution to an ongoing debate. The elusive formula for success is not quite so simple as this government seems to think.
  £5.00, 1998

- **Levelling Down**
  Sean Williams
  ISBN: 1897969759, 37pp, A5
  The School Standards and Framework Bill is immensely centralising, will reduce diversity in education and will restrict parental choice. Its impact will not be, as it claims, to raise standards in education, but to lower them.
  £7.50, 1998

- **The Dearing Report – A Personal Response**
  Anthony O'Hear
  ISBN: 1897969678, 23pp, A4
  The real danger in the Dearing Report is not the proposal to introduce student fees but the more insidious threats to the concept of the traditional university. Professor O'Hear shows that the Report's recommendations must be rejected if the university as a place of scholarship and learning is to survive.
  £7.50, 1997

- **Spelling Standards**
  Jennifer Chew
  ISBN: 1897969503, 15pp, A4
  Standards have fallen in both the long and the short term. The author calls for a return to phonics.
  £5.00, 1996

- **Standards in Arithmetic**
  John Marks
  ISBN: 1897969554, 17pp, A4
  Too many primary school children cannot perform the simplest arithmetical tasks. Standards have fallen far below those found on the continent. They can and must be raised. Out of Print
  £5.00, 1996

- **Culture in the Classroom**
  Irina Tyk
  ISBN: 1897969511, 10pp, A4
  The headmistress of a North London primary school shows that all children – but particularly those in deprived inner-city areas – respond best to traditional teaching methods.
  £5.00, 1996

- **School Funding: present chaos and future clarity**
  Nick Seaton
  ISBN: 1897969562, 19pp, A4
  The Chairman of the Campaign for Real Education demonstrates that the lack of transparency of education budgets would be unacceptable in the private sector. Practical steps on how to achieve clarity are recommended.
  £7.00, 1996

- **Reading Fever: why phonics must come first**
  Martin Turner and Tom Burkard
  ISBN: 1897969570, 33pp, A4
  The authors address the causes of the low standards prevalent in Britain's primary schools and put forward practical recommendations on how to reverse the situation.
  £7.00, 1996

- **An Education Choice: a collection of the CPS' educational pamphlets**
  ed. Sheila Lawlor
  ISBN: 1897969333, 358pp, A5
  Principal topics in this 350-page book include the raising of educational standards, the proper teaching of history and English, the training of teachers, the 'inspecting of inspectors', the introduction of more market mechanisms in the Universities – and above all questions of choice versus collectivism in all aspects of education.
  £15.00, 1995

- **City Technology Colleges**
  David Regan
  ISBN: 187025698X, 48pp, A5
  The author examines the success of technology colleges in developing balanced curricula with an emphasis on the latest technology, in creating new educational opportunities and in establishing links between industry, colleges and local communities.
  £3.50, 1990

- **Teachers Mistaught**
  Sheila Lawlor
  ISBN: 1870265475, 48pp, A5
  Sheila Lawlor recommends abolishing the PGCE, and replacing the BA Ed. by a certificate as a qualification not only for primary teachers but for those hoping to follow other careers. Teachers should be trained 'on the job' in classrooms.
  £4.95, 1990

- **Raising Educational Standards**
  Sir Cyril Taylor
  ISBN: 1870265610, 51pp, A5
  The Chairman of the CTC Trust recommends that Grant Maintained Schools should be allowed to become Grammar Schools or CTCs; school hours be increased; attainment standards be clarified; BTEC diplomas be accepted more freely; transfers of academic credit be facilitated; and closing down of surplus school places be hastened.
  £7.95, 1990

- **LEAs Old and New: a view from Wandsworth**
  Edward Lister
  ISBN: 1870265904, 28pp, A4
  The present surplus of school places creates market conditions which can lead to more variety. All schools should be given self-governing status. Schools should be given more opportunity to open, close or change character. Local authorities should only be educators of the last resort.
  £4.95, 1991

- **Inspecting Schools, breaking the monopoly**
  John Burchill
  ISBN: 1870265750, 13pp, A4
  No one LEA or HMI inspectorate should enjoy a monopoly. Not every LEA need maintain an inspectorate in the present way; nor may some of today's inspectors be suitable in the future. Competing inspectorates should operate as consultants, licensed to inspect schools under clear criteria.
  £3.95, 1991

- **Father of Child Centredness – John Dewey and the ideology of modern education**
  Anthony O'Hear
  ISBN: 1870265653, 48pp, A5
  A century ago in the US, teaching began to be about the present and the future, not the past: about problem-solving, not perspective. Professor O'Hear calls for a radical review of such mischievous theories and shows why and how education should become more didactic, less child-centred, more authoritative, less Deweyesque.
  £5.95, 1991

- **Reading, Learning and the National Curriculum.**
  Martin Turner
  ISBN: 1870265920, 18pp, A4
  Too little emphasis in the National Curriculum is laid on learning to read. Assessment should be by pencil and paper. Attainment targets should be simpler. Contract for design of pilot tests, and external marking and reporting, should be tendered for by independent bodies.
  £6.95, 1991

- **Of Universities and Polytechnics**
  Enoch Powell
  ISBN: 1870265807, 9pp, A4
  Enoch Powell regrets that the distinction between the two has ended. 'It is a grave national misfortune to be governed by those who do not know what a university is.' Polytechnics are meant to cater for activities which follow and obey market forces, the workings of the market; none the worse for that, but they are not universities
  £2.95, 1991

- **End Egalitarian Delusion: different education for different talents**
Canon Peter Pilkington
ISBN: 1870265769, 34pp, A5
We lack a single vocational/technical qualification commanding a respect equivalent to A-levels. We should develop one, and brave the wrath of those who oppose any separation of vocational/technical and academic. This would also safeguard against dilution of our academic standards.
£5.95, 1991

- **Inspecting the School Inspectors**
Sheila Lawlor
ISBN: 1897969082, 32pp, A5
Schools should be allowed to choose their own independent inspectors from a registered list; this would introduce an element of competition into the measurement of 'the first and central task of a school – its academic standards and record'.
£4.95, 1993

- **An Entitlement to Knowledge**
Anthony O'Hear
ISBN: 1897969007, 29pp, A5
A principal duty of the new School Curriculum and Assessment Authority must be to guarantee the entitlement to knowledge of every pupil. This need in no way derogates from the creation of diversity and choice, on which the success of the educational reforms must also be judged.
£5.95, 1993

- **Testing Time – the Dearing Review and the future of the National Curriculum**
John Marenbon
ISBN: 1897969120, 16pp, A5
The Curriculum needs thorough, not piecemeal, reform. It should be minimal, setting out only fundamental areas of knowledge which everyone agrees that schoolchildren should master: basic reading and writing, basic numeracy, elementary science, one foreign language.
£3.95, 1993

- **The Dearing Debate – assessment and the National Curriculum**
ed. Sheila Lawlor
ISBN: 1897969147, 36pp, A5
How far should the Government go in pruning the National Curriculum? Should teacher assessment or formal tests or both be used to measure standards? Sir Ron Dearing defends his approach to the National Curriculum against three of his major critics.
£5.00, 1993

- **Vanishing Worlds – spoken English, the GCSE and the National Curriculum**
Colin Butler
ISBN: 1897969201, 16pp, A4
The inclusion of spoken English for separate assessment in the National Curriculum is a mistake. Verification and effective moderation are simply not possible. While continuing to be taught, spoken English should no longer be an examined part of the GCSE.
£3.95, 1994

- **Opting for Freedom – a stronger policy for grant maintained schools**
Brian Sherratt
ISBN: 1897969228, 23pp, A5
The headmaster of a GM school explains how interest groups have exploited the Government's hesitancy over promoting grant-maintained status. The author argues that the Government should loosen the constraints placed on GM schools so as to make diversity and choice in education a reality.
£5.00, 1994

- **Nursery Choices – the right way to pre-school education**
Sheila Lawlor
ISBN: 1897969295, 39pp, A5
Who should run Nursery schools? The State (through the LEAs) or the parents? Sheila Lawlor re-examines the arguments from the social as well as the educational points of view.
£5.00, 1994

3. The Economy

- **The War of Independence**
Lord Saatchi & Peter Warburton
ISBN 1897969910, 43pp, A4
Why is it that taxes are always going up and yet the government never seems to have enough money to spend on things like health and education? The authors propose an overhaul of the tax and benefits system: a clearing up of the overlap between taxes and benefits and echanging the complex web of reliefs, allowances, credits and tax breaks for lower rates for all.
£7.50, 1999

- **Serious Damage: the Withholding Tax & the City of London**
Richard Baron
24pp, A4
The withholding tax would drive the London bond market offshore. In addition the Government's failure to veto the tax has sent a clear message to the City institutions: their interests are negotiable. City institutions can and will move their London operations if they feel that their interests are better understood elsewhere.
£5.00, 1999

- **Handicap, Not Trump Card: The Franco–German Model isn't Working**
Keith Marsden
ISBN 1897969961, 28pp, A4
The French and German Finance Ministers recently declared their confidence in the European model: it was a 'trump card, not a handicap'. Why then, asks Keith Marsden, is unemployment so much higher in France and Germany than in Britain or the USA?
£5.00, 1999

- **A Market Under Threat: How the European Union Could Destroy the British Art Market**
David Heathcoat-Amory MP
ISBN: 1897969740, 18pp, A5
Britain's art market is a great national asset. Now it is under threat, not from competitive pressures, but from two tax initiatives being proposed by Brussels: the imposition of VAT at 5% on works imported from outside the EU; and a levy (the droit de suite) which would be payable whenever most 20th century works of art

are re-sold. Either of these two taxes will have a severe effect on the attractiveness of Britain as an international art centre. Together they would destroy it. For art is mobile: buyers and sellers of art will simply go to
those cities (such as New York) where such taxes do not apply.

£5.00, 1998

- **Miracle or Mirage? Britain's Economy seen from Abroad**
  Keith Marsden
  ISBN: 1897969570, 51pp, A4

  Britain's economy is flourishing. That is the only conclusion which can be drawn from an impartial analysis
  of the international data. Yet, writes Keith Marsden, a renowned international economist based in Geneva,
  the achievements of recent Conservative administrations are under threat – from both the Labour Party and
  from Brussels.

  £7.50, 1997

- **The Key to Higher Living Standards**
  Walter Eltis
  ISBN: 1897969481, 31pp, A5

  The leading economist demonstrates that economic policies since 1979 have led to a higher increase in living standards in the UK than in any of our European competitors. Such growth can only be maintained if
  government expenditure as a proportion of GDP is, at the very minimum, contained.

  £7.50, 1996

- **Public Spending – a 20-year plan for reform**
  Patrick Minford
  ISBN: 1897969392, 27pp, A5

  Professor Minford proposes a thoroughly radical reform in fiscal policy; he insists that only by bringing about
  a sea-change in our cultural attitudes towards welfare will we be able to cope with the demographic and economic imperatives to come.

  £3.95, 1995

- **Pensions in the 21st Century**
  John MacGregor
  ISBN: 1897969481, 41pp, A5

  The former Chief Secretary to the Treasury demonstrates that the success of pension reform in the last 15
  years is threatened by an over-regulated supervisory regime. A new code, designed to encourage appropriate
  investment, should replace the present one at the earliest opportunity.

  £5.95, 1996

- **Exploding Wealth for All**
  George Copeman
  ISBN: 1897969998, 36pp, A4

  The Deputy Chairman of the Wider Share Ownership Council makes recommendations for encouraging all
  companies to set up one of the many Revenue-approved schemes for employee share ownership.

  £3.50, 1990

* **Giving More Ways to Encourage Donations to Charities**
Nicholas True
ISBN: 1870265793, 44pp, A5
Nicholas True recommends that once-only gifts should be eligible for relief; donations should be 'rollable-forward'; limits on payroll giving should be abolished; rules on VAT for corporate gifts in kind should be eased, and that the duty of the Charities Commission to report should be stronger.
£4.95, 1990

* **For a Stable Pound**
Tim Congdon
ISBN: 1870265955, 43pp, A5
It is not good enough to accept a 'fairly low' inflation rate. An independent Bank of England would help to attain really stable prices. Tim Congdon recommends an Act for its establishment. Under the Act the Governor would be selected by and be responsible to Parliament; and be obliged to achieve price stability by a specific Date
£7.50, 1991

* **What's wrong with Capital Gains Tax?**
Tom Griffin
ISBN: 1870265866, 32pp, A4
CGT is almost wholly a political tax, levied for appearance's sake. It does mischief, since it reduces the rewards for enterprise and risk-taking. At the very least it should be ameliorated, for example reducing the rate to 15% and granting rollover reliefs.
£4.95, 1991

4. International Affairs

* **Kosovo: Law & Diplomacy**
Mark Littman QC
ISBN: 190321900, 59pp, A4
The British Government claimed throughout the Kosovo war that its actions were in accordance with international law. Mark Littman demonstrates that this is simply not the case. Moreover, the NATO action was also unnecessary and unsuccessful in achieving its stated humanitarian objectives.
£7.50, 1999

* **Fifty Years of Failure**
Peter Bauer & Cranley Onslow with a reply by Clare Short
The Jubilee 2000 campaign for Third World debt cancellation is misguided: it favours the incompetent and the dishonest. A radical revision of aid policy is required. Instead of being linked to per capita income, aid should be given to those governments which pursue domestic and foreign polcies likely to promote the welfare of their people.
£7.50, 1999

* **Ken Costa**
ISBN: 1870265505, 39pp, A5
The director of a leading City bank recommends: that the EU Committee on South Africa be invigorated; that South Africa be admitted into international finance organisations; and that the South African Reserve Bank become independent.
£4.95, 1990

- **The Democratic Revolutions – popular capitalism in Eastern Europe**
John Redwood MP
ISBN: 1870265378, 28pp, A5
John Redwood looks at ways forward to land reform and to free markets in agricultural produce; the mechanics of privatisation in state industries; the introduction of sound money and currency convertibility; and the drawing-up of a framework of law to guarantee basic rights.
£4.95, 1990

- **Arms and Men: equipment, organisation, morale**
Julian Brazier MP
ISBN: 1870265564, 37pp, A4
Defence expenditure must not be further whittled down. But a reduction in tanks might allow for more Apache helicopters. An MoD co-ordinating body should decide about other trade-offs; excellence must be given priority, for which sake conditions of service should be urgently improved.
£4.95, 1990

- **Imperatives of Defence**
General Sir David Fraser
ISBN: 1870265661, 18pp, A4
General Fraser insists that defence decisions be taken in a large community of peoples. A European defence policy must nurture high technology development. A commission post dealing with procurement must be established immediately.
£3.95, 1990

- **Soviet Calculations: the shifting correlation of forces**
James Sherr
ISBN: 1870265874, 16pp, A4
James Sherr argues that the Soviets will continue to follow the doctrine of 'correlation of force'; we must appreciate that unless we maintain firm military disciplines in Europe, the European status quo may not endure. Our capabilities must allow us to counter any resurrected use of force.
£3.95, 1991

- **Croatia at the Crossroads**
President Tudjman
ISBN: 1870265718, 14pp, A4
In his CPS lecture the President stated 'it is incumbent on Great Britain to apply pressure especially on the Serbian Government to recognise the right of self-determination of all nations within Yugoslavia'. He steered away from ethnic questions towards democratic ones, as embodied in Croatia's new constitution.
£3.95, 1991

- **The Role of Religion in the Fall of Soviet Comuunism**
Canon Michael Bourdeaux
ISBN: 1869900641, 28pp, A5
The links between the KGB and parts of the hierarchy of the Moscow Patriarchate remain in place. The old guard still holds sway, and believes that it has a mission to curtail the missionary endeavours of the Roman Catholic and evangelical churches.
£5.95, 1992

- **America and Britain, is the relationship still special?**
Anthony Hartley
ISBN: 1897969198, 39pp, A5

The durability of the 'special relationship' is due to the many levels at which it operates. It can survive occasional disputes and poor relations between governments. Britain's competing European and American ambitions should be looked on, robustly, as sources of strength.

£6.95, 1994

- **The Challenge for Europe**
Mart Laar, Prime Minister of Estonia
ISBN: 1897969236, 16pp, A4

A preface by Baroness Thatcher endorses this view from the Baltic. Mart Laar insists that success in the ex-communist states can come only from political stability, liberalised economy, strict finance, reined-in government expenditure, market competition and the forming of a wide and deep layer of private ownership.

£4.50, 1994

- **An Awful Warning: the war in ex-Yugoslavia**
Christopher Cviic
ISBN: 1897969244, 46pp, A5

Instead of recognising that the war in ex-Yugoslavia stemmed from Serbian expansionism, Western policy-makers have treated it as a civil war, excusing themselves from serious military intervention. UN sanctions have helped the aggressors to seize and to hold territorial spoils.

£6.95, 1994

5. European Union

- **The European Commission: Administration or Government?**
Tom King
ISBN 1897969989
23pp, A5

The fall of the Santer Commission showed clearly that the Commission – and the institutional structure of the Union as a whole – needs radical reform. Tom King argues that the Commission needs to be de-politicised and must concentrate on the proper administration of the Union's activities.

£7.50, 1999

- **Britain's Place in the World**
Crispin Blunt MP
ISBN 1897969856
31pp, A5

Britain has a choice: it can join EMU or it can renegotiate its relationship with Europe and build on its traditional links with the US and the Commonwealth. But what it cannot do is postpone the decision any longer. An early, decisive national referendum is vital.

£7.50, 1998

- **A Market Under Threat: How the EU could destroy the British art market**
  David Heathcoat-Amory MP
  ISBN 1897969740
  18pp, A5

  Britain's art market is a great national asset. Now it is under threat, not from competitive pressures but from two tax initiatives being proposed in Brussels: the imposition of VAT and the droit de suite. Either of these would have a sever effect on the attractiveness of Britain as an international art centre. Together they would destroy it.

  £5.00, 1998

- **Britain's Final Choice: Europe or America?**
  Conrad Black
  ISBN 1897969783
  28pp, A5

  Britain has a choice. It can join social democratic, centralising Europe. Or it could consider joining NAFTA: an expanded free trade bloc would share Britain's belief in the free market, low taxation and low social spending. And unlike the EU, a free trade bloc would not impinge on British sovereignty.

  £5.00, 1998

- **Further Considerations on EMU**
  Dr Walter Eltis
  ISBN: 1897969732, 28pp, A5

  There are fundamental economic obstacles to British membership of EMU. And should the UK want to join a currency which will be particularly vulnerable to financial strains during the next few years? For international markets will still be able to bet on a break-up of the euro by buying and selling bonds denominated in national currencies. With the grave problem of increasing structural unemployment in continental Europe, some governments may be tempted to question the constraints of EMU membership. The pressures on EMU could thus prove to be unsustainable.

  £7.50, 1998

- **From Maastricht to Amsterdam**
  Martin Howe QC
  ISBN: 1897969651, 27pp, A5

  The Treaty of Amsterdam presents a giant stride towards the creation of a European superstate. In four key areas – border controls, employment and social policy, human rights and the creation of a legal personality for the EU – the Treaty represents a surrender of Britain's independence.

  £7.50, 1997

- **The Future of Europe**
  Michael Howard QC MP
  ISBN: 1897969678, 27pp, A5

  In order to cater for the different aspirations, economies and customs of the Member States, the EU must develop a flexible approach, an approach which will allow each nation state to decide for itself those areas in which to co-operate. Variable geometry must mean that countries should be allowed to repatriate control of wholly domestic matters.

  £6.00, 1997

- **The Creation and Destruction of EMU**
  Dr Walter Eltis
  ISBN: 189796966X, 18pp, A5
  Can EMU survive its three-year transition period during which the Euro will be freely exchangeable with national currencies? Dr Walter Eltis, the leading Oxford economist, identifies a crucial weakness: if there is any question that EMU will fracture during the transition period, then speculators will convert Italian or Spanish debt into D-mark denominated bonds. Should EMU go ahead, then the speculators will lose nothing. But should it collapse, there "will be staggering opportunities for profit".
  £7.50, 1997

- **Labour's Federal Agenda for Europe**
  The European Research Group
  ISBN: 1897969414, 45pp, A5
  Labour Party policies on Europe are exposed for the first time; it can now be shown that, if such policies were implemented, Britain as an independent nation-state would cease to exist. Instead, it would be member of a high-spending, protectionist trading bloc. Britain's constitutional and commercial interests would be damaged irreparably.
  £5.95, 1996

- **Reccommendations for the IGC: opposing views**
  Martin Howe & Michael Welsh
  ISBN: 1897969457, 45pp, A5
  Martin Howe and Michael Welsh propose two radically different negotiating positions for Britain. Should we resist what Martin Howe sees as a "drift to union" – or should we, as Michael Welsh argues, try to counter Europe's bureaucratic centralising tendencies by enthusiastically supporting intergovernmentalism?
  £5.95, 1996

- **Less than meets the Eye, the modest impact of CAP reform**
  Gale Johnson
  ISBN: 1897969341, 53pp, A5
  The CAP has proved a most inefficient way of raising farm incomes. But it has raised the price of land. Future reforms should take note that despite immense costs borne by taxpayers it has failed to achieve one fundamental purpose: preventing a decline in rural employment.
  £5.95, 1995

- **Monetary Union; Issues and Impact**
  Sir Leon Brittan
  ISBN: 1870265467, 21pp, A5
  The author argues that the principal objective of EMU should be to benefit business, which must be allowed to operate within the most competitive environment possible. Price stability is the key to work towards which a flexible central bank should be set up as soon as possible
  £3.95, 1990

- **EMU Now? The Sudden Leap Assessed**
  Tim Congdon
  ISBN: 1870265572, 32pp, A5
  Tim Congdon argues that the costs of a single currency would be heavy; against its few benefits (such as the ending of currency conversion costs) must be set the upheaval of existing contracts. Above all, the dangers of increased unemployment through the loss of the option to devalue.
  £4.95, 1990

- **A Cautionary tale of EMU**
Andrew Tyrie
ISBN: 1870265726, 44pp, A5
Politics are the key. The trade-off is between French desire to gain influence over the Bundesbank, and German hopes of greater political union. Britain should concentrate on pragmatic arguments, stressing that the economic pros and cons of EMU are much exaggerated.
£5.95, 1991

- **A Maastricht Phrasebook**
Charles Moore
ISBN: 1870265912, 15pp, A5
Euroterminolgy creates euromuddle. Phrases such as 'qualified majority voting', 'communautaire', 'subsidiarity' and so on, are glib disguises and excuses for not thinking. We must guard simple English with greater vigilance, if we wish to guard our independence.
£3.95, 1991

- **Monetary Policy After Maastricht**
Martin Howe
ISBN: 1869990110, 19pp, A4
Martin Howe concentrates on the legal implications of Maastricht affecting Britain's scope for action in monetary and exchange rate policy. He concludes that the Treaty will render the opt-out of Stage 3 monetary union to be 'so unattractive that the option looks unreal'.
£4.95, 1992

- **The Resistable Appeal of Fortress Europe**
Martin Wolf
ISBN: 0844738719, 69pp, A5
The Maastricht Treaty reinforced Europe's protectionist and centralising tendencies: a trend likely to be imitated in other parts of the world. 'Naive mercantilists' on both sides of the Atlantic may well put at risks all that has been achieved by the last half-century's trade liberalisation.
£6.95, 1994

- **Britain and the Community**
Nevil Johnson
ISBN: 1897969058, 47pp, A5
Britain's vision must be based on an open Commonwealth of Europe: an association of states co-operating in the maintenance and strengthening of a single market. But we must stay true to our very different political culture and legal traditions.
£6.95, 1993

6. Social Policy

- **The Benefit of Experience**
David Willetts MP
10pp, A4
The working families tax credit is fundamentally flawed. David Willetts demonstrates that the tax credit would both put women at a disadvantage and would increase administrative burdens on business. Willetts concludes that the tax system and the benefit system work on different principles. Just as Wilson and Heath failed to integrate the systems, so will Gordon Brown.
£5.00, 1998

- **Are Families Affordable?**

Patricia Morgan

ISBN: 1897969449, 49pp, A5

Working families with children are over-represented in all poverty statistics – and this is in part the fault of the current tax system which discourages responsible parenting and incentivises lone parents. Patricia Morgan concludes with a call for a radical overhaul of the current system.

£5.95, 1996

- **Rewards of Parenthood**

Lord Joseph

ISBN: 1870265459, 16pp, A4

We should re-examine the disadvantages suffered by mothers who choose to stay at home when their children are young. Governments should also encourage voluntary bodies which provide help to parents in raising their children; and make modest contributions towards some of the overheads.

£2.25, 1990

- **Happy Families? Four points to a Conservative family policy**

David Willetts

ISBN: 1870265629, 38pp, A5

David Willetts recommends improved benefits for under-fives: paid for by not uprating the child benefit for older children. Child tax allowances should also be brought back in preference to cutting income tax. Regulatory and tax burdens should be lightened on private child care.

£5.95, 1990

- **The Importance of Parenting**

Lord Joseph

ISBN: 1870265971, 19pp, A4

The upbringing of children deserves greater priority, for the sake of all our futures. The great voluntary bodies might do even more to support parents living with their children at home; we must always look out for new ways to spread the blessing of good parenting

£3.90, 1991

- **The Social Market containing some ideas from Germany**

Lord Joseph

ISBN: 1869990250, 24pp, A5

It was the policy of letting the market work, subject to law and competition, that brought the shambles of defeated, hungry, bombed West Germany back to life. Her post-war history, with its successes and now its problems, has much to teach us.

£5.95, 1992

- **The Crisis of the Welfare State: ethics and economics**

Michael Novak

ISBN: 1897969155, 16pp, A4

Close attention to personal responsibility and civil society should take centre stage. If social justice is a virtue, it must be practised only by individuals as a virtue. Every citizen must think for himself. But the mediating institutions of a civil society must also be strengthened.

£4.95, 1993

- **Privatise the Prosecutors**
Christopher Frazer
ISBN: 1897969171, 32pp, A5
The system of bringing accused people to trial must undergo major reform. This should involve the appointment of high street solicitors as local Crown prosecutors operating under clear national standards.
£6.95, 1993

- **Divorce Dissent**
Ruth Deech
ISBN: 189796918X, 23pp, A5
The 1993 Green Paper threatened several counter-productive changes: more divorces at higher cost, and more children suffering the traumatic effects of broken marriages. The Government should review recent legislation in order to strengthen marriage
£5.00, 1994

- **Social Work or Crime Prevention: a better future for crime probation**
David Coleman
ISBN: 1897969368, 32pp, A4
The training and practice of social workers should be devolved to their parent services which care for children, mental health, the elderly − starting with an audit commission review.
£3.95, 1995

7. The Constitution

- **The Bogus State of Brigadoon**
Bill Jamieson
ISBN 1897969775
48pp, A5
Soctland is at a crossroads. Either it can choose the economics or redistribution as proposed by the SNP and the Labour Party. Or it can resist the siren calls of separatism and adopt an agenda which accepts devolution and which advocates competition in tax policy with the benefits of economy of scale which the Union can offer.
£7.50, 1998

- **Lords A'Leaping**
Edward Heathcoat Amory
ISBN 1897969791
35pp, A5
The Conservatives need to put bold plans of their own for the House of Lords. It should be replaced by a Senate, elected by a system of proportional representation, and with powers to delay the passage of legislation for two years. Such a chamber would enjoy the legitimacy to hold a government properly to account.
£7.50, 1998

- **A Federal Britain – no longer unthinkable**
  John Barnes
  ISBN: 1897969708, 59pp, A4
  Labour's devolution proposals are fundamentally unstable. Yet the Union must be preserved. John Barnes argues that the best way of ensuring the survival of the Union is to embrace a codified structure which will enable a proper dispersal of powers to provincial parliaments.
  £9.00, 1998

- **Electoral Reform: the risks of unintended consequences**
  Nevil Johnson
  ISBN: N/A, 14pp, A4
  On this submission to the Independent Commission on the Reform of the Voting System, the author argues that adopting any system of proportional representation will change not just the way we vote but the whole political culture of Britain. Power would gravitate to political parties; the geographical link with constituencies weakened; the ability to identify responsibility (and allocate blame) for policies diminished. The first past the post system must therefore be retained.
  £5.00, 1998

- **Think Minister . . .**
  Prof Philip Norton
  ISBN: 1897969589, 41pp, A5
  While the constitutional framework of the United Kingdom is fundamentally healthy, there is a crisis in the way that government works. New pressures on ministers – including those from Brussels – need to be countered. Above all, government must learn to look ahead not to the next press release but to the next five years.
  £7.50, 1997

- **The End of the Peer Show?**
  Simon Heffer
  ISBN: 1897969600, 43pp, A5
  The purpose of any reform of the House of Lords should be the better governance of Britain. Simon Heffer demonstrates that current proposals to abolish the voting rights of the hereditary peerage would not fulfil such a purpose. The effectiveness of the House of Lords should not be undermined in the name of ideological purity.
  £7.00, 1997

- **Sense on Sovereignty**
  Noel Malcolm
  ISBN: 1870265963, 30pp, A5
  Sovereignty implies the exercise of plenary, exclusive authority in a legal order. Delegating some functions of State does not derogate from this, provided it does not entail setting up a constitutional authority higher than the State's own constitution. We must not confuse concepts of authority and power – else we shall risk losing sovereignty.
  £5.95, 1991

- **The Political Consequences of PR**
  Nevil Johnson
  ISBN: 189990250, 31pp, A5
  PR may be 'fairer', but it makes life safer for politicians and reduces their career risks. A secure place for life in a party oligarchy is unhealthy. Our system of relative majority voting induces some responsibility in those we elect – what they gain they may well lose.
  1992

- **The Constitutional Mania**
  Kenneth Minogue
  ISBN: 1897969 104, 37pp, A5
  Constitutional reform is a chimera. Finding a very common expression in the demand for PR and a written Bill of Rights, it may spring from impoverished national self-esteem. Its character also has much in common with misguided and over-ambitious rationalist ideologies.
  £6.95, 1993

8 Privatisation

- **The Performance of Privatised Industries Volume I: The Question of Safety**
  National Economic Research Associates (NERA)
  ISBN: 1897969422, 41pp, A4
  A detailed study showing the impact of privatisation on safety standards. For employees, consumers and the general public, the evidence is that safety has improved.
  £20.00, 1996

- **The Performance of Privatised Industries Volume II: The Effect on the Exchequer**
  National Economic Research Associates (NERA)
  ISBN: 189796949X, 35pp, A4
  An analysis of the inflows and outflows to the Treasury; it shows that the Exchequer has benefited to the tune of £9 billion p.a. – with over half of all proceeds being from sources other than the proceeds of privatisation.
  £20.00, 1996

- **The Performance of Privatised Industries Volume III: Total Factor Productivity**
  National Economic Research Associates (NERA)
  ISBN: 1897969546, 27pp, A4

- **The Performance of Privatised Industries Volume IV: Prices and Quality**
  National Economic Research Associates (NERA)
  ISBN: 1897969597, 48pp, A4
  A detailed statistical analysis of how the consumer has benefited from lower prices and higher quality of service from the privatised industries.
  £20.00, 1997

- **The impact of privatisation on total factor productivity**
  £20.00, 1997

- **Liberate the Tube!**

  Stephen Glaister & Tony Travers

  ISBN: 1897969309, 85pp, A5

  The best solution for an ailing system involves splitting up the underground into ten separate line business-es, each with full commercial responsibility; these should be sold to private operators or run on a franchise basis, with capital grants partly financed under a new scheme.

  £6.95, 1995

- **Charging for Roads**

  Michael Schabas

  ISBN: 189796935X, 22pp, A4

  Banded charges should be applied to the entire road network, not just to motorways – even extended onto urban and local roads. Properly targeted, it would encourage road users to make fewer road journeys and con-sider the alternatives. This would reduce both road congestion and an undue expansion of the network.

  £3.95, 1995

- **Pleasure and Profit from Canals**

  Keith Boyfield

  ISBN: 1870265513, 34pp, A5

  British Waterways should be split into three: a trust charged with conservation and improvement of ameni-ties; a development company with a commercial remit; and a regulatory body. The trust would own 49% of the development company, be represented on its board, and share in its profits.

  £4.95, 1990

- **Freeing the Phones**

  William Letwin

  ISBN: 1870265823, 41pp, A5

  Competitive entry into the telecom networks should be made still easier. But while BT remains the domi-nant supplier the regulatory regime should not be relaxed; although, like benevolent despots, regulators should leave the scene as soon as circumstances permit.

  £7.95, 1991

- **A New Direction for the Post Office**

  Peter Warry

  ISBN: 187026570X, 26pp, A4

  Competition should be brought into the Royal Mail by franchising the services of its 64 districts. A Director General of Posts should ensure an integrated service from pillar-box to doormat, and a uniform stamp price. The aim is to open the way to management buyouts of the districts.

  £4.95, 1991

- **Competitive Coal**

  Colin Robinson & Alan Sykes

  ISBN: 1870265556, 36pp, A5

  Once privatised, coal must compete with imports, not rely on protection. Government should sell pits by tender, region by region. All restrictions on private mines should be lifted at once. British Coal should ask the private sector to bid for any pit which it contemplates closing.

  £5.95, 1991

- **What's Good for Woods**
  Robert Rickman
  ISBN: 1869990102, 48pp, A5
  The Forestry Commission woodlands of natural beauty and value to our heritage should be transferred to local authorities. Commercial woodlands should be sold into private hands..
  £6.95, 1991

- **The Disease of Direct Labour**
  Michael Ivens
  ISBN: 1869990153, 25 pp, A4
  Few commercial companies act as their own builders, cleaners, caterers etc. Direct labour organisations in local and national government lead to inefficiency and extra cost. Michael Ivens estimates that, if competition were extended to the provision of most general (non-medical) services, savings might amount to £500m.
  £4.95, 1992

- **Privatisation Everywhere**
  John Moore MP
  ISBN: 186999020X, 36pp, A5
  State ownership of industry is necessarily inefficient – the priorities of politicians being different from those of business managers; nationalised industries have neither the stick of failure, nor the carrot of self interest. And the benefits of privatisation spread beyond economic efficiency.
  £6.95, 1992

9. Employment Policy

- **The Price of Fairness**
  Parick Minford & Andrew Haldenby
  ISBN: 1897969929
  21pp, A4
  The costs of the Government's labour market reforms will impose additional costs of up to £2.7 billion per year on business and will put 860,000 out of work. Moreover the climate of business retrenchment and caution which will be caused will mean that the damage is lasting.
  £5.00, 1999

- **Four Failures of the New Deal**
  Damien Green MP
  ISBN: 1897969848
  13pp, A4
  Green argues that the New Deal is bad for the young, for business, for other unemployed groups and for the taxpayer. There is no evidence that it is proving any more effective in finding jobs than previous schemes. And it is more expensive than these schemes in terms of cost per job.
  £5.00, 1998

- **The Unhelping Hand**
  Diana Rowan
  ISBN: 1869990250, 24pp, A4
  Government should confine itself to providing the 'level playing field', nurturing a well-educated population, ensuring open trade, enforcing anti-trust laws; and (only when market forces are inadequate) funding basic research. This (and not the 'myth of MITI') is the background to Japanese industrial strength.
  £4.95, 1992

- **Return to Work**
  Anthea Zeman
  ISBN: 1870265521, 31pp, A4
  Proceedings should be modified in order to clarify matters for claimants. Anthea Zeman suggests a pilot scheme should try out a 'small earnings option' to encourage more claimants to return to work via part-time employment. This might enable many to end their dependency on benefit, and lead to better things for them
  £3.95, 1990

- **Towards an Employee's Charter**
  Nicholas Finney & Graham Brady
  ISBN: 1870265858, 36pp, A5
  The European Social Chapter should be resisted if only because it imposes collectivism. It is important to strengthen individual employment contracts; and never to fall into the trap of (so-called) legally enforceable collective bargaining. Another step in labour reform should be to impose a cooling-off period of more than seven days.
  £5.95, 1990

10. Trade Policy

- **Trade Policy Review 1996/1997**
  Ed. by Dr Brian Hindley
  ISBN: 1897969619, 56pp, A4
  Patrick Messerlin on European Film Policy; Tim Josling on a new agricultural trade policy for the EU; Brian Hindley on the problems of EU anti-dumping rules; and Richard Rosecrance on the rise of the virtual state.
  £10, 1997

- **Trade Policy Review 1995**
  Brian Hindley & Deepak Lal
  ISBN: 1897969376, 70pp, A5
  This collection of essays analyses the state of global free trade in 1995 with particular reference to EU Trade Policy, the dangers of US regionalism and the growth of Free Trade Areas
  £6.95, 1995

- **Trade Policy Review 1994**
  Brian Hindley, Deepak Lal & Patrick Messerlin
  ISBN: 1897969252, 63pp, A5
  Members of the EU must unite (if in nothing else) at least in moving GATT from the periphery to the centre of its trade policies. So insists Professor Messerlin, while Brian Hindley in a separate article warns that some of the recent anti-dumping negotiations shows that GATT can be misused for protectionist measures.
  £6.95, 1994

- **Out of Sight, Out of Mind – the Dangerous Neglect of Britain's 'Invisibles'**
Bill Jamieson
ISBN: 1897969260, 31pp, A5

The DTI should be recast to take into account the changing balance in the domestic economy. Also, there is an urgent need to ease the burden of regulatory compliance – if cost-sensitive exchange, equity market and investment management business is not to be driven away.

£5.95, 1994

- **The Goldsmith Fallacy – why open trade and GATT are best**
Brian Hindley
ISBN: 1897969287, 36pp, A5

Abandoning the goal of global free trade and abolishing GATT would depress European living standards, and create chaos in international economic relations. There are problems caused by the rapid growth of emerging economies, but protectionism will not solve them.

£5.00, 1994

- **The Mystery of Japanese Growth**
Ramesh Ponnuru
ISBN: 1844739391, 61pp, A5

Japan's economic success is not due to government intervention, but the avoidance of burdens on the private sector: a light regulatory environment, low taxes on individuals and dividends, fierce competition, and high savings. Intact families and strong education also play a great part.

£5.95, 1995

11. Micellaneous

- **Courting Mistrust: The Growing Culture of Litigation**
Frank Furedi
ISBN 1897969953
47pp, A5

A culture of compensation has Britain firmly in its grasp. This incisive analysis of the problem shows that the cost to society has now reached some £6.2 billion per year. Further damage is caused by the need to avoid litigation and the undermining of trust which follows directly from the flight to the law.

£7.50, 1998

- **Left Home: the myth of Tory abstensions in the Election of 1997**
Tim Hames & Nick Sparrow
ISBN 189796983X
15pp, A4

Many Tories took comfort from a view that it was Tory abstentions that caused the landslide defeat in 1997: such voters would not be too hard to win back. This pamphlet explodes that myth. A huge number of former Conservative voters positively endorsed another party. The Tory Party will have to work very hard if it is to win them back.

£5.00, 1998

- **A Better Deal for London**

  Jeffrey Archer

  ISBN: 1897969716, 25pp, A5

  Only 75% of what Londoners pay in London is returned to the capital in the form of government spending. Yet not all Londoners are rich – the capital is over-represented in many of the key indicators of deprivation. So should London subsidise the rest of the country tot he extent that it suffers itself?

  £7.50, 1998

- **A Better BBC**

  Damian Green

  ISBN: 1870265777, 42pp, A5

  Neither subscription nor advertising are good substitutes for the licence fee. Damian Green proposes a mixed method of funding. A new Public Service Broadcasting Authority would collect the licence fee, for the support of all quality broadcasting – at first giving the BBC the highest percentage of income.

  £5.95, 1991

- **NIMBYism: The disease and the cure**

  Richard Ehrman

  ISBN: 1870265475, 52pp, A5

  Richard Ehrman looks towards better design, better compensation for those affected by development and an imaginative approach to new villages (rather than the creation of large towns and estates). We must find ways to build without wrecking our countryside and cities.

  £4.95, 1990

- **Looking over the Jargon Wall**

  John Redwood

  ISBN: 1897969279, 15pp, A5

  In his time as Secretary of State for Wales, John Redwood found that far too often submissions were 'prey to the new jargon-ridden world of consulting, advising, networking...' He gives examples and pleads for simplicity of thought and clarity of expression.

  £5.00, 1994

- **Local Limits – cutting the costs of good councils**

  Edward Lister

  ISBN: 1897969325, 40pp, A5

  Radical policies in Wandsworth have cut costs, improved standards and brought electoral success. Competitive tendering should be the rule in every council, DLOs disbanded and the split between provider and purchaser compulsory. Capping and the uniform business rate should both be abolished.

  £5.00, 1995

12. 2000 Publications

- **The Great and Good**

  Martin McElwee

  ISBN: 1903219035

- **The Five per cent Solution**

  Keith Marsden

  ISBN: 1903219043

- **Leviathan at Large**
  Martin McElwee & Andrew Tyrie MP
  ISBN: 190321906X

- **The Bad Samaritan**
  Lord Saatchi & Peter Warburton
  ISBN: 1903219094

- **A Raw Deal for Lone Parents**
  David Willits MP & Nicholas Hillman
  ISBN: 1903219124

- **Mr Blair's Poodle**
  Andrew Tyrie MP
  ISBN: 1903219124

- **What are Special Educational Needs?**
  Dr John Marks
  ISBN: 1903219124

- **Towards a Treaty of Commerce**
  Keith Marsden
  ISBN: 1903219140

- **The Price of Peace**
  Michael Gove
  ISBN: 1903219159

- **Freedom for Schools**
  Sean Williams
  ISBN: 1903219086

- **Nice and Beyond the Parting of the Ways**
  Christopher Booker
  ISBN: 1903219183

- **Second Amongst Equals**
  Tessa Keswick
  ISBN: 1903219191

- **The Betrayed Generations**
  John Marks
  ISBN: 1903219191

- **Unfair Funding**
  Nick Seaton
  ISBN: 1903219205

- **Things can only get different?**
  Robert Tyrrell
  ISBN: 190321921

Centre for Reform

Objectives

The Centre for Reform is a public policy think tank pursuing the values of the Liberal Democrats, but open to all those who wish to debate social, economic and political reform. The Centre publishes pamphlets of a range of issues, and facilitates debates through seminars, conferences and informal policy articles in its newsletter.

History

Ten years on from the formation of the Liberal Democrats, the Centre for Reform was established to provide a powerful source of the new ideas that will be required in the century ahead. Firmly in the centre of Britain's strong tradition of progressive, reforming, liberal democratic thought; undeprinned by the independence that allows free thinking to flourish; the Centre intends to be out in front in the articulation of new approaches and new solutions to the many problems of the age.

The Centre was launched at the Liberal Democrat Spring Conference in Southport on 14 March 1998. Its office in Westminster opened a month later.

Publications

- **Saving our future: disaffection with schools**

  Analyses recent debates on dissatisfaction in schools with the various measures that have been put forward to tackle it.

  Richard Grayson & John Howson

  ISBN: 1902622006

  September 1998, £8.00

- **Identity and Politics**

  A Discussion with Michael Ignatieff & Sean Neeson

  ISBN: 1902622014

  November 1998, £6.00

- **Britain's Constitutional Revolution**

  Challenges for the English Regions

  If we accept that there is a strong case for regional government in the English regions, what form should it take, what powers should it have, and how should it fit in with other existing levels of government?

  Dick Newby

  ISBN: 1902622049

  November 1998, £5.00

- **Liberal Democrats and the 'Third Way'**

  William Wallace and Neil Stockley, with a foreword by Diana Maddock

  ISBN: 1902622022

  December 1998, £8.00

- **Alternative Currencies, Alternative Identities.**

  The development of local currencies is used to look at the state of our communities and local economies, and how we can rebuild them in the face of the modern pressures that seem to be unravelling them.

  David Boyle

  ISBN: 1902622030

  March 1999, £7.00

- **Tax and the Euro**

  Argues that fears of the EU forcing us to raise taxes overall are ill-founded, the need for harmonisation in EMU is limited and that the proposed withholding tax is based on mistaken premises and, if implemented, would damage not only the city but the EU as a whole.

  Dick Taverne

  ISBN: 1902622057

  May 1999, £6.00

- **Preparing for EMU: A Liberal Democrat Approach**

  The government should make a firm and formal 'declaration of intent' to join EMU, subject to an early referendum to give British membership democratic legitimacy. Such a commitment would send positive signals to the rest of Europe and focus attention on the large potential costs of exclusion.

  Vincent Cable

  ISBN: 1902622065

  May 1999, £6.00

- **Funding Federalism**
  How other countries fund their governments.
  Margaret Sharp, Nick Bromley & Richard Grayson, with Ryan White and Jay Liotta September 1999
  ISBN: 1902622073
  £12.00

- **A New Future for the Basic State Pension**
  A solution that for the same long term costs as the Government's proposals, will achieve a better balance between encouraging people to save for their own retirement and looking after the poor in retirement.
  Alison Dash & Steve Webb
  ISBN: 1902622081
  August 1999, £10.00

- **Power in the Community: a vision of local government**
  The main aim of local government should be to empower local people, through devolution below local council levels to all community groups.
  Jackie Ballard et al
  ISBN: 190262209X
  September 1999, £6.00

- **Directors' Remuneration in the Privatised Utilities**
  History of the debate over utility company regulation and analysis of the current position regarding director's pay.
  Paul Hodgson, Archy Kirkwood & Trevor Smith
  ISBN: 1902622111
  September 1999, £10.00

- **Energy: Clean & Green by 2050**
  Argues for the need for a long-term energy policy for the UK. Based on examination of the future direction and development of energy sources for electricity generation. Aims to set out policy directions to demonstrate that electricity generation can be clean, green and lean by 2050, and is both feasible and highly beneficial.
  Laura Brodie & Andrew Stunnell
  ISBN: 190262212X
  October 1999, £6.00

- **Why Trust has no Part in Modern Politics**
  New thinking that builds upon voter distrust, through measures such as the independent costing of election manifestos, the establishments of citizens contracts, and the introduction of voting for policies in addition to voting for parties or candidates.
  Andrew Tucker
  ISBN: 190262212X
  October 1999, £6.00

- **Beyond Citizen's Britain**

  British politics has changed fundamentally since Paddy Ashdown set out his case for a different sort of politics in 1989. However, the role of the third party may still prove to be as the provider of a radical agenda.

  Alison Holmes

  ISBN: 1902622138

  November 1999, £8.00

- **"God Bless the Prince of Wales" Wales' Royal Prerogative: Do we still need a Prince of Wales?**

  A brief history of the post and looking in some detail at what Wales gains from this position. With a modern system of political government in the form of the National Assembly, the central conundrum of the monarchy's place in Wales is addressed.

  Russell Deacon and Steve Belzak

  ISBN: 1902622146

  May 2000, £6.00

- **Asylum: a balanced view**

  By providing detailed informatin this pamphlet raises the standards of the debate surrounding asylum-seekers in Britain.

  Jane Coke, Georgina Dobson, Nick Hardwick, Kate Harris, Richard Kemp, Sandy Ruxton and Graham Watson MEP. Introduction by Simon Hughes MP.

  ISBN 1902622154

  July 2000, £8.00

- **The Invisible Revolution: The Globalisation of Power and its consequences for our politics at home and abroad**

  Paddy Ashdown sets out his beliefs on the paradigm shift in politics taking place over the next twenty years. He paints a picture of a world that is rapidly changing and to which many politicians are unable or unwilling to respond.

  Paddy Ashdown. Foreword by Lord Dahrendorf.

  ISBN: 1902622189

  August 2000, £8.00

- **To the Power of Ten**

  A book by the ten Liberal Democrat MEPs about the reality of power and decision-making at a European level. The European style differs radically from the British parliamentary system, and co-operation not confrontation is the defining characteristic.

  Edited by Graham Watson MEP & Joanna Hazelwood

  ISBN: 1902622170

  September 2000, £9.99

- **Women, Children and Poverty: Values and Visions**

  A party political debate on the 'feminisation of poverty', and its effects on women, children and families. The focus is on long-term values and visions of a society based on a 'gendered political economy', where women are 'equal but different' and the roles of mothers and carers are more highly valued.

  ISBN: 1902622197

  Barbara Lindsay

  £10.00

- **The Unification of Europe? An Analysis of EU Enlargement**

  Brings together the insights of a wide range of experts on the EU's institutions and policies, on the diverse countries in the accession process, on Russia and Ukraine and on the Mediterranean, providing the reader with a broad picture of the changing political kaleidoscope and the issues which will come increasingly to the fore over the years ahead.

  Edited by Charles Jenkins

  ISBN: 1902622162

  September 2000, £9.99

- **The Leaf and the Law: The Case for the Legalisation of Cannabis**

  The former Chief Constable of Gwent argues that the harm done to society by the illegal supply of cannabis is caused by its prohibition. Based on existing policies in a number of European countries, a practical regime is devised which also meets the UK's international obligations.

  Francis Wilkinson

  ISBN: 1902622200

  October 2000, £6.00

- **Making MPs Work for Our Money: Reforming Parliament's role in Budget Scrutiny**

  It is argued that central to Parliament's decline is the failure of MPs to perform their historic function of challenging Government demands for tax and spending. Drawing on the experience of the US, Sweden and New Zealand, it proposes a wide range of practical changes.

  Edward Davey

  ISBN 1902622219

  December 2000, £10.00

Centre for Scottish Public Policy

Address	20 Forth Street
	Edinburgh
	EH1 3LH
Tel	0131 477 8219
Fax	0131 477 8220
Email	none
Website	none
Director	Gerry Hassan
Conference Officer	Pat Herd
Research & Admin Assistant	Amy Jones

Objectives

The Centre for Scottish Public Policy is an independent centre-left think tank which aims to develop Scottish based solutions for the new politics of the Scottish Parliament. The Centre provides an independent forum for organisations and individuals to develop ideas which can be drawn upon by Government and other policy makers. The Centre is independent of political parties; radical and open to relevant policy debate whatever its source. It aims to ensure that the policy debate reflects the distinctive concerns of Scottish society and seeks to involve all sections of civil society in its work, including the voluntary sector, business, trade unions, the education sector and public bodies.

The Centre organises conferences, seminars and training events. It publishes reports and shorter briefing documents and carries out research both in-house and commissioned.

Publications

- **Upskilling Scotland**
  Dr. Ewart Keep
  May 2000, ISBN 1873118201
  Price £10.00
  How Scotland can develop a more effective skills strategy.

- **A Different Future: A Modernisers' Guide to Scotland**
  November 1999, ISBN 0114972311
  Price £10.99
  Over 30 contributions from leading commentators including Scottish Government Minister, academics and independent experts.

- **A Guide to the Scottish Parliament: The Shape of Things to Come.**
  Editor Gerry Hassan
  March 1999, ISBN 011497231
  Price £6.99
  A definitive and informed overview of the context, organisation and likely operations of the Socttish Parliament.

- **Parliamentary Practices in Developed Parliaments**
  December 1998, ISBN 0748072454
  Price £6.00
  Research commissioned by The Scottish Office examining procedures, committee structures, executive scrutiny, equal opportunities and lobbying devolved European regions, Canada & Australia. Published by The Stationery Office.

- **New Scotland New Europe: Scotland & the Expanding European Union**
  Mark Lazarowicz
  September 1998, ISBN 1873118198.
  Price £10.00
  A collection of papers examining Scotland's future involvement in the EU at a time of major change.
  Proportional Representation & Local Democracy
  January 1998. ISBN 187311818X. Price £3.00

- **A Parliament for the Millennium**
  July 1997, ISBN 1873118163
  Price £8.00
  A report by the Advisory Committee on Telematics for the Scottish Parliament.

- **Working for Sustainability: An Enviornmental Agenda for the Scottish Parliament**
  August 1997, ISBN 1873118171
  Price £10.00

- **Key Questions for a Scottish Parliament: Education & Training Commission**
  March 1997, ISBN 1873118120
  Price £10.00

- **Quangos: Policy Proposals for a Scottish Parliament**
  1997, ISBN 1873118104
  Price £10.00

- **Scots Law and the Scottish Parliament**
  1997, ISBN 1873118147,
  Price £10.00

- **Equal Opportunities under a Scottish Parliament**
  1997, ISBN 1873118147
  Price £10.00

- **Scotland's Place in Europe**
  1997, ISBN 1873111815
  Price £10.00

- **To Make the Parliament of Scotland a Model for Democracy**
  Bernard Crick & David Millar
  October 1995, reprinted 1997, ISBN 1873118090
  Price £5.00
  The definitive publication on proposed standing orders for a Scottish Parliament

Demos

Address	The Mezzanine
	Elizabeth House
	39 York Road
	London
	SE1 7NQ
Tel	020 7401 5330
Fax	020 7401 5331
Email	mail@demos.co.uk
Website	www.demos.co.uk
Director	Tom Bentley
Deputy Director	Beth Egan
Business Manager	John Holden
Research Associates	Helen Wilkinson
	Perri 6
	Ian Christie
Chair of Trustees	Ian Hargreaves
Number of Employees	13
Cost of Subscription	£125 Libraries, £100 Institutions, £50 Individuals

History

Demos is an independent think tank and research institute based in London. Launched in 1993, its role is to help reinvigorate public policy and political thinking which were felt to have become too short-term, partisan and out of touch with an increasingly complex society.

In its first five years, Demos has pursued an original and eclectic research agenda. Working closely with businesses, local authorities, voluntary organisations and other like-minded bodies, we have helped to revitalise political and social debates. We have carried out innovative and rigorous social research, working with leading thinkers from across Britain and the across the industrialised world on reports designed to influence key decision makers. Our aim has been to produce radical and fresh analysis of the problems facing advanced societies – and also to develop solutions.

Demos's approach is different from other think-tanks and research institutes in that it:

- maintains independent status, publishing authors as diverse as Philip Dodd (Battle over Britain) and Roger Scruton (Animal Rights and Wrongs), and including figures such as Anita Roddick (co-founder of The Body Shop) and Sir Douglas Hague (former advisor to Margaret Thatcher) on its advisory council

- is committed to long term perspective using its innovative Serious Futures methods of forecasting and scenario building.

- works closely with the people likely to be affected by policy proposals through focus groups, surveys and polls, analysis of values and in-depth interviews

- links theory and ideas to the practical work of people from all walks of life, including the professions, business and commerce, academia and the public sector

- acts as a bridge between different disciplines and between business, non-profit organisations and public policy makers.

Over the next five years Demos will continue to operate at the leading edge of ideas. We will further develop our links with partners in Europe, North America and around the world while our research agenda will increasingly focus on the ways in which individuals, communities and organisation can thrive in the face of the big challenges of the next century. Demos seeks to act not only as a think-tank but also as a 'do-tank'.

Publications

Books

- **Creating Wealth from Waste**
  Robin Murray
  ISBN 1 898309 07 9 £11.95 A5 pbk 171pp
  Sets out why the UK has failed to make a leap towards intensive recycling and sets out a zero waste programme for the UK.

- **The Creative Age**
  Kimberley Seltzer & Tom Bentley
  ISBN 1 898309 70 1 £9.95 A5 pbk 91pp
  Argues that creativity can be learned, presenting pioneering examples from education, communities and business.

- **Destination Unknown: engaging with the problems of marginalised youth**
  Tom Bentley & Ravi Gurumurthy
  ISBN 1 898309 29 9 £9.95 A5 pbk 91pp
  A ground breaking report setting out a detailed national picture of the numebrs of young people who are not in work, full time education or training and not claiming benefits.

- **Governing in the Round: Strategies for Holistic Government**
  Perri 6, Diana Leat, Kimberley Seltzer & Gerry Stoker
  ISBN 1 898309 02 7 £9.95 A5 pbk 96pp
  Sets out principal lessons from early experiences of holistic working in government, identifying achievements and problems and detailing how public managers can develop strategies for holistic working.

- **The Good Life**
  Ian Christie & Lindsay Nash
  ISBN 1 898309 06 X £9.95 168pp
  Argues that it is time to bring back the idea of the good life back into our public conversation.

- **Family Business**
  Helen Wilkinson
  ISBN 1 841800 05 8 £9.95 233pp
  Globalisation & radical changes in gender roles are changing the worlds of work and family.

- **An Inclusive Future? Disability, Social Change & Opportunities for Greater Inclusion by 2010**
  Ian Christie & Gavin Mensah-Coker
  ISBN 1 841800 00 7 £11.95 A5 pbk 110pp
  Shows the potential to harness mutual interests of the disabled and non-disabled.

- **The Independents: Britain's New Cultural Entrepreneurs**
  Charles Leadbeater & Kate Oakley
  ISBN 1 898309 96 5 £9.95 pbk 76pp
  Charts the rise of the cultural industries of design, fashion & multimedia and internet service industries.

- **Living Together: Community Life on Mixed Tenure Estates**
  Ben Jupp
  ISBN 1 898309 15 9 £9.95 A5 pbk 103pp

- **The Real Deal**
  ISBN 1 898309 88 3 £11.95 pbk 139pp
  What young people really think about government, politics and social exclusion.

- **To Our Mutual Advantage**
  Charles Leadbeater & Ian Christie
  ISBN 1 898309 84 1 £9.95 A5 pbk
  Surveys the current state of mutuals in the UK in sectors such as finance, childcare, health and social housing.

- **After Social Democracy: politics, capitalism and the common life**
  John Gray
  ISBN 1 898309 52 3 £5.95 A5 pbk 62pp
  This pathbreaking new essay shows why social democracy has become obsolete, and why a 'communitarian liberalism' is now needed to succeed it. 'Fascinating' *Guardian*

- **Alone Again: ethics after certainty**
  Zygmunt Bauman
  ISBN 1 898309 40 X £5.95 A5 pbk 48pp
  An account of why the old ethical arguments no longer stand up, and of how we should think about the new ethical landscape in which we live. 'A brilliant moral tract.' *Independent*

- **Animal Rights and Wrongs (2nd ed)**
  Roger Scruton
  ISBN 1 898309 19 1 £7.95 A5 pbk 113pp
  Roger Scruton sets out a compelling account of how we should think about the morality of our relationships to other animals. This second edition also contains a provocative essay on hunting.

- **The Audit Explosion**
  Michael Power
  ISBN1 898309 30 2 £5.95 A5 pbk 60pp
  Offers a comprehensive critique of the spread of auditing in both the public and private sectors and shows how to achieve a better balance between audits and other forms of accountability.

- **The Battle over Britain**
  Philip Dodd
  ISBN 1 898309 26 4 £5.95 A5 pbk 52pp
  The author examines what it means to be British, and how the British see themselves, arguing that Britain now needs to remake and rediscover its identity.

- **BritainTM: renewing our identity**

  Mark Leonard

  ISBN 1 898309 78 7 £5.95 A5 pbk 75pp

  This report examines how corporate identity techniques could be used to 'brand' Britain and sets out some of the themes that might shape Britain's identity in the future.

- **The British Spring: a manifesto for the election after next**

  Geoff Mulgan, Perri 6 et al.

  ISBN 1 898309 43 4 £5.00 pbk 58pp

  Drawing on examples from around the world, Demos' manifesto sets out what could be done in Britain over the next decade to tackle problems such as crime and unemployment.

- **Business Ethics: the new bottom line**

  Sheena Carmichael

  ISBN1 898309 61 2 £5.95 pbk 63pp

  Showing why ethical confusions can be so costly to business, the author explains how firms can bring greater clarity and coherence to the ethical choices they and their employees make.

- **Civic Entrepreneurship**

  Charles Leadbeater & Sue Goss

  ISBN 1898309 39 6 £9.95 pbk 80pp

  Sets out vivid case studies showing how innovative management by 'civic entrepreneurs' can bring about dramatic improvements in schools, policing, local government and health services.

- **The Common Sense of Community**

  Dick Atkinson

  ISBN 1 898309 80 9 £5.95 pbk 63pp

  Presents a practical vision for revitalising local communities, based on the development of clusters of local self-governing institutions working together, such as schools, housing associations and voluntary organisations.

- **The Creative City**

  Charles Landry and Franco Bianchini

  ISBN1 898309 16 7 £5.95 pbk 60pp

  Argues that cities now need to mobilise creativity not only to achieve competitiveness in the new high value-added industries but also to better solve social problems.

- **An End to Illusions**

  Alan Duncan

  ISBN 1 898309 05 1 £5.95 pbk 64pp

  A forensic study of recent economic policy and a set of recommendations for microeconomic reform. Alan Duncan is Conservative MP for Rutland and Melton.

- **The Family in Question**

  Stein Ringen

  ISBN 1 898309 69 8 £7.95 pbk 60pp

  A radical analysis of the role of the family in modern society. Professor Ringen proposes new approaches to child allowances and argues for more democracy within the family including votes for children.

- **The Freedom of the City**
  Ken Worpole & Liz Greenhalgh
  ISBN 1 898309 08 6 £5.95 51pp

  This book draws on a series of pathbreaking studies of town centres, libraries and parks which argue that the key to safe and enjoyable public spaces is to make them full of activity.

- **Freedom's Children: work, relationships and politics for 18-34 year olds in Britain today**
  Helen Wilkinson & Geoff Mulgan
  ISBN 1 898309 27 2 £9.95 pbk 160pp

  Drawing on extensive new data from the British Household Panel Study and MORI Socioconsult, this report describes in detail the lifestyles and values of the 18-34 year old generation.

- **The Future of Privacy: Volume 1**
  Perri 6
  ISBN 1 898309 44 2 £19.95 336pp

  At the close of the century, huge flows of personal data are the life-blood of the new economy – with serious implications for privacy. This book analyses the forces – technological, economic, political and cultural – shaping the future of privacy.

- **The Future of Privacy: Volume 2**
  Perri 6
  ISBN 1 898309 49 3 £19.95 128pp

  Each of us appears on hundreds of databases held by government agencies, businesses and charities. This book reviews what is known about public concerns about how information is stored and used and presents survey findings which reveal for the first time the dimensions of public trust in the handling of personal information.

- **The Governance Gap: quangos and accountability**
  John Plummer
  ISBN 0 904677 60 5 £8.50 pbk 123pp

  An extensive survey of Britain's quangos – unravelling the inconsistencies in accountability arrangements and the emphasis on upwards accountability to Whitehall rather than downwards to voters and citizens.

- **Guaranteed Electronic Markets: the backbone of a twenty first century economy?**
  Wingham Rowan
  ISBN 1 898309 09 4 £14.95 A5 pbk 72pp

  Guaranteed Electronic Markets sets out a new dimension of electronic trade, conceptualising a vast digital marketplace where anyone could sell their goods and services, thus benefiting a wider community than large corporations.

- **Holistic Government**
  Perri 6
  ISBN 1 898309 04 3 £9.95 pbk 84pp

  The author calls for radical reform to make government more holistic, preventive, outcome-oriented and culture-changing, setting out a series of recommendations for making government more effective and more coherent.

- **Life after Politics: new thinking for the 21st century**
  Geoff Mulgan, ed
  ISBN 0 006387 55 1 £7.99 (Fontana Press) pbk 458
  Bringing together some of the best of Demos' work since its launch in 1993, this comprehensive anthology of essays provides an invaluable source for thinking about how politics and society are developing.

- **Modernising Public Appointments**
  John Viney & Judith Osborne
  ISBN 1 898309 71 X £5.95 pbk 70pp
  Based on a study of the existing system of making public appointments, the authors set out proposals for modernisation, introducing modern business practice to the world of the public sector.

- **The Mosaic of Learning: schools and teachers for the next century**
  David Hargreaves
  ISBN 1 898309 45 0 £5.95 pbk 58pp
  A long overdue agenda for achievable change in schools, the author shows how schools can again become sources of satisfaction for those who teach and learn.

- **No Turning Back: generations and the genderquake**
  Helen Wilkinson
  ISBN 1 898309 75 2 £7.95 pbk 87pp
  This report sets out the implications of the genderquake – the shift in power from men to women and the fast-changing values of the younger generation of 18-34 year olds.

- **On the Cards: privacy, identity and trust in the age of smart technologies**
  Perri 6 & Ivan Briscoe
  ISBN 1 898309 72 8 £9.95 pbk 128pp
  The UK's first comprehensive report on the technological, economic and social dimensions of smart cards and the challenge they pose to existing rules on information and data protection.

- **Open wide: futures for dentistry in 2010**
  Perri 6 with Ben Jupp and Tom Bentley
  ISBN 1 898309 03 5 £14. 95 pbk 207pp
  This is the most comprehensive recent study of the long term future of this politically sensitive health care industry.

- **The Other Invisible Hand: remaking charity for the 21st century**
  Geoff Mulgan and Charles Landry
  ISBN1 898309 81 7 £9.95 pbk 133pp
  Argues that the laws and financial mechanisms which govern the world of charity are antiquated, cumbersome and inflexible, and makes the case for an historic new settlement to encourage voluntary action.

- **The Parenting Deficit**
  Amitai Etzioni
  ISBN 1 898309 20 5 £5.95 pbk 71pp
  Argues that the movement first of men, and more recently of women, out of the home and into work has left a serious deficit of parental care.

- **Park Life: urban parks and social renewal**
  Liz Greenhalgh and Ken Worpole
  ISBN 1 873667 86 8 £20 pbk 99pp
  The final report of the extensive study undertaken by Comedia in association with Demos into the use of Britain's urban parks.

- **A Piece of the Action: employee ownership, equity pay and the rise of the knowledge economy**
  Charles Leadbeater
  ISBN 1 898309 68 X £14.95 pbk 75pp
  This report proposes entrepreneurial employee ownership; equity pay schemes; and the use of employee ownership to create more participatory management and reform corporate governance.

- **The Post-modern State and the World Order**
  Robert Cooper
  ISBN1 898309 62 0 £5.95 pbk 50pp
  This essay argues that in the wake of the cold war, world affairs are being shaped by a new division between the 'pre-modern' areas, the 'modern' nation states and the 'post-modern' areas.

- **Public, Private or Community: what next for the NHS?**
  Chris Ham
  ISBN 1 898309 23 X £8.95 pbk 80pp
  A hard-headed look at the affordability, financing, coverage, organisation and control of the National Health Service.

- **Reconnecting Taxation**
  Geoff Mulgan & Robin Murray
  ISBN 1 898309 00 0 £5.95 pbk 60pp
  A detailed analysis of the current tax crisis offering a wide range of new ideas for tax policy, focusing in particular on new forms of hypothecation and corporate taxation.

- **Rediscovering Europe**
  Mark Leonard
  ISBN 1 898309 54 X £5.95 pbk 68pp
  The European Union is less popular than it has been for a generation. It's core mission and institutions have become detached from the Europe found in people's everyday lives. The author offers a radical approach to legitimacy, using new data and analysis to highlight seven narratives which could reconnect the EU with the priorities and values of its citizens.

- **The Rise of the Social Entrepreneur**
  Charles Leadbeater
  ISBN 1 898309 53 1 £9.95 pbk 115pp
  This report examines the growing band of social entrepreneurs who are working at the grass roots of the welfare system in the space between the public and private sector.

- **Sharper Vision**
  Ian Hargreaves
  ISBN 1 898309 25 6 £5.95 pbk 66pp
  A powerful argument for radically altering the BBC's funding base and ownership structure to enable it to compete effectively in the world's emerging multimedia markets.

- **The Substance of Youth: the role of drugs in young people's live today**
  Perri 6, Ben Jupp, Helen Perry & Kristen Lasky
  ISBN1 859350 38 0 £11.95 pbk 58pp
  Available only from Joseph Rowntree Foundation, York
  This detailed study of young people's views on and experiences of drug use finds that the stereotypes of drug users, on which many of Britain's drug policies are based, can be misleading.

- **Time Out: the costs and benefits of paid parental leave**
  Helen Wilkinson with Stephen Radley, Ian Christie, George Lawson & Jamie Sainsbury
  ISBN 1 898309 58 2 £12.95 pbk 218pp
  This study shows how a new scheme of parental leave could be introduced into the UK with substantial benefits for parents and children, and manageable costs for business, employees and the government.

- **Tomorrow's Women**
  Helen Wilkinson & Melanie Howard
  ISBN 1 898309 48 5 £9.95
  What will women's lives look like in 2010? Drawing on a detailed analysis of the major trends in demography, economics, technology, values, politics and culture, this report sets out where women are headed.

- **Transforming the Dinosaurs: how organisations learn**
  Douglas Hague
  ISBN1 898309 10 8 £5.95 59pp
  An analysis of how institutions can transform their cultures, setting out a series of proposals for introducing greater dynamism and learning capacity into schools, universities, the civil service and companies.

- **Turning the Tide: crime, community and prevention**
  Jon Bright
  ISBN 1 898309 33 7 £12.95 pbk 128pp
  Jon Bright argues for a crime management policy that emphasises prevention, setting out what can be done to stop people drifting into crime and to make crime more difficult to commit.

- **Values Added: how emerging values could influence the development of London**
  Ben Jupp & George Lawson
  £10.00 pbk 51pp
  An in-depth study of the values and beliefs of Londoners, drawing on surveys, group discussions and interviews, offering a number of challenges for policy makers thinking seriously about the future of London.

- **The World's New Fissures**
  Vincent Cable
  ISBN1 898309 35 3 £5.95 pbk 90pp
  An account of the new worldwide dividing lines in politics and the implications of the new politics of identity which are having such an impact on issues such as free trade and migration.

Arguments – This is a series of shorter papers.

- **Access Denied? Preventing information exclusion**
  Danny Kruger
  ISBN 1 898309 24 8 £4.95 46pp
  The author explores the effect of the digital revolution on social divisions, arguing that policies to prevent information exclusion could help the unemployed and low-waged overcome existing disadvantages.

- **Big is Beautiful: bringing East Central Europe into the European Union**
  Perri 6
  ISBN 1 898309 41 8 £4.95 pbk 72pp
  Explains the arguments for and against including countries of East and Central Europe in the European Union, concluding in favour of enlargement.

- **The Building Society Bounty: the case for member philanthropy**
  David Shutt
  ISBN 1 898309 57 4 £4.95 pbk 18pp
  David Shutt argues that those who benefit from building society conversions should be encouraged to give a percentage of their windfall to a 'community bounty' to be used for local community projects.

- **Careerquake: policy supports for self-managed careers**
  AG Watts
  ISBN 1 898309 18 3 £4.95 pbk 42pp
  Argues that there is a lack of adequate supports to enable people to realise their career aspirations. New foundations are needed, including flexible learning systems, common qualifications and lifelong access to career guidance.

- **Civic Spirit: the big idea for a new political era**
  Charles Leadbeater
  ISBN 1 898309 93 0 £4.95 pbk 38pp
  The days of 'there is no such thing as society' are over – the author argues that mutuality could be the idea which shapes politics in the years ahead.

- **Democracy in the Digital Age**
  Lord Freeman
  ISBN 1 898309 14 0 £4.95 pbk 28pp
  Giving specific examples, the author sets out how government can use IT to become more open and efficient, provide better information to citizens and allow more effective expression of political opinions.

- **Easternisation: the rise of Asian power and its impact on the west and on our own society**
  David Howell
  ISBN 1 898309 76 0 £4.95 pbk 24pp
  The author argues that the West needs to learn from the success of East Asian societies not only in industry but also in education and welfare.

- **Escaping Poverty: from safety nets to networks of opportunity**
  Perri 6
  ISBN 1 898309 88 4 £7.95 pbk 52pp
  Bringing together a wide range of evidence, the author argues that 'active labour market policies' ignore the importance of social networks for helping people to get work and get out of poverty.

- **Family Learning: the foundation of effective education**
  Titus Alexander
  ISBN 1 898309 98 1 £7.95 pbk 57pp
  The author presents a long-term strategy for developing family learning including national media campaigns to raise the profile of family learning, strengthening family learning support networks and partnerships between schools and parents.

- **Holding Back the Years: how Britain can grow old better in the twenty first century**
  Diana Leat & Perri 6
  ISBN 1 898309 73 6 £7.95 pbk 38pp
  Britain's services for the elderly are inefficient and put most of their effort into care instead of prevention. The authors propose a single purchasing system to buy cure, care and community services.

- **In Whose Service? Making community service work for the unemployed**
  Ivan Briscoe
  ISBN 1 898309 56 6 £4.95 pbk 70pp
  Briscoe finds the schemes for national and community service in Britain and the US wanting, and suggests that the emphasis on community service needs to be linked to the self-interest of the unemployed.

- **Netstate: Creating electronic government**
  George Lawson
  ISBN 1 898 309 34 5 £7.95 pbk 59pp
  George Lawson uses evidence from around the world to show how government can harness the forces of the technological revolution to become more creative, smarter, enterprising and trustworthy.

- **Relative Values: Support for relationships and parenting**
  Ed Straw
  ISBN 1 898 309 64 7 £4.95 pbk 43pp
  In this important publication from Demos in association with Relate, Ed Straw argues for far greater priority for investment in building successful family relationships and preventing family breakdown.

- **Restoring Public Trust: a governance act for public bodies**
  Norman Warner
  ISBN 1 898309 47 7 £4.95 pbk 62pp
  In the wake of a fall in public trust in government institutions, this report sets out a blueprint for reform of public governance, making the case for a new Governance Act.

- **Revolutionising Share Ownership: the stakeowner economy**
  Jeffrey Gates
  ISBN 1 898309 77 9 £4.95 pbk 32pp
  Jeffrey Gates shows how wider ownership of capital resources can play a vital role in simultaneously improving social cohesion, fiscal health, environmental sustainability and international competitiveness.

- **The Self-policing Society**
  Charles Leadbeater
  ISBN 1 898309 87 6 £4.95 pbk 35pp
  Sets out a number of ways in which society could better deal with crime, including repopulating public spaces, bringing back the police box, enabling informal policing and prioritising public crime concerns.

- **Single Rate Tax: the path to real simplicity**
  Nigel Forman
  ISBN 1 898309 13 2 £4.95 pbk 32pp
  Puts the case for further radical tax reform, proposing that the priority now should be to simplify the tax system. This argument shows how flat taxes would work in Britain.

- **The Society of Networks: a new model for the information superhighway and the communications supermarket**
  by Geoff Mulgan and Ivan Briscoe
  ISBN 1 898309 32 9 £4.95 pbk 52pp
  Makes the case for a new form of ownership for the main communications infrastructure, involving service providers in an open association.

- **Taking Tax out of Politics: seven maxims for tax policy in the late 1990s**
  Sir Douglas Hague & Geoff Mulgan
  ISBN 1 898309 86 8 £4.95 18pp
  Tax is the most fiercely contested issue in Western politics. The authors set out seven maxims to define tax policies in the years ahead, arguing in particular for widening the tax base and lowering rates.

Project Reports

- **How are Charities Accountable?**
  John Plummer
  ISBN 1 898309 97 3 £9.95 pbk 97pp
  A study of the approaches to governance and accountability developed by twelve major charities in Britain
  This report contains the most detailed survey yet on how charities are accountable to their various stakeholders and to the causes they serve.

- **Parental Leave: the price of family values?**
  Helen Wilkinson, Ivan Briscoe & Martin Kaye
  ISBN 1 898309 67 1 £4.95 pbk 77pp
  This study contains a detailed analysis of why parental leave is becoming a key policy issue, through an extensive survey of parental leave in sixteen countries, and an assessment of the lessons to be learned.

- **Politics Without Frontiers: the role of political parties in Europe's future**
  Mark Leonard
  ISBN 1 898309 63 9 £9.95 pbk 92pp
  The author shows how Europe's citizens feel more distant than ever from political decision making, and argues how an effective link can be provided between the public and decision makers.

- **The Proposal: giving marriage back to the people**
  Helen Wilkinson
  ISBN 1 898309 28 0 £4.95 pbk 66pp
  Drawing on historical evidence and international examples, this report argues that the institution of marriage can be revived if the institution itself is brought up to date.

- **Saving Sense: a new approach to encourage saving**
  Ben Jupp
  ISBN 1 898309 38 8 £9.95 pbk 66pp
  This report discusses the growing importance of savings for both retirement and short-term needs and shows why current policies to encourage saving are failing.

Commentaries – These short papers are produced at short notice and are a response to current political debate.

- **The Athenian Option: radical reform for the House of Lords**
  Anthony Barnett and Peter Carty
  £2.95
  Establishes principles and advocates practical experiments for setting up a new more popular second chamber. The report suggests creating PP – people's peers – chosen in the same way as jurors through the electoral roll to scrutinise legislation.

- **Britain: the California of Europe? What the UK can learn from the West Coast**
  Charles Leadbeater
  £2.95
  California provides an example of how Britain might flourish in the next century. The author argues that its development of the 'knowledge economy', based on IT and services, can and should be pursued in Great Britain.

- **Employee Mutuals: the 21st century trade union?**
  Geoff Mulgan & Tom Bentley
  ISBN 1 898309 92 2 £5
  As the jobs market becomes more insecure and self-employment increases, a new way to empower workers is needed. Employee mutuals that manage workers, provide occupational benefits and offer professional training could be one solution.

- **Fair Game: tackling monopoly in sports broadcasting**
  Julian LeGrand & Bill New
  £2.95
  This report argues that the government must take urgent action to safeguard key sporting events. It recommends a new body, the Sports Broadcasting Regulator, which would act as a 'viewer's referee', controlling pricing and preserving the crown jewels of British sport for the nation.

- **Making Europe Popular: the search for European identity**
  Mark Leonard
  £2.95
  An interim report on the European Union's failure to engage with the citizens of its member states and measure it could take to help foster European identity.

- **Mistakeholding: whatever happened to Labour's big idea?**
  Charles Leadbeater and Geoff Mulgan
  £2.50
  A critique of the principles of stakeholding and recommendations to help create a more flexible and entrepreneurial model of stakeholding.

- **Reasonable force: the place of compulsion in securing adequate pensions**
  Benn Jupp
  £2.95
  Drawing on the experiences of other countries, the author explores the options for pension reform and makes recommendations for achieving target pensions through a form of compulsory saving.

- **Soft sell or hard policies: how can the parties best appeal to women?**
  Helen Wilkinson and Shelagh Diplock
  £2.95
  Analysis of how the main parties approach women voters and women's recent voting patterns; highlights policies that are especially important to women.

2000 *Publications*

- **Entrepreneurship and the Wired Life**
  Fernando Flores & John Gray
  ISBN: 1 841800 20 1

- **The Third Way to a Good Society**
  Amitai Etzioni
  ISBN: 1 841800 30 9

- **Working Together: creating a better environment for cross sector partnerships**
  Ben Jupp
  ISBN: 1 841800 25 2

- **The Post-modern State and the World Order, 2nd Edition**
  Robert Cooper
  ISBN: 1 841800 10 4

- **Futures for Dentistry**
  Tom Bentley & Ben Jupp
  ISBN: 1 841800 15 5

- **Patient Power: choice for the NHS**
  Peter Lilly
  ISBN: 1 841800 35 X

- **People before Structures**
  Paul Bricknell
  ISBN: 1 841800 80 5

- **Enterprise Learning**
  Matthew Horne
  ISBN: 1 8410406

- **Linking Home and School**
  Ken Worpole
  ISBN: 1 841800 50 3

European Policy Forum

Address	125 Pall Mall
	London
	SW1Y 5EA
Tel	020 7839 7565
Fax	020 7839 7339
Email	epfltd@compuserve.com
Website	None
President	Graham Mather MEP
Director	Frank Vibert
Executive Secretary	Alison Denyer
Research Assistant	James Temple-Smithson
PA to the President	Dawn Hawkins
Number of Employees	5
Cost of Subscription	N/A
How to Order	By Post, Phone or Fax
Credit Cards	Visa, Mastercard

History and Objectives

The European Policy Forum was created in 1992 in order to develop a new agenda of ideas for Britain and Europe.

The EPF is a non-partisan combination of discussion forum, channel for international contacts, and think tank. It brings together policymakers, scholars, companies and business organisations. It does not have a corporate view but encourages thinking on market led solutions to public policy problems and decentralised solutions to institutional questions

Since its foundation the EPF has established a programme of events in London, Brussels and elsewhere in Europe , as well as an active publications programme. It has established a profile as a source of new ideas on public policy and institutions in Britain and Europe with a special interest in regulatory, institutional and constitutional economics.

Publications

Regulatory/Competition Policy

- **Competition Policy in the Community**
  Diana Rowen, December 1992 (£5.00)

- **The Future of Industry Regulation in the UK – A Report of an Independent Inquiry**
  Dr Cento Veljanovski, January 1993 (£10.00)

- **Technology Policy and EC Competitiveness**
  Diana Rowen, April 1993 (£5.00)

- **The Need for a Regulatory Charter**
  Dr Cento Veljanovski, August 1993 (£5.00)

- **Power in Perspective – Players, Performers, Prospects and Potential Privatisations**
  Keith Boyfield, July 1994 (£20.00)

- **Telecommunications Regulation in the UK**
  Maev Sullivan & John Prior, July 1994 (£5.00)

- **Fresh Approaches to Regulating Media**
  Professor John Kay, June 1995 (£5.00)

- **The Hidden Costs of Regulation in Europe**
  Peter Stein, Thomas Hopkins, Roland Vaubel, September 1995 (£7.50)

- **Report by the Commission on the Regulation of Privatised Utilities**
  EPF/Hansard Society, January 1997 (£30.00)

- **Privatisation: A Prize Worth Pursuing?**
  Keith Boyfield, May 1997 (£30.00)

- **Reforming Regulation "One Agency; One Law"**
  Dr Cento Veljanovski January 1998 (£5.00)

- **Better Regulation of Utilities in Europe**
  D Dimitrakopoulos, L Miles, E Page, R Wurzel, Centre for European Union Studies, University of Hull,
  September 1998 (£15.00)

- **New Ideas on Competition & Regulation**
  Dr Cento Veljanovski & Professor Patrick Dunleavy, October 1999 (£10.00)

Economics & Finance

- **Unravelling the Rouble Regime**
  Jozef M van Brabant, November 1992 (£5.00)

- **Britain, Europe and the Square Mile**
  Report by Matthew Bishop, Evan Davis and Phedon Nicolaides commissioned from the Forum by the
  Corporation of London.

- **The Independence of the Bank of England and the Maastricht Treaty**
  Frank Vibert, May 1993 (£5.00)

- **Paths to Monetary Union, Views of the Future of EMU**
  Walter, Mentré, de Maigret, Salin and Flemming, December 1993 (£7.50)

- **Accounting Standards Applicable to State Owned Enterprises in the European Union**
  Professor Simon Archer, January 1994 (£5.00)

- **Proto-EMU as an Alternative to Maastricht**
  Dr John Williamson, July 1995 (£5.00)

- **European Competitiveness and Employment Generation**
  Prof Walter Eltis, November 1995 (£10.00)

- **Economic and Legal Aspects of the Transition to Economic and Monetary Union**
  Dr Andrew Sentance, December 1995 (£10.00)

- **Will there be a Monetary Union and Should Britain join?**
  Prof Walter Eltis, December 1995 (£5.00)

- **Europe's Unemployment Problem: Lessons from the German Labour Market**
  Dr Steven Englander PhD, February 1996 (£5.00)

- **Liberalisation of Financial Services**
  Stephen Woolcock, October 1997 (£10.00)

- **Sense on EMU**
  Andrew Tyrie MP February 1998 (£10.00)

- **How to Share the Burden of the EU Budget**
  Rebecca Stokes, May 1998 (£10.00)

- **Is Britain Inflation-Prone?**
  David Kern and Giles Keating, August 1998 (£5.00)

- **Is Tax Competition Harmful?**
  Keith Marsden, December 1998 (£15.00)

Institutional/Constitutional Issues

- **Decentralising Power in Europe**
  Frank Vibert, May 1992

- **The UK Presidency**
  Frank Vibert, June 1992

- **Reforming Select Committees**
  David Hencke et al, July 1992

- **Protocol on the Application of Subsidiarity in the European Community**
  Sept 1992

- **Subsidiarity: No Panacea**
  Andrew Tyrie & Andrew Adonis
  December 1992 (£5.00)

- **Modernising British Government**
  Rt Hon John Patten MP and Frank Vibert, March 1993 (£5,00)

- **Britain and the Future Europe**
  Sir Michael Jenkins KCMG, October 1993 (£5.00)

- **A Proposal for a European Constitution – Report of the European Constitutional Group, December 1993 Summary**
  (£10.00)

- **The Future Role of the European Commission**
  Frank Vibert, May 1994 (£7.50)

- **Solving Britain's Euro Crisis**
  Graham Mather, January 1995 (£5.00)

- **A Core Agenda for the 1996 IGC**
  Frank Vibert, May 1995 (£12.50)

- **The Developing Role of the European Court of Justice**
  Various contributors, August 1995 (£25.00)

- **The European Court of Justice: A Case Study in Judicial Activism**
  Sir Patrick Neill QC, August 1995 (£10.00)

- **Westminster and Europe: Proposals for Change: The Role of National Parliaments in the EU**
  Graham Leicester (£7.50) (EPF/Hansard Society)

- **The Case of Belgium (Proportional Representation)**
  Prof Lieven de Winter, July 1997 (£10.00)

- **Brussels on Britain: the UK in Europe viewed from Brussels**
  Introduced by Graham Mather MEP, Graham Watson MEP and Richard Corbett MEP Survey report by James Temple-Smithson (£10.00)

Accountability & Roles of Central/ Local Government

- **Accountability to the Public**
  Papers by Prof John Stewart, Prof Norman Lewis & Diane Longley, December 1992 (£5.00)

- **Responsibility, Accountability & Standards in Government – Memorandum to the Treasury & Civil Service Select Committee of the House of Commons**
  Graham Mather, March 1993

- **How to Reinvent British Government**
  Prof Norman Lewis, May 1993 (£7.50)

- **The Local Government Review Itself Reviewed**
  Prof John Stewart, July 1993 (£5.00)

- **Making Good Government Seem Easy, Lessons from New Zealand's Economic & Policy Reforms**
  Graham Mather, October 1993 (£5.00)

- **Civil Service Numbers: Analysis and Proposals**
  Jonathan Smith & David Gold, October 1993 (£5.00)

- **Independent Local Government**
  Graham Allen MP, November 1993 (£5.00)

- **The Local Government Review, A Crisis of Credibility**
  Steve Leach, November 1993 (£5.00)

- **Better Legislation**
  Graham Mather, January 1994 (£5.00)

- **The New Local Governance**
  Michael Clarke et al, February 1994 (£7.50)

- **Changing the Machinery: A Perspective of Market Reforms in Government**
  Sir Duncan Nichol, April 1994 (£5.00)

- **Reforming Government in Practice, Lessons & Prospects**
  Speeches by Sir Roger Douglas & Dr Graham Scott, May 1994

- **Civil Service Reform: A Case for More Radicalism**
  Barry Legg MP, November 1994 (£5.00)

- **Britain's Civil Service and the Machinery of Government**
  Graham Mather, December 1994 (£5.00)

- **The Public Works Directive: A Study of its implications for Local Authorities & Contractors**
  Matthew Perry, April 1995 (£7.50)

- **Leaks by Civil Servants**
  Graham Mather, September 1995 (£7.50)

- **Leaks by Civil Servants: The Picture in 1995**
  Graham Mather, December 1995 (£7.50).

- **Leaks Continue**
  Graham Mather, December 1995 (£7.50)

- **A Better Machine: Government for the 21st Century**
  Sir Peter Kemp and David Walker, May 1996 (£7.50)

- **Leaks by Civil Servants: The Picture in 1996**
  Graham Mather, December 1996 (£10.00).

- **Leaks by Civil Servants: The Picture in 1997**
  Graham Mather, March 1998, (£10.00).

- **Re-Building Trust? Central-local relationships and the new Millennium**
  Michael Clark July 1998 (£10.00)

- **New Labour – A Third Way?**
  Lord Plant of Highfield July 1998 (£10.00)

Home Affairs / Social Policy

- **Reforming the BBC**
  Chris Hopson, November 1992 (£5.00)

- **Crime in Britain**
  Dr David Pyle, May 1993 (£5.00)

- **Prospects for Trade Unions in Britain**
  Graham Mather, September 1993 (£5.00)

- **The Journey Into Work (A bright future?)**
  by Royston Flude, May 1999 (£10.00)

- **Rights and the Free Market**
  Graham Mather, September 1999 (£7.50)

- **The Single Market for European Advertisers**
  Keith Boyfield, May 2000 (£25.00)

Defence

- **The Eurovision Defence Contest**
  George Brock, November 1993 (£5.00)

International Trade / Investment

- **Making Sense of European Trade Administration**
  Alex McLoughlin, December 1995 (£5.00)

- **Free Investment: The Next Stage for Global Free Trade**
  Frank Vibert, December 1996 (£5.00)

Insurance / Pensions / Health

- **A Health Cheque for All, Proposals for a Mixed Market in Healthcare**
  Mark Bassett, January 1994 (£7.50)

- **A Mixed Market in Healthcare**
  Prof Benito Arrunada, Mr Brendan H Devlin, Prof Fleix Gutzwiller, Prof Chris Ham, Prof Hans Maarse, Dr Blaise Martin, Dr Hans Wenkebach, November 1995 (£10.00)

- **Private vs. Public Healthcare in Germany: A model for other countries**
  Dr Wilfried Prewo, January 1997 (£5.00)

- **The Insurance Solution**
  Philip Booth and Gerry Dickinson, July 1997 (£15.00)

- **The "Myth" of National Insurance**
  Rosalind Stevens-Ströhmann, October 1997 (£5.00)

- **Insurance Regulation in the UK**
  Mike Kipling and Rosalind Stevens-Ströhmann, November 1997 (£5.00)

- **Tax Treatment of Savings for Pension Products in the EU**
  Dr Ann Robinson, November 1997 (£5.00)

- **Product Developments in the UK Insurance Industry**
  Harry Taylor, November 1997 (£10.00)

- **Insurance – the Solution to Welfare Problems?**
  Various contributors, May 1998, (£10.00)

Agriculture

- **British Farming – A Vision of the Future**
  Ben Gill CBE, November 1998 (£5.00)

- **Reform of the Common Agricultural Policy, The Use of Exit Bonds**
  Philip Poole, December 1993 Out of Stock

- **Reforming the European Union's Common Fisheries Policy**
  Dr Federico Foders, February 1994 (£5.00)

- **Toward a CAP for the next century**
  Prof Stefan Tangermann & Prof Josling, April 1995 (£10.00)

Enlargement of the European Union

- **Switzerland and Europe: Problem or Pattern**
  Professor Clive Church, November 1993 (£7.50)

- **What is the chance for democracy in Central and Eastern Europe?**
  Prof Richard Rose, November 1994 (£7.50)

- **Perspectives in Europe**
  Various contributors including Prof Helen Wallace,
  January 1996 (£7.50)

- **Europe: Time for Pragmatism**
  Graham Leicester and Miguel Herrero de Minon
  March 1996 (£7.50)

- **Structured Flexibility in the EU**
  Frank Vibert, August 1996 (£12.00)

Fabian Society

Address	11 Dartmouth Street
	Westminster
	London
	SW1H 9BH
Tel	020 7222 4900
Fax	020 7976 7153
Email	info@fabian-society.org.uk
Website	www.fabian-society.org.uk
General Secretary	Michael Jacobs
Research Director	Gavin Kelly
Conference Director	Ben Egan
Finance Officer	Margaret McGillen
Membership Officer	Giles Wright
Administration Officer	Cyril O'Keefe
Administration Officer	Tina Howes
Number of Employees	8
Cost of Membership	Corporate £200, Individual £31.00 (waged), £14.00 (unwaged)
How to order	By post or phone

History

The Fabian Society is Britain's oldest think tank. Concerned since its foundation with evolutionary political and economic reform, and progressive social change, the Fabian Society has played a central role for more than a century in the development of political ideas and public policy on the left of centre. It is unique among think tanks in being a democratically constituted membership organisation. Its 5,500 members engage in political education and argument through the Society's publications, conferences and other events, its quarterly journal Fabian Review and a network of local societies and meetings.

The Fabian Society was founded in 1884, taking its name from the Roman General Quintus Fabius, who was known as Cunctator from his strategy of delaying his attack until the right moment. Leading figures in the early years included Beatrice and Sidney Webb, George Bernard Shaw and H G Wells. The Society has no collective policy, beyond the broad aims of democratic socialism and the promotion of human rights both nationally and internationally.

The Society was one of the founders of the Labour Party, and it has remained affiliated to the Labour Party. At the 1945 landslide victory, the Parliamentary Labour Party was said to "look just like an enormous Fabian School". Leading figures in the post-war years included Clem Attlee, Hugh Gaitskell, Harold Wilson, Tony Crosland, Denis Healey, Tony Benn and Shirley Williams.

At the even greater landslide of 1997, almost 200 Fabians were elected, and twenty out of twenty-two Cabinet members are Fabians including Tony Blair, Goirdon Brown and Robin Cook. Leading academics include Raymond Plant, Ben Pimlott and David Marquand.

Today, the Fabian Society aims to be a "critical friend" of the Labour Government.

Objectives

To contribute to a renaissance of political ideas on the left of centre; to their coherence and relevance, and to the commitment of the public to them.

To help influence the philosophy and policy of the Labour Government and through this to contribute to its re-election.

To help raise public debate and public understanding of political issues in general, particualkrly among Fabian Society and Labour Party members, and among young people.

Publications

Pamphlets

- **538 Sustainable development: Greening the economy**
  Michael Jacobs
  ISBN: 0716305380
  July 1990, £5.00, 28pp
  Sustainability requires a new set of economic objecives, and constraints on the market economy. Government action is required to achieve change on the scale needed, and to mitigate inequitable effects.
  paperback, A5

- **539 Controlling inflation: Two views**
  Gerald Holtham and Neil MacKinnon
  ISBN: 0716305399
  July 1990, £5.00, 36pp, paperback, A5

- **540 After the Cold War: Building on the Alliances**
  Mike Gapes
  ISBN: 0716305402
  Sept 1990, £5.00, 28pp, paperback, A5

- **541 Quotas now: Women in the Labour Party**
  Rachel Brooks, Angela Eagle, Clare Short
  ISBN: 0716305410
  Sept 1990, £5.00, 24pp, paperback, A5

- **542 A public services pay policy**
  William Brown and Bob Rowthorn
  ISBN: 0716305429
  November 1990, £5.00, 20pp
  Calls for a Pay Advisory Commission, on the model of ACAS, to provide the data on which comparability exercises and pay negotiations can be carried out.
  paperback, A5

- **543 A European Environment Charter**
  Nick Robins
  ISBN: 0716305437
  January 1991, £5.00, 24pp

Outlines the case for an Environment Charter, on the lines of the Social Charter, to specify rights and obligations of the Community, member states and individuals. Also calls for an accompanying action programme of measures

paperback, A5

- **544 Targeting competitive industries**
P A Geroski and K G Knight
ISBN: 0716305445
April 1991, £5.00, 20pp
To develop competitive advantage, clusters of geographically concentrated industrial activity should be encouraged. The unevenness of economic development must be accepted. Policy needs to be sector-specific and locally
paperback, A5

- **545 Making a minimum wage work**
Fred Bayliss
ISBN: 0716305453
May 1991, £5.00, 20pp
Argues in favour of a minimum wage. It could have major benefits for the low paid, without sparking off adverse economic consequences, provided that it is introduced gradually and the correct steps are taken to mitigate its effects.
paperback, A5

- **546 South Africa: Out of the laager?**
Martin Plaut
ISBN: 0716305461
May 1991, £5.00, 25pp,
Clearly explains recent changes and prospects for peace, and argues that despite recent problems, the underlying pressures on both the Government and the ANC make a negotiated settlement likely.
paperback, A5

- **547 Economic Short Termism: A Cure for the British Disease**
David Pitt-Watson
ISBN: 071630547X
July 1991, £5.00, 25pp,
If the problem of short-termism in British industry is to be solved, we must first tackle the failings of both the City and industrial management.
paperback, A5

- **548 The USSR and the West: A Medium-Term Strategy**
Adrian Hyde-Price
ISBN: 0716305488
July 1991, £5.00, 21pp
The West needs a medium-term strategy to bridge the gap between short-term considerations of whether to aid the Soviet Union and long-term visions of a common European home.
paperback, A5

- **549 Quality, equality, democracy: Improving public services**
Margaret Hodge
ISBN: 0716305496
September 1991, £5.00, 24pp
Drawing on her experience as leader of Islington Council, Margaret Hodge argues that empowerment must be about decentralisation and democratisation of public services.
paperback, A5

- **550 Labour's First Year: A sense of socialism**
Simon Crine
ISBN: 071630550X
September 1991, £5.00, 24pp
Outlines a programme which a Labour government could enact in its first year, taking account of financial and possible parliamentary constraints. (Foreword by Chris Smith MP)
paperback, A5

- **551 Reviving the Regions**
Jim Taylor
ISBN: 0716305518
November 1991, £5.00, 24pp
Proposes a series of fiscal measures to encourage regional economic performance, and the diversion of public resources away from already-congested areas.
paperback, A5

- **552 A National Housing Bank**
Stephen Merrett and Ross Cranston
ISBN: 0716305526
January 1992, £5.00, 20pp
Need for good quality rented accommodation, from local authorities, housing associations and private landlords. A national Housing Bank would provide finance.
paperback, A5

- **553 Labour's Choice: The Fabian debates**
John Smith, Bryan Gould, Margaret Beckett, John Prescott
ISBN: 0716305534
June 1992, £5.00, 25pp
Key speeches from the candidates in the leadership and deputy leadership elections.
paperback, A5

- **554 The Name of the Rose**
David Lipsey
ISBN: 0716305542
July 1992, £5.00, 24pp
What should the long-term aims of the Labour Party be? Discussion of market economics; alliance with Liberal Democrats; change of name.
paperback, A5

- **555 Southern Discomfort**
  Giles Radice
  ISBN: 0 7163 0555 0
  Sept 1992, £5.00, 25pp
  Attitudes to Labour in southern marginal constituencies.
  paperback, A5

- **556 Social justice, Labour and the new Right**
  Raymond Plant
  ISBN: 0716305569
  February 1993, £5.00, 20pp
  Examines the concept of social justice, criticises the New Right's theories, and argues for the creation of a new redistributive consensus.
  paperback, A5

- **557 Making sense of pensions**
  Frank Field and Matthew Owen
  ISBN: 0716315577
  March 1993, £5.00, 20pp
  Explains the different types of pension; how pension schemes work; who controls them; how flexible they are; how they are funded.
  paperback, A5

- **558 What's wrong with Fabianism**
  David Piachaud
  ISBN: 0715305585
  June 1993, £5.00, 20pp
  Criticises Fabians' preference for state action, their static view of society, and arrogance; recommends a new "opportunities" policy for all: a commitment to full employment, better education, redistribution of wealth.
  paperback, A5

- **559 All for One: The future of the unions**
  Philip Bassett and Alan Cave
  ISBN: 0716305593
  July 1993, £5.00, 28pp
  How the trade unions can recover from their declining influence and membership
  paperback, A5

- **560 More Southern Discomfort a year on – taxing and spending**
  Giles Radice and Stephen Pollard
  ISBN: 0716305607
  September 1993, £5.00, 20pp
  Surveys the attitudes of key swing voters in the South of England, concentrating on taxation and benefits; suggests ways in which Labour can win them over.
  paperback, A5

- **561 Beyond the Town Hall: Reinventing Local Government**
Margaret Hodge and Wendy Thompson
ISBN: 0716305615
February 1994, £5.00, 24pp
The local community should be given more power; this change requires structural changes also in central government.
paperback, A5

- **562 What Price A Safe Society?**
Tony Blair and 1994 Fabian New Year School
ISBN: 0716305623
April 1994, £5.00, 40pp
Crime and punishment: the need for a new approach
paperback, A5

- **563 Fair Is Efficient: A socialist agenda for fairness**
Gordon Brown
ISBN: 0716305631
April 1994, £5.00, 26pp
Far from socialism and equality being the cause of inefficiency, they are the pre-requisites of economic efficiency.
paperback, A5

- **564 Towards a Social Economy: Trading for a social purpose**
Peter Welch and Malcolm Coles
ISBN: 071630564X
May 1994, £5.00, 20pp
Argues for organisations trading for a social purpose, which are in neither the public nor the private sector; as recommended by the European Commission.
paperback, A5

- **565 Socialism**
Tony Blair
ISBN: 0716305658
July 1994, £5.00, 7pp
Outlines the history of socialist ideas in 20th C Britain, rejects Marxist analysis, and argues that ethical socialism has re-emerged as the unifying feature of socialism.
paperback, A5

- **566 Infertility, feminism and the new technologies**
Sally Keeble
ISBN: 0716305666
July 1994, £5.00, 20pp
Freedom for women has to be the ability to say yes, as well as no, to having children.
paperback, A5

- **567 Reforming Welfare: American lessons**
Simon Crine
ISBN: 0716305674
September 1994, £5.00, 28pp
Analyses Clinton's attempts to reform welfare, and argues that universal benefits are the most efficient means of relieving poverty.
paperback, A5

- **568 Any Southern Comfort?**
Giles Radice and Stephen Pollard
ISBN: 0716305682
September 1994, £5.00, 16pp
Third report on floating voters' attitudes in Southern England; presents a more encouraging picture of Labour's standing.
paperback, A5

- **569 Beyond the patronage state**
Tony Wright
ISBN: 0716305690
February 1995, £5.00, 32pp
Reveals the growth of quangos and the abuse of patronage; and offers a comprehensive package of reform.
paperback, A5

- **570 The Nation's Health**
Hugh Bayley
ISBN: 0715305704
June 1995, £5.00, 28pp
Proposes three principles for the NHS: equity, efficiency and accountability. Rejects the internal market, but accepts the shift in power from hospitals to doctors.
paperback, A5

- **571 Let us face the future: the 1945 anniversary lecture**
Tony Blair
ISBN: 0716305712
August 1995, £5.00, 16pp
The lessons of 1945; New Labour, eternal values. Fabian lecture celebrating the 1945 election victory.
paperback, A5

- **572 Against a single currency**
Roger Berry
ISBN: 0716305720
November 1995, £5.00, 24pp
The Future of Europe debate; monetary union.
paperback, A5

- **573 For a single currency**
  Keith Hill
  ISBN: 0716305739
  November 1995, £5.00, 24pp
  The Future of Europe debate; monetary union.
  paperback, A5,

- **574 Health Crisis – What Crisis?**
  Hugh Bayley
  ISBN: 0716305747
  April 1996, £5.00, 30pp
  Proceedings of the Fabian/SHA New Year Conference, 1996
  paperback, A5

- **575 Global Business: Global Rights**
  Denis MacShane
  ISBN: 0716305755
  June 1996, £5.00, 28pp
  Argues for a social clause in all major international trade agreements which guarantees a set of minimum standards for employees worldwide.
  paperback, A5

- **576 Long to reign over us?**
  Paul Richards
  ISBN: 0716305763
  August 1996, £5.00, 25pp
  The monarchy should continue, but it should be stripped of its remaining powers, democratised and given a purely ceremonial role.
  paperback, A5

- **577 New questions for Socialism**
  Chris Smith
  ISBN: 0716305771
  October 1996, £5.00, 16pp
  A vision of a new libertarian democratic socialism, committed to tackling poverty and recognising the benefits of collective action
  paperback, A5

- **578 No more Big Brother**
  Paul Corrigan
  ISBN: 071630578X
  November 1996, £5.00, 12pp
  Labour should change the nature of local government from service provider to service watchdog.
  paperback, A5

- **579 Who Wins Dares: New Labour – New Politics**
  Tony Wright
  ISBN: 0716305798
  March 1997, £5.00, 16pp
  The radicalism that changed the Labour Party must now change the country, and the way it is governed.
  paperback, A5

- **580 Low Cost Socialism**
  Gordon Marsden
  ISBN: 0716305801
  July 1997, £5.00, 32pp
  Articles by Bernard Crick, Anne Campbell MP, Andrew Adonis, Caroline Abrahams, Karen Grudzien and Jeremy Beecham
  paperback, A5

- **581 Labour's next steps: Tackling social exclusion**
  Peter Mandelson
  ISBN: 071630581X
  September 1997, £5.00, 10pp
  Announcement of the Social Exclusion Unit to tackle poverty; based on Labour's vision of a modern, competitive, socially cohesive country.
  paperback, A5

- **582 Information Age Government: Delivering the Blair Revolution**
  Liam Byrne
  ISBN: 0716305828
  November 1997, £5.00 40pp
  Argues that Labour must automate, integrate and devolve the civil service organisations, and describes how Labour can harness the power of business, new technology and local leaders to do so. Reprint of DP38
  paperback, A5

- **583 Creative futures: Culture, identity and national renewal**
  Chris Smith, Trevor Phillips, Bridget McConnell, Jude Kelly
  ISBN: 0716305836
  December 1997, £5.00, 28pp
  The Labour Government is refashioning Britain's sense of national identity and is putting a new emphasis on culture and the arts.
  paperback, A5

- **584 Arms and the man: Renewing the armed services**
  Eric Joyce
  ISBN: 0716305844
  March 1998, £10.00, 30pp
  The services must root out prejudice based upon gender, race and class, and must adapt to a modern environment. (Second edition of DP37)
  paperback, A5

- **585 High Time or High Tide for Labour Women?**
Maria Eagle and Joni Lovenduski
ISBN: 0716305852
March 1998, £5.00, 30pp
Positive action is still needed to ensure proper equality of male and female representation in parliament and in local government.
paperback, A5

- **587 Reforming the Lords and Changing Britain**
John Osmond
ISBN: 0716305879
September 1998, £5.00, 32pp
Argues for a reformed Upper Chamber that would be representative of the nations and regions of the United Kingdom

- **588 The Third Way: New Politics for a New Century**
Tony Blair
ISBN: 0716305887
September 1998, £4.00, 20pp
Tony Blair sets out his vision of the Third Way as a modernised social democracy, passionate in its commitment to social justice and the other goals of the centre-left, but flexible, innovative and forward looking in the means to achieve them.

- **589 Must Labour Win?**
David Marquand
ISBN: 0716305895
December 1998. Price £5.00, 16PP
Argues for a left of centre politics based upon pluralism rather than centralism, and rejects the 'winner takes it all' mentality of 20th century British politics.

- **590 Is New Labour Working?**
Various authors
ISBN: 0716305909
August 1999, £5.00, 58pp
Seven Government Ministers set out what they have been doing in their first two years, what their plans are, and why. Seven independent commentators evaluate their performance and suggest new directions for policies.

- **591 Environmental Modernisation: The new Labour Agenda**
Michael Jacobs
ISBN: 0716305917
October 1999, £5.00, 50pp
Argues that environmental issues can be understood in terms of the key trends of the modern world – globalisation, individualisation, and rising inequality. It shows how the environment can be incoprorated into New Labour's Third Way, and sets out a far reaching policy agenda.

- **592 Modern Socialism**
Lionel Jospin
ISBN: 0716305925
November 1999, £5.00, 16pp
The French Prime Minister sets out his philosophy of socialism in the modern world. He describes social-
ism as a way 'of putting the market economy at the service of the people'.

- **593 Citizens and Taxes**
Selina Chen
ISBN: 0716305933
December 1999, £5.00, 28pp
A more democratic and accountable state requires governments to justify their taxing and spending decisions
more clearly to their citizens.

- **594 Is the Party Over?**

Paul Richards

£6.95

- **595 Making Flexibility Work**

Denis MacShane and Chris Brewster

£10.00

- **596 Winning for Women**

Harriet Harmen and Deborah Mattinson

£6.00

- **597 Closing the Casino: Reform of the global financial system**

John Grieve Smith

£6.00

- **598 Coping with post-democracy**

Colin Crouch

£6.95

Fabian Discussion Papers

- **DP 1 Telecommunications in the UK**

  Nicholas Garnham

  Date: October 1990 Price £: 5.00 Pages: 24 ISBN: 0 7163 3009 1

  British Telecom should be broken up into ten regional companies, to improve services and management efficiency. Labour should abandon its commitment to introduce a national broad-band fibre optic network,
  which would be expensive

  Format: paperback, A4

- **DP 2 The Hidden Wiring**

  Peter Hennessy

  Date: November 1990 Price £: 5.00 Pages: 12 ISBN: 0 7163 3010 5

  If Parliament is to function effectively, a vigorous Opposition, well-resourced select committees and 'awk-
  ward' backbenchers are all essential. This underlines the need to get the right calibre of individual.

  Format: paperback, A4

- **DP 3 East meets West: Policies for a Common European Home**

  Kevin Featherstone and John Hiden

  Date: January 1991 Price £: 5.00 Pages: 20 ISBN: 0 7163 3001 6

  The EC needs to define its Ostpolitik, which must include a timetable for East European states to join the
  Community. The EC would be better able to help, and to absorb new members, if it speeded up the process
  of its own

  Format: paperback, A4

- **DP 4 The democratic deficit and the European parliament**

  Juliet Lodge

  Date: March 1991 Price £: 5.00 Pages: 20 ISBN: 0 7163 3002 4

  Governments operating within the EC framework are not subject to adequate democratic scrutiny. Attempts
  to plug this deficit by increasing the involvement of national parliaments are misplaced.

  Format: paperback, A4

- **DP 5 Regulation and ownership of the major utilities**

  Michael Waterson

  Date: May 1991 Price £: 10.00 Pages: 21 ISBN: 0 7163 3003 2

  Regulation is necessary to prevent abuse of natural monopolies, but the type of regulation appropriate
  depends on the specific industry.

  Format: paperback, A4

- **DP 6 Labour's Environment Protection Executive**

  Ann Taylor

  Date: July 1991 Price £: 5.00 Pages: 20 ISBN: 0 7163 3004 0

  Gives details of the structure, powers and responsibilities of Labour's proposed Environment Protection
  Executive, and explains how it will interact with local authorities and other existing institutions.

  Format: paperback, A4

- **DP 7 Accounting for change: Proposals for reform of Audit and Accounting**
Austin Mitchell, Anthony Puxty, Prem Sikka, Hugh Willmott
Date: August 1991 Price £:10.00 Pages: 32 ISBN: 0 7163 3005 9
Puts forward a series of proposals to reform accountancy and audit, including the creation of a single, independent regulatory body, and the expansion of corporate reports to include information on environmental policy and health.
Format: paperback, A4

- **DP 8 Labour and Whitehall: A Fabian Enquiry into the Machinery of Government**
Stephen Tindale (ed)
Date: September 1991 Price £: 5.00 Pages: 32 ISBN: 0 7163 3006 7
Discusses issues such as low outside advisers can best be deployed in Whitehall, how the higher civil service can be made more representative, and how executive agencies can delive Labour's programme.
Format: paperback, A4

- **DP 9 Disarmament in a changing world**
Caroline Kennedy, Colin McInnes, Len Scott
Date: October 1991 Price £: 5.00 Pages: 24 ISBN: 0 7163 3007 5
Calls for the UK to participate in future START talks and to press for Soviet and US concessions on deployments of Anti-Ballistic Missiles.
Format: paperback, A4

- **DP10 A New Model Army: Towards a European defence community**
Calum Macdonald
Date: November 1991 Price £: 5.00 Pages: 36 ISBN: 0 7163 3008 3
Argues the economic and political case for replacing national armed forces with European ones.
Format: paperback, A4

- **DP11 Regional Power and Local Government in Europe**
Mike Lee and Jonathan McLeod
Date: November 1991 Price £: 5.00 Pages: 24 ISBN: 0 7163 3011 3
Looks at the financing of local and regional government in East and West Europe, and draws conclusions for Britain.
Format: paperback, A4

- **DP12 Beyond Economics: European Government after Maastricht**
Stephen Tindale and David Miliband
Date: November 1991 Price £: 5.00 Pages: 25 ISBN: 0 7163 3012 1
Looks at the structure of European institutions which will be needed to take the EC beyond economic integration to joint action in the face of common political problems.
Format: paperback, A4

- **DP13 Towards a wider, deeper, federal Europe**
David Martin
Date: December 1992 Price £: 5.00 Pages: 24 ISBN: 0 7163 3013 X
Enlargement of the European Community is both inevitable and desirable. Discusses which states should be included, and when.
Format: paperback, A4

- **DP14 Euro-Monetarism Why Britain was ensnared and how it should escape**
Edward Balls
Date: December 1992 Price £: 7.50 Pages: 24 ISBN: 0 7163 3014 8
Calls for a non-monetarist but pro-European alternative to Britain's damaging boom-bust cycles, including an independent UK central bank, a policy for profits and pay, and a medium term industrial strategy.
Format: paperback, A4

- **DP15 Taxing the speculator: The route to forex stability**
Ruth Kelly
Date: May 1993   Price £: 7.50 Pages: 28 ISBN: 0 7163 3015 6
Analyses the nature of foreign exchange speculation and proposes an international transactions tax to foster a more long term outlook by the markets.
Format: paperback, A4

- **DP16 Private Pensions for All: Squaring the circle**
Frank Field and Matthew Owen
Date: July 1993   Price £: 10.00 Pages: 24 ISBN: 0 7163 3016 4
Since the State will not be able to afford good state pensions for all, the role of the State should be to design a legal framework to achieve universal private pensions.
Format: paperback, A4

- **DP17 The Active Society: Defending Welfare**
Malcolm Wicks
Date: October 1994 Price £: 10.00 Pages: 25 ISBN: 0 7163 3017 2
Sets out social policy guidelines based on the core values of liberty, equality and community, with citizenship as the unifying concept.
Format: paperback, A4

- **DP18 Hedging our future: Regulating the derivative markets**
Ruth Kelly and Alastair Hudson
Date: November 1994 Price £: 15.00 Pages: 16 ISBN: 0 7163 3018 0
Shows how government policies can be undermined by financial markets, and proposes ways to regulate derivative markets.
Format: paperback, A4

- **DP19 Reforming the Commons**
Derek Fatchett
Date: November 1994 Price £: 10.00 Pages: 16 ISBN: 0 7163 3019 9
Argues that an incoming Labour government, committed to democratic change, can only achieve that objective if it is prepared to make its own executive powers more subject to control by Parliament.
Format: paperback, A4

- **DP20 Report of the Fabian Business Seminar on Health**
Neil Stewart (intro)
Date: June 1995   Price £: 15.00 Pages: 28 ISBN: 0 7163 3021 0
April 1995 seminar on the internal market, trusts and GP fundholding.
Sponsored by Bayer plc.
Format: paperback, A4

- **DP21 Labour and schools: Creating a local democratic framework**
  Fiona Mactaggart, Ian Wilson, John Denham
  Date: June 1995   Price £: 15.00 Pages: 25 ISBN: 0 7163 3020 2
  Three alternative suggestions for local accountability.
  Format: paperback, A4

- **DP22 The future of pensions: Revitalising Nat Insurance**
  Peter Townsend And Alan Walker
  Date: September 1995 Price £: 10.00 Pages: 28 ISBN: 0 7163 3022 9
  Recommends an improved form of National Insurance and SERPS as the most efficient and equitable way
  forward.
  Format: paperback, A4

- **DP23 Accountability not ownership: Labour and the NHS**
  Kathy Jones
  Date: December 1995 Price £: 10.00 Pages: 26 ISBN: 0 7163 3023 7
  Argues that the quality of service is more important than the name of the provider. Private provision does
  not mean the end of free healthcare.
  Format: paperback, A4

- **DP24 Corporate governance matters**
  Austin Mitchell and Prem Sikka
  Date: April 1996   Price £: 20.00 Pages: 32 ISBN: 0 7163 3024 5
  Companies have been hit by scandals, frauds and regulatory failure. The authors argue that companies should
  be run as communities in partnership with all their stakeholders.
  Format: paperback, A4

- **DP25 A partnership democracy for Europe**
  David Martin
  Date: April 1996   Price £: 7.50 Pages: 12 ISBN: 0 7163 3025 3
  Suggests ways in which the European Union could be made more democratic
  Format: paperback, A4

- **DP26 Left out of Europe?**
  Denis MacShane
  Date: September 1996 Price £: 10.00 Pages: 28 ISBN: 0 7163 3026 1
  Argues for a positive European economic agenda based on a package of reforms which recognise the close
  economic ties that Britain has with Europe; shows that EMU could have a beneficial impact on the British
  economy.
  Format: paperback, A4

- **DP27 Europe after Major: Can Labour make a difference?**
  Graham Leicester
  Date: September 1996 Price £: 10.00 Pages: 18 ISBN: 0 7163 3027 X
  Argues for entry into EMU and greater European integration.
  Format: paperback, A4

- **DP28 Earth, wind and fire: Utility regulation under new Labour**
  John Dickie
  Date: October 1996 Price £: 10.00 Pages: 24 ISBN: 0 7163 3028 8
  The regulatory framework for utilities is in disarray. Labour should embrace efficiency regulation, and recognise that profits based on real efficiency improvements best serve the public interest.
  Format: paperback, A4

- **DP29 Destiny not defeat: Reforming the Lords**
  Lord Desai & Lord Kilmarnock
  Date: January 1997 Price £: 5.00 Pages: 12 ISBN: 0 7163 3029 6
  Calls for radical change in the powers, shape and structure of the upper house of Parliament
  Format: paperback, A4

- **DP30 Hand in glove: Private sector delivering public goods**
  Jake Arnold-Forster, Mike Lee, Jon McLeod
  Date: January 1997 Price £: 15.00 Pages: 20 ISBN: 0 7163 3430 5
  New approaches to private-public partnerships. Argues for less, not more, interference by central government.
  Format: paperback, A4

- **DP31 Twelve good neighbours: The citizen as juror**
  Anna Coote & Deborah Mattinson
  Date: March 1997 Price £: 5.00 Pages: 16 ISBN: 0 7163 3031 8
  Advocates citizens' juries to enhance local decision-making and to increase a sense of involvement.
  Format: paperback, A4

- **DP32 More than the flower show: Elected mayors and democracy**
  Margaret Hodge, Steve Leach, Gerry Stoker
  Date: March 1997 Price £: 10.00 Pages: 30 ISBN: 0 7163 3032 6
  Covers the issue of elected mayors from theory to practice; considers alternative systems and suggests a model.
  Format: paperback, A4

- **DP33 Tough on crime, tough on the causes**
  Alun Michael
  Date: March 1997 Price £: 10.00 Pages: 46 ISBN: 0 7163 3033 4
  A collection of essays with imaginative new ideas on tackling crime and its causes. Authors: Robert Reiner, John Smith, Chris Stanley, Jon Bright, Gareth Williams, Colleen Atkins, Paul Cavadino, Chris Holtom, Rita Stringfellow.
  Format: paperback, A4

- **DP34 The cross we bear – electoral reform for local government**
  Andrew Adonis and Stephen Twigg
  Date: May 1997 Price £: 5.00 Pages: 12 ISBN: 0 7163 3034 2
  Argues for a system of Single Transferable Voting in local elections to make councils more representative.
  Format: paperback, A4

- **DP35 Labour and Europe: Proposals for government**
  Denis MacShane
  Date: May 1997   Price £: 10.00 Pages: 36 ISBN: 0 7163 3035 0
  A collection of essays by Denis MacShane, Neil Kinnock, Bob Bischof, Christopher Haskins, Chris Golden, Paul Gillespie, Bill Shannon, and Graham Leicester
  Format: paperback, A4

- **DP36 Sold short:Government and retailing**
  Ian Corfield & Peter Welch
  Date: June 1997   Price £: 15.00 Pages: 32 ISBN: 0 7163 3036 9
  A properly regulated retail sector is the bedrock of economic growth.
  Format: paperback, A4

- **DP37 Arms and the man: Renewing the armed services**
  Eric Joyce
  Date: July 1997   Price £: 10.00 Pages: 24 ISBN: 0 7163 3037 7
  The services must root out prejudice based upon gender, race and class, and must adapt to a modern environment.
  Format: paperback, A4

- **DP38 Information Age Government: Delivering the Blair Revolution**
  Liam Byrne
  Date: October 1997 Price £: 15.00 Pages: 30 ISBN: 0 7163 3038 5
  Argues that Labour must automate, integrate and devolve the civil service organisations, and describes how Labour can harness the power of business, new technology and local leaders to do so.
  Format: paperback, A4

- **DP39 The Last Rotten Borough [The Corporation of London]**
  Malcolm Matson
  Date: November 1997 Price £: 15.00 Pages: 20 ISBN: 0 7163 3039 3
  Exposes the anti-democratic and elitist practices of the Corporation of London; recommends its abolition, and the transfer of its assets to the new Greater London Authority.
  Format: paperback, A4

- **DP40 Defence for the 21st century: Towards a post-Cold War force structure**
  Malcolm Chalmers
  Date: November 1997 Price £: 10.00 Pages: 30 ISBN: 0 7163 3040 7
  The UK's heightened commitments to international peacekeeping and peace enforcement require changes in the structure and equipment of our armed forces, within a reduction of overall defence spending.
  Format: paperback, A4

- **DP41 Turning Houses into Homes**
  Nic Frances
  Date: January 1998 Price £: 6.00 Pages: 16 ISBN: 0 7163 3041 5
  Proposals for a national policy framework for furnished housing
  Format: paperback, A4

- **DP42 The Rule of Lawyers**
  Arun Arora & Andrew Francis
  Date: May 1998   Price £15.00 Pages: 20pp ISBN 0 7163 3042 3
  Proposes the creation of a new, genuinely independent regulatory body for the legal profession
  Format: paperback, A4

- **DP43 Getting Real: Improving Teenage Sexual Health**
  Alison Hadley
  Date: June 1998 Price £:15.00 Pages: 20 ISBN: 0 7163 3043 1
  The government should improve teenage sexual health by generating a climate of openness, providing free information and access to confidential advice.
  Format: paperback, A4

- **DP44 Modernising Criminal Justice: Opportunities for Labour**
  Neil Addison
  Date: July 1998 Price £:15.00 Pages: 20 ISBN: 0 7163 3044 X
  Advocates a unified Ministry of Criminal Justice, bringing together police, Crown Prosecution Service and probation and prison services; new powers for coroners and juries; and the wholesale codification of criminal law
  Format: paperback, A4

- **DP45 Representatives of the People? The Constituency Role of MPs**
  Greg Power
  Date: October 1998 Price £:15.00 Pages: 25 ISBN: 0 7163 3045 8
  Argues that much constituency work should be handed over to a more powerful system of ombudsmen. All backbench MPs should be on select committees, srutinising legislation and holding the executive to account.
  Format: paperback, A4

- **DP46 Time Pays Off Off**
  Anne Gray
  Date: February 1999 Price £: 15.00 Pages: 40 ISBN: 0 7163 3046 6
  How reductions in working time can create jobs and promote lifelong learning.
  Format: paperback, A4

- **DP47 The Net Effect**
  Charles Doyle and Hugh Morris
  Date: March 1999   Price £15.00 Pages: 34 ISBN: 0 7163 3047 4
  Rethinking the regulatory role of the nation state in the global electronic economy.
  Format: paperback, A4

- **DP48 Enabling Government: Joined up Policies for a National Disability Strategy**
  Marilyn Howard
  Date: July 1999 Price £: 15.00 Pages: 36 ISBN: 0 7163 3048 2
  Proposes changes to the structure of central government to allow departments to work together and to devise policies which address the causes of social exclusion.
  Forma: paperback, A4

Fabian Specials

- **A new constitution for the Labour Party**
  Peter Archer
  Date: June 1993 Price £: 5.00 Pages: 28 ISBN: 0 7163 4017 8
  Suggests a new constitution for the Labour Party, starting with a new statement of aims and objectives.
  Format: paperback, A5

- **Bridging the NHS Treatment Gap**
  Stephen Twigg MP and Neil Stewart
  Date: July 1997   Price £: 10.00 Pages: 20 ISBN: 0 7163 4038 0
  The time between proving that a drug works and administering it to patients should be reduced.
  Format: paperback, A4

- **Britain under the Tories: Facts for socialists 1997**
  Melissa Robinson and Peter Metcalfe
  Date: April 1997   Price £: 5.00 Pages: 20 ISBN: 0 7163 4036 4
  The essential facts about the Conservative government's record – the economy, employment, tax, business, poverty, crime, health, education, housing.
  Format: paperback, A5

- **Changing Work**
  John Jackson and David Souter
  Date: July 1996   Price £: 20.00 Pages: 66 ISBN: 0 7163 4024 0
  Report on an enquiry chaired by John Jackson. Argues for a new approach to employment relations, based on commonality of interests and partnership. Aims to increase productivity, and to improve the quality of working life.
  Format: paperback, A4

- **D-I-Y Britain**
  Lindsay Mackie
  Date: March 1997   Price £: 5.00 Pages: 24 ISBN: 0 7163 4035 6
  A Fabian Special published in conjunction with CSV: ideas about getting young people involved as volunteers – in education, the health service, social service.
  Format: paperback, A5

- **Election Fever**
  Christopher Bollas
  Date: October 1996 Price £: 5.00 Pages: 13 ISBN: 0 7163 4026 7
  Examines the theatrical and psychological nature of political campaigning.
  Format: paperback, A5

- **Wherever Next? The Future of Europe**
  Liz Kendall (ed.)
  Date: February 1996 Price £: 7.95 Pages: 36 ISBN: 0 7163 4023 2

- **Report of the proceedings of the Fabian/Guardian Conference on Europe, 2**
December 1995.
Format: paperback, A5

- **Facts for socialists**
Giles Wright
Date: March 1991   Price £: 5.00 Pages: 32 ISBN: 0 7163 4016 X
Page-by-page summaries of the Conservative Government's record on issues such as the economy, education, housing and the environment, and Labour's policy proposals on each. (Foreword by Robin Cook MP.) Illustrated with graphs.
Format: paperback, A5

- **Football United: New Labour, the Task Force and the Future of the Game**
Mark Perryman
Date: September 1997 Price £: 5.00 Pages: 10 ISBN: 0 7163 4039 9
Eleven practical new ideas for the Football Task Force
Format: paperback, A5

- **Jobs and Growth**
Stephen Pollard, Will Hutton, Robert Kuttner
Date: November 1994 Price £: 9.95 Pages: 86 ISBN: 0 7163 4019 4
Practical measures to tackle unemployment and poverty in advanced economies.
Report of Fabian/Unison international seminar, April 1994.
Format: paperback, A5

- **Machinery of Local Government**
Paul Corrigan, Jack Dromey And
Date: February 1998 Price £: 5.00 Pages: ISBN: 0 7163 4040 2
Format: paperback, A4

- **Reform of Direct Taxation: Report of the Fabian Society Taxation Review Committee**
Tony Atkinson
Date: March 1990 Price £: 5.95 Pages: ISBN: 0 7163 3505 0
This report, the first major enquiry into the British tax system since the 1970s, dispels the notion that the Conservatives have delivered real tax cuts.
Format: paperback, A4

- **Ready, steady, go! New Labour and Whitehall**
Peter Hennessy, Rosaleen Hughes, Jean Seaton
Date: April 1997   Price £: 7.50 Pages: 36 ISBN: 0 7163 4037 2
Based on discussions between former civil servants and Labour's frontbench team; givies an insight into the thinking of the Civil Service and provides practical tips for anyone who wants to understand government.
Format: paperback, A4

- **Income and Wealth in the 1980s: 1990 edition**
  Thomas Stark
  Date: July 1990   Price £: 15.00 Pages: 74 ISBN: 0 7163 3000 8
  Uses Government statistics to contradict claims that the poor have done well out of economic growth under the Conservatives.
  Format: photocopy, A4

- **Income and Wealth in the 1980s: 1992 edition (third)**
  Thomas Stark
  Date: October 1992 Price £: 15.00 Pages: 74 ISBN: 0 7163 3506 9
  Uses Government statistics to contradict claims that the poor have done well out of economic growth under the Conservatives.
  Format: paperback, A5

- **Is Equality Dead?**
  Michael Newton, Sean Hall, Bernard Crick
  Date: November 1992 Price £: 5.00 Pages: 22 ISBN: 0 7163 2052 5

- **1992 Webb Essay (under 31) prizewinners' essays, with introduction by Bernard Crick**
  Format: paperback, A5

- **Election 45 Reflections on the Revolution in Britain**
  Austin Mitchell
  Date: July 1995   Price £: 12.95 Pages: 128 ISBN: 1 85725 109 1

- **An Illustrated History of the 1945 Election**
  Format: paperback, A5

- **The New European Left**
  Donald Sassoon et al
  Date: November 1999 Price £: 9.95, Pages 70, ISBN 0 7163 6001 2
  Explores the ideas, policy debates and electoral pressures which are determining the governing agenda in Germany, France, Sweden and the Netherlands.
  Format, paperback

- **Now's the Hour: New Thinking for Holyrood**
  Jack McConnell MSP et al
  Date June 1999   Price £: 5.00 Pages: 26 ISBN: 0 7163 4042 9
  Five leading figures from the Scottish political community set out their priorities and ideas for the new Parliament.
  Format, paperback

- **Modernising Local Government**
  Jack Dromey et al
  Date: February 1998 Price £: 6.00 Pages: 20 ISBN: 0 7163 4040 2
  In exchange for greater powers to raise income, local government must become more accountable to the communities it serves – for its decisions, its performance and the quality of its services.
  Format: paperback

Other

- **BK2 The English Question**
  Edited by Selina Chen and Tony Wright
  £8.95

- **BK3 Paying for Progress: a New Politics of Tax for Public Spending**
  By The Commission on Taxation and Citizenship
  £9.95

- **PR49 A Capital Idea: Start-up Grants for Young People**
  By David Nissan and Julian Le Grand
  £7.50

- **PR50 Votes for All: Compulsory Participation in Elections**
  By Tom Watson and Mark Tami
  £7.50

- **PR51 Plugging the Parent Gap: The Case for Paid Parental Leave**
  By Ruth Kelly
  £7.50

- **SP44 Radicals and Reformers: A Century of Fabian Thought**
  By Mark Thomas and Guy Lodge, with a foreword by Gordon Brown
  £7.50

The Foreign Policy Centre

Address	Elizabeth House
	York Road
	Mezzanine Floor
	39 York Road
	London, SE1 7NQ
Tel	020 7401 5350
Fax	020 7401 5351
Email	info@fpc.org.uk
Website	www.fpc.org.uk
Director	Mark Leonard
Research Director	Sunder Katwala
Senior Researcher	Yasmin Alibhai-Brown
Conference & Events Manager	Kate Ford
Fundraising Manager	Rachel Briggs
Press Officer	Robert Blackhurst
Researcher	Vidhya Alakeson
Advisory Council	Zeinab Badawi, Sir Michael Butler, Professor Fred Halliday, Baroness Helena Kennedy, Lord Levy, Adam Lury, John Lloyd, Lord Paul, Baroness Ramsay
Year of Foundation	1998
Cost of Subscription	£50 (individual), £150 (organisations), £200 (Libraries). Diplomatic forum £500 per year.

History

The Foreign Policy Centre was launched in 1998 by Prime Minister Tony Blair (Patron) and Foreign Secretary Robin Cook (President) to reflect the growing impact of foreign policy on people's everyday lives. Mark Leonard was appointed Director in November 1998 and the Centre's Mission Statement was launched in March 1999.

Objectives

The Foreign Policy Centre is the only London-based think tank set up to look at global solutions to domestic problems. It was launched to revitalise debates and develop a progressive, internationalist approach to issues which cut across borders and government departments. Described by the BBC as 'one of the most important influences on British foreign policy' and the *New Statesman* as 'media-savvy, energetic and original'. The Centre's conferences, seminars, publications and media work are underpinned by a distinctive approach which:

- Learns from international good practice – from Peruvian ways of dealing with the informal economy to Indian drug treatment programmes

- Examines how business, charities, and governments can work together in new types of international institutions and networks to deliver global public goods

- Starts with people's everyday problems and helps them develop their own solutions

- Promotes international engagement, understanding and an outward-looking British identity

- Broadens foreign policy making by bringing policy-makers in government, business, academia, and NGOs together with voices often left out of the debate such and diaspora groups, local communities and ordinary citizens.

Recent and current work includes groundbreaking studies of European public opinion, EU reform, multiculturalism and British identity, NGO rights and responsibilities, humanitarian intervention, the identities of corporations and their role in global and local governance, the future of the Commonwealth, the changing nature of kidnapping, and the cleaning-up global sport.

Publications

- **The Future Shape of Europe**
  Mark Leonard (editor) – supported by Adamson BSMG Worldwide
  November 2000
  £9.95
  Joschka Fischer, Tony Blair, Guiliano Amato, Hubert Vedrine and Anna Lindh show that European goverments are grappling with the central question of European reform and legitimacy in a new way. Other contributors, such as Anthony Giddens, Jan Zielonka, Alison Cottrell, Ben Hall and Mark Leonard look at what a new case for Europe will mean in practice.

- **Democratising Global Sport**
  Sunder Katwala
  September 2000
  £9.95
  How the governance of international sport can cope with an age of globalisation, commercialisation and accountability – proposing reforms to better reconcile the interests of athletes, supporters, sponsors, broadcasters, officials and the game as a whole in the spirit of fair play.

- **NGO Rights and Responsibilities: A new deal for global governance**
  Michael Edwards in association with NCVO
  July 2000
  Argues that we need to move beyond the blame-game over the failure of internationl governance and work out what the new rules of the road are. Innovative reform proposals set out a reform agenda for NGO accountability and show how international organisations can become more effective and incluseive by channelling NGO energies democratically and to the genuine benefit of those excluded from global progress.

- **How to Win the Euro Referendum: Lessons from 1975**
  Robert Worcester
  June 2000
  £9.95
  An examination of the decisive factors in the 1975 referendum and the lessons which can be learnt for the Europe debate today. Britain's future relationship with Europe and how we citizens will make up our minds about it.

- **The Postmodern State and the New Order**
Robert Cooper in association with Demos
June 2000
£8.95
A second edition of the ground-breaking analysis of how pre-modern, modern and post-modern states co-exist and interact in the post-Cold War world. The new edition offers new material on Kosovo, Sierra Leone and the role of democracy and religion in international politics.

- **Going Public: Diplomacy for the Information Society (interim report)**
Mark Leonard and Vidhya Alakeson
May 2000
£9.95
Global transformations in security, sovereignty and economics mean that diplomats must deal with a new global society where power and influence depend as much on values and reputation as on military might.

- **After Multiculturalism**
Yasmin Alibhai-Brown
May 2000
£9.95
Our approach to national identity, race and public culture needs to be fundamentally rethough, it is argued. We must create new ways of talking about who we are, and what this will mean in specific policy areas if the coming battles over political culture and naational identity are to have a progressive outcome.

- **Re-engaging Russia**
John Lloyd in accociation with BP Amoco
March 2000
£9.95
An important attempt to redefine the way that western countries seek to promote their values and engage with other societies.

- **New Visions for Europe: The Millennium Pledge**
Mark Leonard, Vidhya Alakson and Stephen Edwards
November 1999
£2.95
Europe is more integarted and successful than it has ever been, but many of its citizens know very little about it and feel disconnected from its institutions. To feed into the debate about reconnecting the EU with its citizens, the FPC has produced a Millennium Pledge which it is asking Heads of Government to sign.

- **Reinventing the Commonwealth**
Kate Ford and Sunder Katwala
095355984X
November 1999
£9.95
Sets out a reform agenda for the Commonwealth for the 21st Century.

- **Trading Identities: Why Countries and Comapnies are Becoming More Alike**
  Wally Olins
  0953559831
  October 1999
  £9.95
  As countries develop their national brands to compete for investment, trade and tourism, mega-merged global companies are using nation-building techniques to achieve internal cohesion across cultures and are becoming ever more involved in providing public services like education and health. What do these trends mean for the new global power balance?

- **Network Europe**
  Mark Leonard
  0953559823
  September 1999
  £9.95
  Mark Leonard sets out a radical new agenda for European reform, arguing that pro-Europeans must reshape the European debate if Europe is to be both effective and popular. Instead of the tradional federalist reform agenda the EU should learn from successful network models of business organisation and introduce elements of direct democracy to reconnect with its citizens.

- **Globalization: Key Concepts**
  David Held, Anthony McGrew, David Goldblatt and Jonathan Perraton
  0953559807
  April 1999
  £4.95
  Globalization is the buzz-word of the age – but how many people understand it? This authoritative guide thrahes out what it really means and argues that we need to rethink politics to keep up with the changing shape of power.

Hansard Society

Address	St Philips Building North
	Sheffield Street
	London
	WC2A 2EX
Tel	020 7955 7478
Fax	020 7955 7492
Email	hansard@hansard.lse.ac.uk
Website	www.hansardsociety.org.uk
Chairman	Dr David Butler CBE
Vice Chairmen	Austin Mitchell MP
	Rt Hon Gillian Shephard MP
	Lord Holme of Cheltenham
	John Tominson MEP
Director	Shelagh Diplock
Director of Studies	Dr Stephen Coleman
Adminstrative Officer	Ralph Allen
Number of Employees	3
Cost of Membership	£15 individual, £350 corporate
Cost of Subscription	£40 individual UK, £45 individual EU, £55 individual worldwide, £35 Schools

History

The Hansard Society for Parliamentary Government was established in 1944 when Parliamentary democracy was in a minority as a form of government in world terms. The first subscribers, Churchill and Attlee, were not joining a club, but rather supporting the cause of parliamentary democracy when it was seen top be threatened by Fascism and Communist dictatorship.

Objectives

The Hansard Society's core belief is that an effective Parliamentary system is central to a successful denocracy and it works to promote knowledge of and interest in the principles and practices of parliamentary democracy.

Many modern commentators argue that the main threat to parliamentary democracy today lies in its own lack of effectiveness and slowness to modernise. The Hansard Society today stimulates positive engagement in the debate about issues relating to modern parliamentary democracy and supplies a significant platform for the debate on changes which will make Parliament more effective and thus strengthen the democratic process.

The Hansard Society is a non-party organisation supported by the Speaker, Party Leaders, MPs, Peers, journalists and academics. The Society's activities range from Mock Elections in Schools to research, on-line debates, conferences, study days and publications. Two major programmes were launched in 1999: Parliament and Electronic Media and Parliamentary Reform.

Publications

- **The Report on the Commission on Women on Top**
  ISBN: 0900432217
  £7.50 (£6 to members), 1990

- **Cameras in the Commons**
  Alistair Heatherington, Kay Weaver and Michael Ryle
  ISBN: 0900432225
  £10.00 (£8 to members), 1990

- **Agenda for Change: The Report of the Commission on Election Campaigns**
  ISBN: 0900432233
  £10.00 (£8.50 to members, £7.50 to Schools), 1991

- **Making the Law: The Report on the Commission on the Legislative Process**
  ISBN: 0900432241
  £16.00 (£12 to members, £13.50 to Schools), 1993

- **The Report of the joint Hansard Society/European Policy Forum Commission on the Regulation of Privatised Utilities**
  ISBN: 0900432276
  £30.00 (£22.50 to members, £24 to Schools), 1997

King Hall Papers

- **What Price Hansard?**
  Anthony Lestor QC, Lindsay Mackle and Michael Renshall
  ISBN: 090043225X
  £1.00, 1994

- **Women at the Top: Progress After Five Years.**
  Prof Susan McRae
  ISBN: 0900432268
  £5 (£3 to members, £4 to Schools), 1996

- **Televised Leader's Debates: An Evaluation and a Proposal**
  Dr Stephen Coleman
  ISBN: 0900432055
  £5 (£3 to members, £4 to Schools), 1997

- **Westminister and Europe: Proposals for Change**
  Graham Leicester
  ISBN: 0900432055
  £7.50 (£3 to members, £5 to Schools), 1997

- **The Case for an Electoral Commission : Keeping Election Law up-to-date**
  David Butler
  ISBN: 0900432101
  £5 (£3 to members, £4 to Schools), 1998

- **The Deregulation Procedure: An Evaluation**
  David Miers
  ISBN: 0900432527
  £5.00, 1999

- **The Future of Parliament: Reform of the Second Chamber**
  Donald Shell and Philip Giddings
  ISBN: 0900432535
  £5.00, 1999

- **The Consequences of Devolution**
  Edited by Philip Norton
  ISBN: 090432314
  £5.00, 1998

- **Parliament in the Age of the Internet**
  Edited by Stephen Coleman
  ISBN:0199224226

- **Published with Oxford University Press**
  ISBN: 019224226
  £14.99, 1999

- **The Electronic Media, Parliament & the People – Making Democracy Visible**
  Stephen Coleman
  £5.00, 1999

- **Media Coverage of Parliament**
  David McKie
  ISBN: 0900432500
  £5.00, 1999

- **Election Call - A Democratic Forum?**
  Stephen Coleman
  ISBN: 0900432519
  £5.00, 1999

- **Televised Leaders' Debates: An Evaluation and a Proposal**
  Stephen Coleman
  ISBN: 0900432004
  £5.00, 1999

- **Watching Parliament on TV – the views from Scotland, England, Wales and Northern Ireland**
  ISBN: 0900432608
  £5.00, June 2000

- **New Media and Social Inclusion**
  Dr. Stephen Coleman and Emilie Normann
  ISBN: 0900432659
  £7.50, July 2000

- **Systematic Scrutiny: Reforming the Select Committees**
  Alex Brazier
  ISBN: 0900432705
  £7.50, July 2000

- **Creating a Working Parliament: Reform of the Commons Chamber**
  Greg Power
  ISBN: 0900432802
  £7.50, October 2000

- **Under Pressure: Are we getting the most from our MPs?**
  Greg Power
  ISBN: 0900432756
  £10.00, October 2000

- **Parliament and the Public Purse: Improving Financial Security**
  Alex Brazier
  ISBN: 0900432853
  £7.50, November 2000

- **Women at the Top 2000: Cracking the public sector glass ceiling**
  Dr. Karen Ross
  ISBN: 090043261
  £7.50, December 2000

- **I Spy Strangers**
  Jackie Ashley
  £1.00, 2000

- **Sounding out the Public**
  Dr. Stephen Coleman
  £1.00, 2000

Parliamentary Affairs

- **The Quango Debate**
  Edited by FF Ridley and David Wilson
  ISBN: 019922238X
  £10.99

- **British Government and Politics since 1945: Changes in Perspective**
  Edited by FF Ridley and Michael Rush
  ISBN: 0199222398
  £13.99

- **Sleaze: Politicians, Private Interests and Public Reactions**
  Edited by FF Ridley and Alan Doig
  ISBN: 0199222738
  £10.99

- **Women in Politics**
  Edited by Joni Lovenduski and Pippa Norris
  ISBN: 0199222754
  £12.99

- **Under the Scott-Light: British Government seen through the Scott Report**
  Edited by Brian Thompson and FF Ridley
  ISBN: 0199222789
  £12.99

- **Britain Votes 1997**
  Edited by Pippa Norris and Neil T Gavin
  ISBN: 019922322
  £12.99

Institute for Public Policy Research

Address	30–32 Southampton Street
	London
	WC2E 7RA
Tel	020 7470 6100
Fax	020 7470 6111
Email	postmaster@ippr.org.uk
Website	www.ippr.org.uk
Director	Matthew Taylor
Director, Human Rights	Sarah Spencer
Senior Economist	Peter Robinson
Director of Social Policy	Lisa Harker
Publications Manager	Helena Scott
Press Officer	Jim Godfrey
Number of Employees	32
Cost of Subscription	Corporate £165
	Library £125
	Individual £99
	Mini £45

History

The IPPR was set up in 1988, and founders included John Eatwell and Clive Hollick. Tessa Blackstone (now an Education Minister) became the first chairman of trustees and the first director was James Cornford, who ran the Institute from an office in Buckingham Gate with Patricia Hewitt (now a Labour MP) as his Deputy Director. Initially, the publishing output concentrated on constitutional reform, education, employment, industry and social policy.

In 1991, the IPPR moved to its present offices in Southampton Street and the Institute started to take on more staff. David Miliband (now a member of the Dowing Street Policy Unit) joined as a researcher for Patricia Hewitt; Dan Corry as Senior Economist and editior of the new quarterly magazine *New Economy*; Anna Coote as Hamlyn Fellow in Social Policy and Sarah Spencer on Human Rights. In December 1992, John Smith MP, then leader of the Labour Party, instigated the Commission on Social Justice, which conducted its wide-ranging review of social and economic change over the next two years. It also employed a number of staff who contributed much to the IPPR.

After the Commission on Social Justice reported in October 1994, the Institute took on different areas of research, expanding its work on human rights, health policy and environmental policy. In 1995 with a new leader for the Labour Party, a new Commission on Public Policy and British Business was established. Its findings have influenced government policy in numerous areas. In 1999 the latest Commission on Private Partnerships was launched.

The Director since 1998 has been Matthew Taylor, who has taken the Institute to its present size of 35 staff and a turnover of £1.2 million.

Publications

Published 1990

- **A Stake in the Company: Shareholding, Ownership and ESOP's**
  James Cornford
  ISBN: 1872452043
  £10.00

- **The Great British Housing Disaster and Economic Policy**
  John Muellbauer
  ISBN: 1872452108
  £7.50

- **European Monetary Union – The Issues**
  Gavyn Davies, David Currie and Neil MacKinnon
  ISBN: 1872452086
  £10.00 out of print

- **Britain's Economic Problems and Policies in the 1990s**
  Ken Coutts, Wynne Godley et al
  ISBN: 1872452124
  £3.00

- **Learning by Right: An Entitlement to Paid Education and Training**
  David Milliband
  ISBN: 1872452558
  £3.00

- **Working Time: A New Legal Framework?**
  Bob Hepple
  ISBN: 1872452140
  £5.00

- **The Time of our Life: Education, Employment and Retirement in the Third Age**
  Tom Schuller and Alan Walker
  ISBN: 1872452116
  £7.50

- **The Future of Jobcentres: Labour Market Policy and the Employment Service**
  Dan Finn and David Taylor
  ISBN: 1872452051
  £5.00

- **Takeovers and Short-termism in the UK**
  Andy Cosh et al
  ISBN: 1872452167
  £7.50

- **The Regeneration Game: A Regional Approach to Regional Policy**
Irene Brunskil
ISBN: 187245206X
£7.50

- **Technology Transfer: Policies for Innovation**
David Milliband
ISBN: 1872452078
£7.50

- **What to do About Water**
Andrew McIntosh
ISBN: 1872452175
£7.50

- **The Family Way: A New Approach to Policy-Making**
Anna Coote, Harriet Harman and Patricia Hewitt
ISBN: 1872452159
£10.00

- **A British 'Baccalaureat': Ending the Division Between Education and Training**
David Finegold et al
ISBN: 1872452094
£10.00

Published 1991

- **What Next? Agencies, Departments and the Civil Service?**
Anne Davies and John Willman
ISBN: 187245240X
£10.00

- **The Constitution of the United Kingdom**
ISBN: 1872452426
£10.00

- **An Experiment in Freedom: The Case for Free Local Authorities in Britain**
John Stewart
ISBN: 1872452329
£3.00

- **Britain, Germany and the New European Security Debate**
Oliver Ramsbotham
ISBN: 1872452272
£10.00

- **Quality and Choice in Housing: A Framework for Financial Reform**
  Stephen Merrett
  ISBN: 187245223X
  £7.50

- **Pay Strategies for the 1990s: Inflation, Jobs and the ERM**
  John Grieve Smith
  ISBN: 1872452213
  £7.50

- **Good Housekeeping: How to Manage Credit and Debt**
  Will Hutton
  ISBN: 1872452221
  £7.50

- **Taxes and Incentives: The Effects of 1988 Cuts in the Higher Rates of Income Tax**
  C.V Brown and C.T Sandford
  ISBN: 1872452205
  £4.50

- **Markets, Politics and Education: Beyond the Education Reform Act**
  David Milliband
  ISBN: 187245280
  £10.00

- **Teachers and Parents**
  Sally Tomlinson and Alec Ross
  ISBN: 1872452353
  £7.50

- **Successful Schools**
  Tim Brighouse and John Tomlinson
  ISBN: 1872452299

- **Assessment in Schools: An Alternative Framework**
  Harvey Goldstein
  ISBN: 1872452302
  £5.00

- **A National Curriculum for All: Laying the Foundations for Success**
  Phillip O'Hear and John White
  ISBN: 1872452310
  £10.00

- **Ecological Food Production: A Food Production Policy for Briatin**
  Michael Begon
  ISBN: 1872452256
  £7.50

- **The CAP and Green Agriculture**
  David Harvey
  ISBN: 1872452248
  £6.00

- **Health before Healthcare**
  Stephen Harrison et al
  ISBN: 1872452345
  £3.00

- **Unnatural Monopolies: Telecommunications in the 1990s**
  Richard Hooper
  ISBN: 1872452191
  £6.00

- **Is Quality Good for You? A critical Review of Quality Assurance in Welfare Services**
  Naomi Pfeffer and Anna Coote
  ISBN: 1872452361
  £10.00

- **Child Care in a Modern Welfare System: Towards A New National Policy**
  B Cohen and N Fraser
  ISBN: 1872452418
  £10.00

- **Equal Rights for Disabled People: The case for a New Law**
  Ian Bynoe, Mike Oliver and Colin Barnes
  ISBN: 1872452434
  £5.00

- **Meeting Needs in the 1990s: The Future for Public Service and the Challenge for Trade Unions**
  Bill Callaghan, Anna Coote et al
  ISBN: 1872452264
  £7.50

- **Unnatural Monopolies: Telecommunications in the 1990s**
  Richard Hooper
  ISBN: 1872452191
  £6.00

Published 1992

- **Swedish Models: The Swedish Model of Central Government**
  Oonagh McDonald
  ISBN: 1872452493
  £5.00

- **Biting the Bullet: A European Defence Option for Britain**
  Malcolm Chalmers
  ISBN: 1872452574
  £10.00

- **Full Employment in the 1990s**
  John Grieve Smith
  ISBN: 1872452485
  £7.50

- **Towards the Renaissance of Private Rental Housing**
  Stephen Merrett
  ISBN: 1872452558
  £5.00

- **Why Britain needs a Minimum Wage**
  Frank Wilkinson
  ISBN: 1872452442
  £5.00

- **Locking the Stable Door: The Ownership and Control of Occupational Pension Funds**
  Bryn Davies
  ISBN: 1872452515
  £5.00

- **Portfolio Management for Not-for-Profit Institutions**
  W B Reddaway
  ISBN: 1872452604
  £5.00

- **Partners in Change: A new Structure For the Teaching Profession**
  Tim Brighouse and Michael Barber
  ISBN: 1872452566
  £5.00

- **Managing Effective Schools: Local Management of Schools and its Reform**
  Elizabeth Monck and Alison Kelly
  ISBN: 1872452477
  £4.00

- **Next Left: An Agenda for the 1990s**
  Tessa Blackstone, James Cornford, Patricia Hewitt and David Milliband
  ISBN: 1872452450
  £5.00

- **Understanding Local Needs**
  Janie Percy-Smith and Ian Sanderson
  ISBN: 1872452590
  £9.95

- **The Welfare of Citizens: Developing New Social Rights**
  Anna Coote
  ISBN: 1854890387
  £9.95

Published 1993

- **Reforming the Lords**
  Anne Davies and Jeremy Mitchell
  ISBN: 1872452655
  £7.50

- **Bankrupt in the Balkans: British Policy in Bosnia**
  Jane Sharp
  ISBN: 1872452620
  £2.95

- **A Game Without Vision: The Crisis in English Football**
  Dan Corry, Paul Williamson with Sarah Moore
  ISBN: 1872452744
  £4.95

- **Economic Integration after Maastricht**
  Gerald Holtham
  ISBN: 1872452663
  £4.95

- **Coming to Terms: Corporations and the Left**
  Roger Warren Evans
  ISBN: 1872452612
  £2.95

- **About Time: The Revolution in Work and Family Life**
  Patricia Hewitt
  ISBN: 1854890409
  £9.95

- **A New Agenda**
  Anne Campbell, Calum MacDonald, Nick Raynsford et al
  ISBN: 1872452701
  £3.95

- **Democracy and the New International Order**
  David Held
  ISBN: 187245271X
  £2.95

- **Better Pensions for All**
  Bryn Davies
  ISBN: 1872452647
  £7.50

Published 1994

- **Ministers and Mandarins**
  William Plowden
  ISBN: 1872452787
  £9.95

- **Money and Votes**
  Martin Linton
  ISBN: 1872452779
  £9.95

- **Paying for Inequality: The Economic Cost of Social Injustice for Inequality**
  Ed. by Andrew Glyn and David Milliband
  ISBN: 185489059X
  £12.95

- **The Reshaping of the German Social Market**
  David Goodhart
  ISBN: 1872452841
  £7.50

- **The Wrecker's Lamp: do currency markets leave our economy on the Rocks?**
  Ruth Kelly and Dan Atkinson
  ISBN: 1872452965
  £4.95

- **Educational Reform and its Consequences**
  Ed. by Sally Tomlinson
  ISBN: 1854890654
  £9.95

- **Rationing Healthcare**
  Stephen Harrison and David J Hunter
  ISBN: 1872452833
  £7.50

- **Strangers and Citizens**
  Ed. by Sarah Spencer
  ISBN: 1854890514
  £14.95

- **Immigration as an Economic Asset: The German Experience**
  Ed. by Sarah Spencer
  ISBN: 1858560101
  £10.95

- **Regulating our Utilities**
  Dan Corry, David Souter and Michael Waterson
  ISBN: 1872452949
  £7.50

- **Reinventing the Left**
  Ed. by David Milliband
  ISBN: 0745613918
  £11.95

- **Families, Children and Crime**
  Ed. by Anna Coote
  ISBN: 1872452914
  £9.95

- **Escaping from Dependence: Part-time workers and the Self-Employed**
  Joan Brown
  ISBN: 1872452930
  £5.00

- **Is there a Case for a Care Corporation?**
  Anne Davies
  ISBN: 1872452892
  £5.00

- **Drugs and Young People**
  Frank Coffield and Les Gofton
  ISBN: 1872452868
  £4.95

- **Social Justice: Strategies for a National Renewal Commission on Social Justice**
  ISBN: 009951141X
  £6.99

Published 1995:

- **Off our Trolleys: Food Retailing and the Hypermarket Economy**
  Hugh Raven, Tim Lang with Caroline Dumonteil
  ISBN: 1872452981
  £4.95

- **Voices Off: Tackling the Democratic Deficit in Health**
  Liz Cooper, Anna Coote, Anne Davies and Christine Jackson
  ISBN: 1860300022
  £9.95

- **Primary Healthcare**
  Maria Duggan
  ISBN: 1860300006
  £7.50

- **Identity Cards Revisited**
  Madeleine Colvin and Michael Spencer
  ISBN: 1860300073
  £4.95

- **Migrants, Refugees and the Boundaries of Citizenship**
  Sarah Spencer
  ISBN: 1860300146
  £4.95

- **Profiting from the Utilities**
  Ed. by Dan Corry
  ISBN: 1860300081
  £9.95

- **Regulating in the Public Interest: Looking to the Future**
  Ed. by Dan Corry
  ISBN: 1860300014
  £9.95

- **Policy for the Press**
  James Curran
  ISBN: 1860300189
  £4.95

- **New Issues in Universal Service Provision**
  Cristina Murroni and Richard Collins
  ISBN: 1860300162
  £4.95

- **Managing the Information Society**
  Ed. by Richard Collins and James Parnell
  ISBN: 1860300030
  £7.50

- **A Flutter in the Future: Why the National Lottery Needs a Citizen's Jury**
  Elisabeth Kendall and James McCormick
  ISBN: 1860300219
  £4.95

- **Building Social Capital**
Mai Wann
ISBN: 187245299X
£7.50

- **Family and Community Socialism**
Michael Young and A.H Halsey
ISBN: 1860300049
£4.95

- **Employee Training: Unequal Access and Economic Performance**
Stephen Machin and David Wilkinson
A Comprehensive assessment of who receives training at work, what type of employer provides training and who gains from it.
ISBN: 1860300162
£3.95

- **Devolution on Demand: Options for the English Regions and London**
Stephen Tindale
Critically assesses the case for English regional government, and discusses the limits to be set on its fiscal and legislative powers.
ISBN: 1860300065
£4.95

- **Growth with Stability: Progressive Macroeconomic Policy**
Dan Corry and Gerald Holtham
An important contribution to the debate on how to structure macroeconomic policy to promote non-inflationary growth.
ISBN: 186030009X
£7.50

- **Restating the Case for the EMU: Reflections from the Left**
Dan Corry
Demonstrates why the left should welcome EMU, not only in its potential to create jobs and growth, but also in ensuing security, equality and aiding the environment.
ISBN: 1860300138
£4.95

- **Tranformation and Integration: Shaping the Future Central and Eastern Europe**
John Eatwell, Michael Ellman, Mats Karlsson et al
Argues that the future prosperity and security of Europe depends on devising policies which transform the former Communist states into socially just and environmentally sustainable market economies.
ISBN: 1860300111
£12.95

- **Taking Part: Children's Participation inDecision Making**
  Gerison Lansdown
  Makes a powerful case for changes in law and practice to increase children's involvement in decisions which directly affect their lives.
  ISBN: 186030012X
  £4.95

Published 1996

- **Converging Media? Converging Regulation**
  Ed. by Richard Collins
  ISBN: 186030026X
  £4.95

- **Resevoirs of Dogma**
  Ed. by Richard Collins and James Purnell
  ISBN: 1860300200
  £4.95

- **Competitiveness and Corporate Governance**
  Ed. by Andrea Westall
  Discusses the impact of different governance arrangements on corporate performance and the role of public policy in promoting 'good' governance.
  ISBN: 1860300391
  £5.50

- **The Future of UK Competition Policy**
  Robin Aaronson, Gordon Borrie, Martin Cave and David Pitt-Watson
  Four Authors debate the need for, and possible reform, of competition policy reform in the UK including its interaction with European competion regulations.
  ISBN: 1860300332
  £3.95

- **Globalisation: Winners and Losers**
  Marina Wes
  A thorough examination of one of the central dilemmas of our age.
  ISBN: 1860300294
  £3.95

- **Could Finance do more for British Business?**
  Ed. by Simon Milner
  Is finance the cause of, accessory to or innocent bystander in the failings of British industry?
  ISBN: 1860300227
  £5.50

- **About Turn, Forward March with Europe**

  Ed.by Jane M O Sharp

  The end of the Cold War and new economic realities mean that Britain's international role has changed. Defence experts look at Britain's future options for defence and security.

  ISBN: 1854890832

  £16.95

- **Economics and European Union Migration Policy**

  Ed. by Dan Corry

  Looks at what economic research tells us about migration flows and the implications for EU Policy.

  ISBN: 1860300413

  £7.50

- **Playing to Win: the success of UK Motorsport engineering**

  Beverly Aston and Mark Williams

  Analyses the UK's exceptional strength in racing car engineering and examines how public policy can encourage such success in other sectors.

  ISBN: 1860300316

  £7.50

- **Tackling Long-term Unemployment**

  Gerald Holtham and Ken Mayhew

  Advocates a job creation scheme whose aim is to bring the long-term unemployed back into the world of work.

  ISBN: 1860300308

  £4.95

- **University for Industry: Creating a National Learning Network**

  Josh Hillman, with a foreword by Rt Hon David Blunkett MP

  This report sets out the blueprint for the University for Industry, describing in detail what is needed, what sort of organisation it should be and what it should do.

  ISBN: 1860300510

  £7.50

- **Green Tax Reform: Pollution Payments and Labour Tax Cuts**

  Stephen Tindale and Gerald Holtham

  Examines the role which tax reform could play in protecting the environment and creating employment, with proposals of specific tax changes for the UK

  ISBN: 1860300367

  £7.50

- **A Market in Efficiency: Promoting Energy Savings Through Competition**

  Gill Owen

  Considers the impact of competition in the electricity market on energy efficiency and fuel poverty.

  ISBN: 1860300243

  £4.95

- **Social Democracy at the heart of Europe**
  Donald Sassoon
  Looks ways to speed up expansion of the Union to Eastern Europe and argues that integration must be based on a democratic charter.
  ISBN: 1860300405
  £7.50

- **Can We Afford the NHS? Future Challenges in UK Healthcare**
  Cam Donaldson, Anthony Scott, and Sarah Wordsworth
  Assesses the likely impact of new technologies and an ageing population on the NHS and shows that these are not insurmountable problems.
  ISBN: 1860300502
  £4.95

- **New Agenda for Health**
  Anna Coote and David J Hunter
  Sets the Agenda for Healthcare in the 21st century.
  ISBN: 1860300324
  £9.95

- **Rationing and Rights in Healthcare**
  Jo Lenaghan
  Explores the possibility of developing citizen's rights to healthcare.
  ISBN: 1860300383

- **Towards a High Trust NHS: Proposals for Minimally Invasive Reform**
  Stephen Harrison and Peter Lachmann
  Advocates changes designed to restore trust and effectiveness, while minimising current levels of turbulence in the service.
  ISBN: 1860300235
  £4.95

- **A British Bill of Rights (2nd Edition)**
  Anthony Lester, James Cornford, Ronald Dworkin et al
  Drawing on the UN International Covenant on Civil and Political Rights as well as on the European Convention on Human Rights, it sets out a Bill of statutory rights and freedoms which would extend significantly the protection of human rights in the UK.
  ISBN: 1860300448
  £7.50

- **European Union Citizenship: Options for Reform**
  Siofra O'Leary
  Assesses the significance of this new citizenship status within the political and legal context in which it was created and may now develop.
  ISBN: 1860300375
  £9.95

- **Child Protection: The Voice of the Child in Decision Making**
  Gillian Schofield and June Thoburn
  Makes the case for involving children in decisions throughout the child protection system.
  ISBN: 1860300286
  £4.95

- **Health Care Choices: Making Decisions with Children**
  Priscilla Alderson and Jonathan Montgomery
  Explains the importance on involving children in their own health care decisions and proposes law reform and a new code of practice for health care professionals.
  ISBN: 1860300433
  £7.50

- **Energy '98: Competing for Power**
  Ed. by Dan Corry, Chris Hewett and Stephen Tindale
  What will happen when gas and electricity are fully liberalised and how should policy makers respond?
  ISBN: 1860300499
  £7.50

- **New Media New Policies**
  Richard Collins and Christina Murroni
  The first comprehensive analysis of public in UK communications. The authors argue for a single regulator to maintain fair competition, protect the consumer and secure basic communication entitlements.
  ISBN: 0745617867
  £12.95

- **Converging Communications: Public Policy For the 21st Century**
  Christina Murroni, Richard Collins and Anna Coote
  Policy recommendations for UK media and telecommunications in the age of convergence.
  ISBN: 1860300421
  £4.95

- **Talking Dirty: Moral Panic and Political Rhetoric**
  Andrew Ward
  Looks at what can happen when moral rhetoric clouds political discourse and simple answers fail to address the complex influences on people's lives.
  ISBN: 1860300529
  £4.95

- **Beyond the Citizen's Charter**
  Ian Brynoe
  Investigates the achievements of the Citizen's Charter and considers alternatives.
  ISBN: 1860300359
  £7.50

- **Men and Their Children: Proposals For Public Policy**

  Adrienne Burgess and Sandy Ruxton

  Explores the experience of men within families. Suggests change in public policy to accommodate the changing role of men as parents within the changing family structure.

  ISBN: 1860300340

  £7.50

Published 1997

- **Promoting Prosperity: A Business Agenda For Britain**

  Commission on Public Policy and British Business

  After wide consultation with the business, policy-making and academic communities, the Commission identifies current failings and successes in the UK economic performance and sets out a wholly different vision of public policy towards business.

  ISBN: 0099747618

  £8.99

- **Small Firms On-line**

  Gillian Lauder and Andrea Westall

  An investigation of new technology and its applications for the success of small firms. Policy implications stress partnerships betweeen companies, public and private organisations.

  ISBN: 186030043X

  £5.50

- **The Greater London Authority: Principles and Structure**

  Paul Brindley, Wendy Hall and Gerald Holtham

  In depth consideration of the Government's proposals to recreate a London-wide government and to introduce the UK's first directly elected Mayor.

  ISBN: 085283072X

  £9.50

- **Honest Broker or Perfidious Albion?**

  Jane M O Sharp

  Describes Britain's unprincipled pragmatism in the search for a peace settlement in Bosnia, and concludes with suggestions for a more principled foreign policy.

  ISBN: 1860300154

  £7.50

- **Public-Private Partnerships**

  Julian Le Grand, Dan Corry and Rosemary Radcliffe

  The centre-left perspective on the pros and cons of delivering public services in partnership with the private sector.

  ISBN: 1860300588

  £7.50

- **Not "Just Another Accession": The Political Economy of EU Enlargement to the East**
John Eatwell, Michael Ellman, Mats Karlsson et al
ISBN: 1860300553
£7.50

- **Public Expenditure: effective management and control**
Ed. by Dan Corry
Analyses the way spending is planned, delivered, spent, evaluated and controlled, and how this should be reformed.
ISBN: 0030990645
£17.95

- **New Labour at Work**
William McCarthy
Employment will be a key factor for the new government. This report considers how reform can be organised and advocates a new Department of Work for labour market reforms.
ISBN: 1860300596
£7.50

- **Britain in Europe**
Ed. by Elizabeth Barrett and Stephen Tindale
Examines options for the EU in arange of policy areas, including EMU, human rights, environmental policy and issues of institutional reform and flexibility.
ISBN: 1860300618
£7.50

- **Reporting the Public Health**
Anne Davies
Suggests reforms to give annual public health reports a clarity of purpose which could lead to greater impact both locally and nationally.
ISBN: 1860300642
£6.50

- **Children and Crime**
Rob Allen
Looks for a new approach which places victims, famillies and the community at the heart both of decision-making about young offenders and the measures of dealing with them.
ISBN: 1860300472
£7.50

- **Effects of UK Utility Reform**
Eleni Markou and Catherine Waddams Price
The UK has exported both the philosophy and design of its own privatisation experiment to a wide variety of economies and countries over the past decade. This paper assesses the outcome both by reviewing previously published work and through new evidence.
ISBN: 1860300170
£4.95

- **Quality in Broadcasting**
  Ed by Cristina Murroni and Nick Irvine
  A collection of essays bringing together contrasting views on quality from broadcasters, independent producers, regulators and politicians.
  ISBN: 1860300669
  £7.50

- **The Politics of Risk Society**
  Ed. by Jane Franklin
  New patterns of risk and uncertainty threaten the stability of our traditional institutions. With contributions from Anthony Giddens, Ulrich Beck, Patricia Hewitt, Susie Orbach.
  ISBN: 0745619258
  £12.95

- **Equality**
  Ed. by Jane Franklin
  Leading political thinkers explore the idea of equality and its many applications and contexts, including the dialogue between the traditional new left, critical evaluations of the philosophy of the Social Justice Commission, and sexual and cultural equality.
  ISBN: 1860300537
  £11.95

- **Citizens' Juries: Theory into Practice**
  Anna Coote and Jo Lenaghan
  The results of the pilot series of citizens' juries is published for the first time. This report sets out the reasons for experiment.
  ISBN: 1860300545
  £7.50

- **Rights to Fair Treatment**
  Ian Brynoe
  Describes IPPR's pioneering project on the introduction of rights to fair treatment for people using public services.
  ISBN: 1860300456
  £10.95

- **Local routes to Social Justice**
  Ed. by James McCormick and Adrian Harvey
  Continuing the exploration of issues of social justice, this book brings together contributions from leading policy-thinkers on how to extend social justice through local economy, local democracy and local services.
  ISBN: 1860300561
  £4.95

- **Beyond a Halfway Housing Policy: Local Strategies for Regeneration**
  Brendan Nevin and Alan Murie
  Argues that national housing policies based simply on market signals are insufficient, and that the future direction of housing policy should be determined locally by housing partnerships which can negotiate long term funding arrangements.
  ISBN: 186030057X

Published 1998

- **The Entrepreneurial Society**
  Bob Gavron, Marc Cowling, Gerald Holtham and Andrea Westall
  Addresses three crucial areas where policy could help start-up businesses: general business awareness, the range and suitability of finance packages and the impact of public and private business support services.
  ISBN: 1860300634
  £9.95

- **Leading the Way: A New Vision for Local Government**
  Rt Hon Tony Blair MP
  The Prime Minister writes about the clear and strong leadership which should be at the heart of local government's new role.
  ISBN: 1860300758
  £4.99

- **Freedom with Responsibility: Can We Unshackle Public Enterprise?**
  Ed. by Gerald Holtham
  ISBN: 1860300731
  £7.50

- **Stimulating Investment: A Role For Policy**
  Peter Kenway
  Looks at where investment is low, why it is low and what government could start to do about it.
  ISBN: 1860300715
  £4.95

- **Wasted Youth: Raising Achievement and Tackling Social Exclusion**
  Nick Pearce and Josh Hillman
  Examines problems of disaffection and non-participation amoungst 14 to 19 year olds.
  ISBN: 1860300693
  £7.50

- **A Blueprint for a Business Energy Tax**
  Chris Hewett
  Can an industrial energy tax package be designed to protect vulnerable sectors from severe losses in competitiveness, whilst retaining its original environmental benefits?
  ISBN: 1860300790
  £3.00

- **Transport Taxes and Equity**
  Malcolm Fergusson and Ian Skinner
  Discusses whether increasing costs of motoring are regressive for some low income groups and, if so, what policy measures can be implemented to adequaetely compensate those groups.
  ISBN: 1860300782
  £4.95

- **Rethinking IT and Health**

Jo Lenaghan

Collection from eminent contributors on the impact of new information technologies on healthcare.

ISBN: 1860300774

£7.50

- **Brave New NHS? The Impact of the New Genetics on the Health Service**

Jo Lenaghan

Provides analysis of where we are now in the sphere of the new genetics, identifies the key issues and questions for the future, proposes specific policies where appropriate and maps out an agenda for debate.

ISBN: 1860300650

£7.50

- **Why a National Health Service?**

Cam Donaldson

Provides an economic perspective on why a tax-funded health service is the most efficient and equitable system.

ISBN: 1860300812

£7.50

- **A Human Rights Commission– The Options**

Sarah Spencer and Ian Brynoe

Explores the possible roles, functions, powers, structure and cost of a UK Human Rights Commission.

ISBN: 186030060X

£9.95

- **Future.Radio.UK**

Cristina Murroni, Robert King and Nick Irvine

Explores the uniqueness of Radio within the brave new world of multi-channel TV, on-line information and internet broadcasts.

ISBN: 1860300820

£4.95

- **Access Matters**

Cristina Murroni, Richard Collins and Anna Coote

As the European Union opens the communications markets, IPPR looks at EU policies for accessible media systems along with intellectual property and internet controls.

ISBN: 1860300685

£7.50

- **True Colours: Public Attitudes to Multiculturalism an the role of the Government.**

Yasmin Alibhai-Brown

Presents a coherent strategy for the government to affect a redefinition of the British identity for the next century.

ISBN: 1860300677

£7.50

- **Globalisation, Inequality and Social Democracy**
  Frank Vandenbroucke
  It is often said that globalisation has changed our society. This report attempts to disentangle the analysis from the myth-making.
  ISBN: 1860300677
  £7.50

- **The Inclusive Society: Tackling Poverty**
  Ed. by Carey Oppenheim
  Moves the debate about poverty beyond its normal terrain.
  ISBN: 1860300707
  £11.95

- **Building Deliberative Democracy: An Evaluation of two Citizen's Juries.**
  Marion Barnes
  Addresses key questions in the implementation and assessment of Citizen's Juries, and suggests a set of criteria for assessing models of participation.
  ISBN: 1860300871
  £7.50

- **The Complete Parent: Towards a New Vision for Child Support**
  Adrienne Burgess
  Suggests that non-resident fathers should be valued for more than their pay-packets and that policy initiatives should appeal to their sense of price.
  ISBN: 1860300766
  £4.95

- **Paying for Peace of Mind**
  James McCormick
  Explores who is uninsured, why and what the consequences are.
  ISBN: 0853747415
  £14.95

- **Social Policy and Social Justice**
  Ed. by Jane Franklin
  ISBN: 0745619401
  £13.95

- **Welfare in Working Order**
  Ed. by James McCormick and Carey Oppenheim
  Presents a map of the main options for change from people of working age who need to get jobs and keep them to today's retired poor who need higher incomes now.
  ISBN: 1860300626
  £11.95

- **Making Better Decisions**
  Clare Delap
  Reports on reactions to IPPR's pilot Citizen's juries and their implications for democratic practice.
  ISBN: 1860300723
  £4.95

Published 1999

- **Sporting Lives**
  Jim Godfrey
  IPPR presents a way to encourage sport at all levels through government policy, including a national plan for mass participation in sport.
  ISBN: 1860300928
  £6.50

- **Social Capital**
  David Halpern
  Describes how we can use social capital as a yardstick in assessing the success of current policies, and also shows ways to promote it as a strong social glue.
  ISBN: 1860300855
  £6.50

- **Key Issues in Crime Prevention, Crime Reduction and Community Safety**
  Ed. by Scott Ballintyne, Prof Ken Pease and Vic McLaren
  This report demonstrates the theoretical underpinning for developments in community safety and provides a bridge into practical guidance and assistance for practitioners.
  ISBN: 186030088X
  £15.95

- **Agenda for Growth**
  Andrea Westall and Marc Cowling
  Looks at barriers to growth of the micro and small enterprises which form the majority of the British business economy and how to overcome them.
  ISBN: 1860300952
  £10.95

- **Tomorrow's Citizens**
  Ed. Nick Pearce and Joe Halgontera
  With contributions from human rights experts, educationalists and practitioners, this report will examine contemporary concepts of citizenship and their implications for education.
  ISBN: 1860300960
  £9.95

- **Piloting the University for Industry: Report of the North East Project**
  Helen Milner, Josh Hillman, Nick Pearce and Michael Thorne
  Outlines key stages in the project's development; the critical success factors in getting it to work; and its outcomes, achievements and future prospects.
  ISBN: 1860300847
  £7.50

- **A Good Enough Service? Values, Trade-offs & the NHS**
  Bill New
  This paper from the Health Policy Forum describes the core values of the present day NHS and explores the necessity of trade-offs in the future.
  ISBN: 1860300936
  £7.50

- **Managing for Health**
  David J Hunter
  Considers the nature of the management task arising from the new health policy agenda and the style of management best able to address it.
  ISBN: 1860300898
  £7.50

- **Unsafe Streets**
  Scott Ballintyne
  This groundbreaking report looks at the victimisation, offending and police contact of people who sleep rough.
  ISBN: 186030091X
  £6.50

- **Mainstreaming Human Rights in Whitehall and Westminister**
  Ian Brynoe and Sarah Spencer
  Explores the role of government and of Parliament in ensuring that the UK meets international human rights standards.
  ISBN: 186030057X
  £7.50

- **Testing the Waters**
  Chris Hewett
  After the liberalisation in the gas and electricity markets, this report will explore the potential for increased competition in delivery and servicing for the water industry.
  ISBN: 1860300944
  £6.95

Published 2000

- **Fathers Figure**
  Emma Longstaff
  A project report on how fathers networks can help absent fathers play an active role in family life
  ISBN: 1860300901
  £4.95

- **Tomorrow's Citizens**
  Editors Joe Hallgarten and Nick Pearce
  An edited collection of essays on the new curriculum subject of citizenship in schools, addressing both practical and philosophical aspects.
  ISBN: 1860300960
  £8.95

- **Reinventing Social Housing Finance**

  John Hills

  A radical paper from the social housing forum on a new system of financing social housing projects.

  ISBN: 1860301169

  £4.95

- **Ownership for All**

  Gavin Kelly and Rachel Lissauer

  Introducing the concept of asset-based welfare with a universal provision of assets for every child.

  ISBN: 1860301142

  £4.95

- **Knowledge links**

  Steve Lissenburgh and Rachel Harding

  Detailed report on the links between industry and universities, and how this can be mutually beneficial and profitable.

  ISBN: 1860301045

  £10.95

- **New Musical Entrepreneurs**

  Paul Brindley

  Ground-breaking study of the new music industry – where technology has completely re-written the rules of ownership and distribution.

  ISBN: 1860301037

  £9.95

- **The New Partnership Agenda**

  Gavin Kelly

  The Commission on public private partnerships begins its in-depth look at the value of partnerships in government provision. The first issue paper sets out the criteria for partnerships and the agenda for the commission

  ISBN: 1860301185

  £7.50

- **Hard Budgets Soft States**

  John Eatwell et al

  If the former communist states of eastern Europe are about to join the EU, it is time for a root-and-branch reassessment of the welfare state in both east and west.

  ISBN: 1860301061

  £9.95

- **Choice and Diversity: An end to monopoly in social housing**

  John Swinney

  How the allocation of social housing could be made more democratic.

  ISBN: 1860301177

  £4.95

- **From Public to Community Housing: Scottish experiences and prospects**
  Robina Goodlad
  The different system of housing provision in Scotland and the lessons which can be learnt in England and Wales.
  ISBN: 1860301223
  £4.95

- **A New Fares Contract for London**
  Stephen Glaister and Tony Grayling
  looks again at the 'fares fair' system, and argues for a new fares contract for London.
  ISBN: 1860301002
  £10

- **London Transport Agenda**
  Tony Grayling and Robert King
  Looking at new issues for the new assembly and London transport.
  ISBN: 1860301096
  £4.95

- **Getting Partnerships Going: PPPs in transport**
  Steven Glaister, Rosemary Scanlon and Tony Travers
  The alternative to a PPP for the London Underground.
  ISBN: 1860301266
  £7.50

- **A Welcome Engagement : SMEs and social inclusion**
  Ella Joseph
  How corporate engagement by small and medium sized enterprises can make a difference within local communities.
  ISBN: 1860301088
  £8.95

- **Social Housing in the Future: a rural perspective**
  Mark Bevan
  The different issues to be addressed for social housing in rural areas.
  ISBN: 186030124X
  £4.95

- **Who Pays for What in Healthcare?**
  Bill New
  How to decide whether the NHS should separate out its duty of health care from the care for the public.
  ISBN: 1860301282
  £7.50

- **A Healthy Partnership: the future of PPPs in the health service**
  Edited by Rachel Lissauer and Peter Robinson
  Whether PPPs are helpful or productive in providing a better NHS
  ISBN: 1860301290
  £7.50

- **Social Housing in the 21st Century : Learning from Europe**
  Michael Oxley
  International comparisons in the social housing market.
  ISBN: 1860301274
  £4.95

- **A Loving Smack or Lawful Assault**
  Christina M Lyon
  Whether corporal punishment for children by anyone is ever justified, and what effect it might have on their future development
  ISBN: 1860301193
  £8.95

- **Secure Foundations: key issues in crime prevention and community safety**
  Ed. by Scott Ballintyne, Ken Pease and Vic McLaren
  Covers new area of social research in a practical and philosophical way. Community safety is addressed in different ways – through policing, through environmental improvements, through local government.
  ISBN: 186030088x
  £15.95

- **Plane Trading**
  Chris Hewett and Julie Foley
  Addresses the introduction of environmental taxes on aeroplane fuel – currently not taxed for its dangerous emissions.
  ISBN: 1860301339
  £20

- **New Gender Agenda**
  Ed by Anna Coote
  Looks at how feminism should move into the 21st century. Have all the 'battles' been won, and should there be a new vocabulary for equality.
  ISBN: 1860301207
  £10.95

- **Parents Exist,OK!**
  Joe Hallgarten
  Comprehensive research on how parent-school relationships should be used to improve a child's educational chances.
  ISBN: 1860301258
  £10.95

- **Finding the Right Partner: diversity in local ppps.**
  Ed. by Ella Joseph
  Looks at the questions of representation and involvement in partnerships.
  ISBN: 1860301363
  £7.50

- **A learning process: PPPs in education**
  Ed. by Rachel Lissauer and Peter Robinson
  Looks at whether Public Private Partnerships have a place in the future of state-provided education.
  ISBN: 1860301304
  £7.50

- **European Defence: making Europe stronger**
  Peter Truscott
  The introduction of a European defence force under the Helsinki agreement is discussed in its implications for industry, for the British army locally, and the government on a European and global level.
  ISBN: 1 86030 142 8
  £12.95

- **Venturing Forward: the role of venture capital policy in enabling entrepreneurship**
  Rebecca Harding
  Contains international comparisons on small business policies and how government policy can improve the chances of small business.
  ISBN: 186030141X
  £9.95

- **Microentrepreneurs: creating enterprising communities.**
  Andrea Westall, Peter Ramsden, Julie Foley
  How to maintain a commitment to social justice and create an 'enterprise-for-all' society.
  ISBN: 1860301436
  £9.95

- **Right up your Street: partnerships for local policy making and delivery**
  Ella Joseph
  How PPPs can be used to reflect local aims and challenges in the provision of local services.
  ISBN: 1860301371
  £7.50

- **Community Justice: Modernising the Magistracy in England and Wales**
  Andrew S Sanders
  Highlights the importance of public participation in criminal justice and advocates reforms that would substantially increase the number and range of people who could become magistrates.
  ISBN: 1860301231
  £10

- **Any More Fares? Delivering better bus services**
  Ed. by Tony Grayling
  Argues that better bus services are central to a progressive and environmentally sustainable transport policy.
  ISBN: 1860301347
  £14.95

Institute of Economic Affairs

Address	2 Lord North Street
	Westminster
	London
	SW1P 3LB
Tel	020 7 799 3745
Fax	020 7 799 2137
Email	iea@iea.org.uk
Website	www.iea.org.uk
General Director	John Blundell
Editorial Director	Professor Colin Robinson
Dir. Health & Welfare Unit	Dr David Green
Dir. Environment Unit	Roger Bate
Dir. Education & Training Unit	Professor James Tooley
Dir. Trade & Development Unit	Gerald Frost
Asst Dir. Health & Welfare Unit	Robert Whelan
Dir. Environment Unit	Julian Morris
Number of Employees	20
Cost of Subscription	£30.00

History

They very emergence of the IEA serves as a good illustration of one of the central beliefs of classical liberals: that creative developments in society result largely from harnessing the spontaneous forces generated by individuals. In the early days of the Institute three individuals in particualr were important.

In 1945 Antony Fisher went to the London School of Economics to see F A Hayek, having read an abridged version of The Road to Serfdom in the Reader's Digest. Sharing Hayek's belief in the dangers of a growing government power, Fisher was full of determination to embark on a political and parliamentary career. Hayek urged otherwise and persuaded Fisher of the need to establish a body which could engage in research and influence 'intellectual' opinion – to win over the opinion of those in the universities, the schools and the media.

In 1949 Fisher found himself sitting in an audience listening to a lecture given by Ralph Harris, a young economist with similar ideas. The two exchanged addresses at their first meeting and Fisher later recalled that it was that day that he had decided on his first director. By a Trust Deed dated 9 November 1955 there was established '. . . a charitable body to be known as the Institute of Economic Affairs with the object of educating the British public in the knowledge of economic and social problems and their solutions.'

By that time the IEA had already secured its first victory. The Free Convertibility of Sterling by George Winder, with an introduction by Fisher, had sold over two thousand copies in the summer of 1955. This success was built upon as IEA publications achieved growing recognition and a reputation for independent and rigorous analysis.Nevertheless, public opinion was harsh in those early days. The IEA found itself consistently ignored or dismissed as irrelevant by an academia and a media steeped in the sentimentality of collectivism and Keynesianism.

Gradually, supporters from the universities and beyond emerged, drawn out by path breaking studies as Hire Purchase in a Free Society (1958), Advertising in a Free Society (1959), and Resale Price Maintenance and Shoppers' Choice (1960). The publishing programme of the IEA grew apace as did the Institute itself, gaining new staff and moving from Austin Friars in the City to new premises in Hobart Place and, eventually, to Eaton Square in 1961.

In January 1960 the original plan to publish ad hoc titles was shelved and the IEA launched its distinctive series of papers and books. With Seldon's effective management of the growing publishing programme, Harris set out for the universities and schools – a commitment and involvement to students and their teachers that continues to this day.

Harris and Seldon were helped in their task by G E 'John' Blundell who, as Company Secretary from 1962, devoted most of his time to raising the funds needed to enable the IEA to continue with its high quality programmes and to reach the widest possible audiences by providing titles at a price affordable to students and teachers. From the outset the IEA had decided that the importance of its independence was such that it would not seek or accept any support from public sources, relying instead on private means of support from individuals, businesses and trusts and foundations, and on sales of its publications.

Today the IEA is still true to its early ideas although it has seen many positive changes and is now credited with a huge impact on public opinion, both at home and abroad. Having moved to its present home in Lord North Street in 1969, the IEA has since fostered a number of specialist research centres – or 'Units' – under its roof. Each continues to grow in stature.

As Keynes recognised: '. . . the ideas of economists and political philosophers…are more powerful than is commonly understood'. From having been the preserve of the isolated few and to the many unthinkable, the belief in market-based analyses of social and economic problems has, through publication and constant reconsideration, been made thinkable. And yet, but for these chance occurrences and meetings in the early days, the IEA might never have come about. The post-war economic orthodoxy so successfully challenged in the work of the IEA might have remained unchallenged and public opinion might not have been shifted in a quite different direction.

Objectives

The IEA is a research and educational charity (No 235351). Its mission is to improve understanding of the fundamental institutions of a free society with particular reference to the role of markets in solving economic and social problems.

The IEA acheives its mission by organising a high quality publishing programme and conferences and seminars on a range of subjects. It provides outreach to school and college students as well as brokering media introductions and appearances.

Established in 1955 by the late Sir Antony Fisher, the IEA is an educational charity, limited by guarantee. It is independent of any political party or group, and is financed by sales of publications, conference fees and voluntary donations.

In addition to its main series of publications, the IEA also publishes a quarterly journal, Economic Affairs, and has four specialist policy units covering Health & Welfare, Environment, Education & Training and Trade & Development.

The IEA is aided in its work by a distinguished international Academic Advisory Council eminent panel of Honorary Fellows. Together with other academics, they review prosepctive IEA publications, their comments being passed on anonymously to authors. All IEA publications are therefore subject to the same rigorous independent refereeing process as used by leading academic journals.

IEA publications enjoy widespread classroom use and course adoptions in schools and universities. They are also sold throughout the world and are often translated and reprinted.

Since 1974, the IEA has helped to create a world-wide network of 100 similar institutions in more than 70 countries. They are all independent but share the IEA's mission.

Publications

- **What Price Civil Justice?**

  Brian Main and Alan Peacock

  Economic principles are used to explore the efficiency of the civil justice system and ways in which a more innovative regime might be introduced.

  Hobart Paper 139 96pp, ISBN: 0255364296

  January 2000 (pb) £8.00

- **Regulating European Labour Markets**

  John Addison and W Stanley Siebert

  The EU has for many years been involved in action intended to improve working conditions. In this paper some of the likely effects of these attempts are analysed.

  Hobart Paper 138 86pp, ISBN: 0255364202

  February 1999 (pb) £8.00

- **Corporate Governance: Accountability in the Marketplace**

  Elaine Sternberg

  Presents a robust defence of the Anglo Saxon model. Refutes stakeholder theories of corporate governance.

  Hobart Paper 137 134pp, ISBN: 0255364164

  October 1998 (pb) £12.00

- **Dilemma of Democracy**

  Arthur Seldon

  On the nature of over-government

  Hobart Paper 136 116pp, ISBN: 0255364172

  August 1998 £10.00

- **WHO, What and Why? Trans-national Government, Legitimacy and the WHO**

  Roger Scruton

  The WHO is used to attack the ill-conceived and anti-democratic tendencies of trans-national organisations. The growing power of organized groups is such that they have an influence on policy out of all proportion to the extent to which they represent general opinion.

  Occasional Paper 113 64 pp, ISBN: 0255364873

  May 2000 (pb) £8.00

- **Reforming EU Farm Policy: Lessons from New Zealand**

  RWM Johnson, with a commentary by Richard Howarth

  From 1984 New Zealand totally dismantled price support for agricultural products. Evidence is produced showing the effect of this on agricultural productivity and economic growth. This is then examined for lessons for the reform of CAP and European agriculture.

  Occasional Paper 112 84 pp, ISBN: 0255364849

  April 2000 (pb) £8.00

- **Hayek, Currency Competition and European Monetary Union**

  Otmar Issing, with commentaries by Lawrence H White and Roland Vaubel

  The introduction of the Euro triggered '... a kind of Hayekian discovery process' which gives more scope to the private sector to 'enhance the quality of the medium-of-exchange and store-of-value functions of money'.

  Occasional Paper 111 62 pp, ISBN: 0255364814

  March 2000 (pb) £6.00

- **Privatisation, Competition and Regulation**

  Stephen C Littlechild

  1999 Wincott Memorial Lecture reprint. An account of the process of utility privatisation.

  Occasional Paper 110 42 pp, ISBN: 02553694

  February 2000 (pb) £5.00

- **Regulation without the State**

  John Blundell and Colin Robinson

  Exploring the logic of government regulation and the possibilities of alternative voluntary forms of regulation. They aregue there is a remorseless tendency for government regulation to be pushed to levels at which the benefits are well below the resulting costs.

  Occasional Paper 109 42pp, ISBN: 0255364261

  July 1999 (pb) £5.00

- **Morals and Markets**

  Jonathan Sacks

  Jonathan Sacks' 1998 Hayek Lecture

  Occasional Paper 108 (58pp), ISBN: 0255364245

  May 1999, £6.00

- **Does Advertising Increase Smoking?**

  Hugh High

  Argues that there is no evidence that tobacco advertising increases total consumption.

  Occasional Paper 107 118pp, ISBN: 0255364237

  March 1999 (pb) £12.00

- **Understanding the Process of Economic Change**

  Douglass C North

  The 1998 Wincott Memorial Lecture examining the link between national institutions and economic performance.

  Occasional Paper 106 32pp, ISBN: 0255364229

  March 1999 (pb) £4.00

- **Changing Fortune of Economic Liberalism**

  David Henderson

  Exmaines the historical background to modern economic liberalism.

  Occasional Paper 105 132pp, ISBN: 0255364199

  November 1998 (pb) £12.00

- **Regulating Financial Markets**
  George Benston
  Provides a comprehensive critique of the justifications for financial services regulation and provides an innovative proposal for reform.
  Hobart Paper 135 130pp, ISBN: 0255364156
  July 1998 £12.00

- **The Conservative Government's Economic Record: An End of Term Report**
  Twenty-Seventh Wincott Memorial Lecture
  Nicholas Crafts
  Economic historian Professor Nick Crafts gives a wide-ranging assessment of the economic record of the recent Conservative Government.
  Occasional Paper 104 45pp, ISBN: 02553643X
  March 1998 (pb) £4.00

- **Adoption and the Care of Children: The British and American Experience**
  Patricia Morgan
  In this comprehensive study of the state of adoption, Patricia Morgan argues that childcare practice and legislation should be re-organised so that adoption becomes the first, not the last, option for children who cannot live with their parents.
  Choice in Welfare 42 210pp, ISBN: 0255364342
  March 1998 (pb) £9.00

- **Fishing for Solutions**
  Michael de Alessi
  In this book it is argued that the primary cause of fish stock depletion is a lack of ownership. The author argues that the only solution is clearly defined, enforceable and tradeable property rights in fish as shown in the many international examples given.
  Studies on the Environment 11 88pp, ISBN: 025536444X
  February 1998 (pb) £8.00

- **Democratic Values and the Currency**
  Rt Hon Michael Portillo
  In this reprint of his January 1998 lecture to the IEA, Mr Portillo directly addresses the political issues raised by EMU. He considers the project's effects on democracy and concludes that it raises real dangers of conflict in the future. The book also contains a postscript by noted American economist Professor Martin Feldstein.
  Occasional Paper 103 31pp, ISBN: 0255364121
  January 1998 (pb) £4.00

- **Markets in the Firm: A Market-Process Approach to Management**
  Tyler Cowen and David Parker
  In this insightful new book Tyler Cowen and David Parker argue that a number of companies are suffering because many of them are still using 'command and control' management methods which are out of place in today's world. They argue that if firms wish to prosper they need to promote individual discovery, innovation and productivity within their own ranks.
  Hobart Paper 134 92pp, ISBN: 0255364059
  August 1997 (pb) £8.00

- **How Markets Work: Disequilibrium, Entrepreneurship and Discovery**
Israel M Kirzner

Professor Israel M Kirzner, one of the most eminent members of the Austrian School of economics uses his unrivalled knowledge to show how the school relates to the older classical tradition and how it diverges from the mainstream. He also opens the 'black box' of the competitive process and offers insights for anti-trust and other policies.
Hobart Paper 133 78pp, ISBN: 0255364040
June 1997 (pb) £8.00

- **Less Than Zero: The Case for a Falling Price Level in a Growing Economy**
George Selgin

In this radical new work Professor Selgin argues that the aim of those who make monetary policy should be not merely price stability but falling prices when productivity change suggests it.
Hobart Paper 132 80pp, ISBN: 0255364024
April 1997 (pb) £9.00

- **Regulating Pensions: Too Many Rules, Too Little Competition**
David Simpson

Professor David Simpson argues that a multi-tiered bureaucracy is imposing over-prescriptive, costly regulation on the pensions industry but failing to protect investors. Detailed regulation should be avoided, being replaced by '...vigorous competition accompanied by the effective enforcement of laws against fraud and unfair trading'.
Hobart Paper 131 84pp, ISBN: 0255363893
December 1996 (pb) £8.00

- **Trouble in Store? UK Retailing in the 1990s**
Terry Burke and J R Shackleton

After describing current trends, the authors address key questions facing British retailing, including issues of consumer protection, environmental regulation and the development of out-of-town retail centres.
Hobart Paper 130 92pp, ISBN: 0255363745
January 1996 (pb) £8.50

- **Cutting the Costs of Crime: The Economics of Crime and Criminal Justice**
David J Pyle

The author argues that public sector policing has largely failed to prevent crime and catch offenders. Alternative solutions include the encouragement of individuals to buy more protection in the market place, and the extension of the private provision of prison.
Hobart Paper 129 68pp, ISBN: 0255363737
November 1995 (pb) £6.00

- **Accountants Without Standards? Compulsion or Evolution in Company Accounting**
D R Myddelton

Statements of standard accounting practice (SSAPs) should be limited to disclosure requirements for listed companies and should not attempt to prescribe rules on measurement. There is little evidence that the growth of standards has produced any measurable benefits to the public.
Hobart Paper 128 77pp, ISBN: 0255363729
October 1995 (pb) £7.00

- **The Centralisation of Western Europe: The Common Market, Political Integration and Democracy**

  Roland Vaubel

  The emminent German economist Roland Vaubel examines whether or not there is a case for the assumption of greater powers by the EU, arguing that the centralising process stifles competition and leads to a flawed political structure.

  Hobart Paper 127 76pp, ISBN: 0255363436

  February 1995 (pb) £8.00

- **The End of Macro-Economics?**

  David Simpson

  Professor Simpson argues that macro-economics is flawed because it makes unwarranted assertions about relationships between aggregates, assumes their unchanging composition, abstracts from essential elements of economic activity, and uses concepts out of context.

  Hobart Paper 126 79pp ,ISBN: 0255363389

  October 1994 (pb) £7.50

- **Chaos, Management and Economics: The Implications of Non-Linear Thinking**

  David Parker and Ralph Stacey

  The authors explore the application of 'chaos theory' to economic and social systems. They argue that it provides a better explanation of how the world works and consequently has profound implications for the management of business and the economy.

  Hobart Paper 125 111pp, ISBN: 0255363338

  January 1998 (pb) £9.00

- **Winning the War on Drugs: To Legalise Or Not?**

  Richard Stevenson

  Stevenson sets out a case for legalisation "...as a response to drug problems which offers substantial savings and deals directly and swiftly with criminality". The paper also contains commentaries by authors who disagree strongly with Stevenson.

  Hobart Paper 124 92pp, ISBN: 0255363303

  March 1994 (pb) £8.50

- **Whither Sunday Trading? The Case for Deregulation**

  John Burton

  The author argues that the case for deregulation rests on the general principle that the criminal law should not be applied to "mundane transactions between willing participants in which no public harm is involved.

  Hobart Paper 123 96pp, ISBN: 0255363281

  December 1993 (pb) £8.95

- **Federalism and Free Trade**

  Jean-Luc Migue

  Professor Migue provides an exposition of the advantages of free trade, linking it to federalism in which the decision making process is so decentralised that the state has little or no interventionist powers.

  Hobart Paper 122 77pp, ISBN: 0255363206

  May 1993 (pb) £7.95

- **On the Move: A Market for Mobility on the Roads**

  John Hibbs

  Hibbs attacks calls for a "long-term coordinated transport policy" which in practice would mean a yet more politicised transport sector. Instead he favours market solutions to Britain's transport problems, including road pricing and further deregulation.

  Hobart Paper 121 94pp, ISBN: 0255363192

  April 1993 (pb) £8.95

- **Can De-Industrialisation Seriously Damage Your Wealth?**

  A Review of Why Growth Rates Differ and How to Improve Economic Performance

  N F R Crafts

  The author examines the evidence about growth rates in Britain and considers the case for an 'industrial policy' to promote manufacturing industry. He concludes that wide – ranging state intervention may well impose costs which exceed any benefits.

  Hobart Paper 120 92pp, ISBN 0-255 36316-8

  January 1993 (pb) £8.95

- **Have the Banks Failed British Industry?**

  A Historical Survey of Bank/Industry Relations in Britain, 1870-1990

  Forrest Capie and Michael Collins

  In this historical survey spanning 120 years, the authors attempt to find out if there is any truth in the allegation that Britain's economic decline has been exacerbated by the failings of the banking system.

  Hobart Paper 119 79pp, ISBN: 0255363087

  July 1992 (pb) £6.95

- **Training Too Much?**

  A Sceptical Look at the Economics of Skill Provision in the UK

  J R Shackleton

  Shackleton analyses the level of training and education in the economy and the economic benefits it can produce. He concludes that there is probably not a shortfall and that increased state expenditure would benefit only vested interests.

  Hobart Paper 118 86pp, ISBN: 0255363079

  June 1992 (pb) £6.95

- **Competition or Credit Controls?**

  David Llewellyn and Mark Holmes

  The authors analyse arguments for rationing of credit by means other than price. They examine the rationale behind credit controls and their likely effects on a now deregulated financial sector.

  Hobart Paper 117 103pp, ISBN: 0255363001

  October 1991 (pb) £7.95

- **Competition and Choice in the Publishing Industry**

  Walter Allan and Peter Curwen

  The authors examine the defences of the Net Book Agreement both analytically and empirically, coming to the conclusion that justifications for such a restrictive practice are fallacious.

  Hobart Paper 116 78pp, ISBN: 0255362455

  May 1991 (pb) £6.95

- **Beyond Universities: A New Republic of the Intellect**

Sir Douglas Hague

In this richly original paper, Professor Sir Douglas Hague identifies the challenges which universities will have to meet in the future and argues that if these are to be overcome, universities will have to able to survive as 'knowledge-based' industries.

Hobart Paper 115 86pp, ISBN: 0255362447

First Published April 1991

Second Impression September 1996 (pb) £8.00

- **The Economics of Law: An Introductory Text**

Cento Veljanovski

Dr Veljanovski introduces lawyers and economists to economic aspects of legal analysis. Taking the different areas of the law in turn – criminal, tort, regulation and judicial procedure – the author explains the application of economics in a non-technical fashion.

Hobart Paper 114 95pp, ISBN: 0255362277

First Published 1990

Second Impression March 1996 (pb) £8.00

- **Economic Fallacies Exposed**

Geoffrey Wood

This book is a collection of the best "Economic Fallacies" columns from the Institute's journal *Economic Affairs*. Covering an extensive range of economic fallacies in common circulation, these lucid and stimulating columns are invaluable as an aid to teaching.

Occasional Paper 102 110pp, ISBN: 0255364075

November 1997 (pb) £8.00

- **Back from the Brink: An Appeal to Fellow Europeans Over Monetary Union**

Pedro Schwartz

In this succinct and incisive analysis of the proposal for the European monetary union, Pedro Schwartz, the eminent Spanish economist, discusses in detail the 'many pitfalls' before monetary union can come into being.

Occasional Paper 101 30pp, ISBN: 0255364016

February 1997 (pb) £4.00

- **New Zealand's Remarkable Reforms**

Donald T Brash

Over the last few years the once moribund economy of New Zealand has undergone a radical transformation. In this important new book the influential Governor of the Reserve Bank of New Zealand, Dr Donald T Brash, explains how this was achieved and what lessons can be learned by the rest of the world.

Occasional Paper 100 56pp, ISBN: 0255364008

January 1997 (pb) £5.00

- **Better Off Out? The Benefits or Costs of EU Membership**

Brian Hindley and Martin Howe

In this major new study two IEA authors truly 'think the unthinkable'. Contrary to the current orthodoxy they dare to consider the economic consequences of UK secession from the EU. Quantifying the costs and benefits, they assert that UK withdrawal would not have "..dire economic consequences" so talk of economic doom is misplaced.

Occasional Paper 99 95pp, ISBN: 0255363885

October 1996 (pb) £8.00

- **Europe: Political Union Through Common Money?**

  Otmar Issing

  European integration requires ". . . more radical and wide-ranging reflection than is evident in the current debate." If there is no will to proceed to political union under ". . . sufficiently explicit and binding contractual provisions, there can be no confidence that the desired political integration can be realised through the indirect route of monetary union."

  Occasional Paper 98 30pp, ISBN: 025536377X

  March 1996 (pb) Price £4.00

- **Competition Regulation the British Way: Jaguar or Dinosaur?**

  Twenty-Fifth Wincott Memorial Lecture

  Sir Bryan Carsberg

  The author argues that the British system of regulation is too complex and costly, with too much Ministerial interference. The most effective way to regulate is to promote competition and policy should be adapted accordingly.

  Occasional Paper 97 32pp, ISBN: 0255363761

  February 1996 (pb) £4.00

- **Free Trade, 'Fairness' and the New Protectionism**

  Reflections on an Agenda for the World Trade Organisation

  Twenty-Fourth Wincott Memorial Lecture

  Jagdish Bhagwati

  Professor Bhagwati applies his unrivalled knowledge and meticulous analysis to some of the most serious threats to the prized goal of freeing world trade.

  Occasional Paper 96 42pp,ISBN 025536346X

  March 1995 (pb) £4.00

- **The Minimum Wage: No Way to Help the Poor**

  Deepak Lal

  Lal analyses the effects of minimum wages on unemployment and training, and concludes that they increase unemployment and reduce the incentive to acquire skills.

  Occasional Paper 95 38pp, ISBN: 0255363443

  January 1995 (pb) £4.00

- **No, Prime Minister! Ralph Harris Against the Consensus**

  Edited by Colin Robinson

  This volume, published as a tribute to Ralph Harris on his seventieth birthday in December 1994, reproduces thirty of his best short articles.

  Occasional Paper 94 112pp, ISBN: 0255363419

  December 1994 (pb) £10.00

- **European Federalism: Lessons from America**

  Clint Bolick

  The author examines the emerging constitution of the EU and, taking the history of the US as an example, concludes that the EU is very vulnerable to over-centralisation.

  Occasional Paper 93 50pp, ISBN: 0255363362

  July 1994 (pb) £4.50

- **Finance – Villain or Scapegoat?**
Twenty-Third Wincott Memorial Lecture
Harold Rose
Analyses the criticisms that have been made of the British financial system, particularly that of short-termism, and finds them flawed.
Occasional Paper 92 27pp, ISBN: 025536329X
January 1994 (pb) £3.50

- **Europe After Maastricht**
Holger Schmieding
A look at the changing economic and political alignments in Europe after the ratification of the Maastricht Treaty, which predicts an emerging 'variable geometry', with economic and political union seen as distinct and not necessarily related goals.
Occasional Paper 91 49pp, ISBN: 0255363273
November 1993 (pb) £4.95

- **Energy Policy: Errors, Illusions and Market Realities**
Colin Robinson
A comprehensive refutation of the arguments for a government directed 'energy policy', which proposes instead the extension of market forces.
Occasional Paper 90 62pp, ISBN: 0255363265
October 1993 (pb) £4.95

- **Central Bank Independence and Monetary Stability**
Otmar Issing
A Bundesbank board member concludes that, though central bank independence is beneficial, countries usually end up with the inflation rate they really want or deserve.
Occasional Paper 89 36pp, ISBN: 0255363222
June 1993 (pb) £3.95

- **Do Currency Boards Have a Future?**
Twenty-Second Wincott Memorial Lecture
Anna J Schwartz
Looks at the role of currency boards, especially for stabilising the newly free economies of Eastern Europe.
Occasional Paper 88 24pp, ISBN: 0255363125
November 1992 (pb) £2.95

- **Predicting the Unpredictable?**
Science and Guesswork in Financial Market Forecasting
Terence C Mills
The author discusses how research in financial markets has evolved and whether the application of theories can ever be translated into 'excess profits'.
Occasional Paper 87 46pp, ISBN: 0255363109
October 1992 (pb) £3.95

- **Monetarism and Monetary Policy**

  Anna J Schwartz

  Professor Schwartz examines systems of fixed and floating exchange rates and concludes that monetary policy can stabilise the exchange rate or the price level, but not both.

  Occasional Paper 86 40pp, ISBN: 0255363028

  January 1992 (pb) £3.95

- **The Wealth of Nations and the Environment**

  Mikhail S Bernstam

  In a cogent and subtly argued discussion of the relationship between economic growth, environmental problems and property rights, the author shows that the pursuit of profit in a capitalist economy leads to a husbanding of resources.

  Occasional Paper 85 71pp, ISBN: 0255362404

  January 1991 (pb) £6.95

- **Market Socialism: A Scrutiny 'This Square Circle'**

  Anthony de Jasay

  The collapse of communism in Eastern Europe has shattered the intellectual foundation of socialism. Antony de Jasay argues that any attempt to reconstruct it, by combining it with market economics, is destined to fail.

  Occasional Paper 84 36pp ISBN: 0255362323

  First published March 1990

  Second Impression February 1991 (pb) £3.95

- **The Limits of International Co-operation**

  Twentieth Wincott Memorial Lecture

  Deepak Lal

  Professor Lal trenchantly questions the value of co-operation between governments, particularly in the field of macro-economic co-ordination and environmentalism.

  Occasional Paper 83 43pp, ISBN: 0255362269

  January 1990 (pb) £4.00

- **The Poverty of 'Development Economics'**

  Deepak Lal

  In this revised and updated edition of his best selling book, Professor Deepak Lal provides a comprehensive critique of 'development economics'. He exposes many of the myths surrounding the issue of Third World development and in attacking the dirigiste attitudes held by many politicians, journalists, and intellectuals, Lal presents a case for development through the promotion of free trade and liberal economics.

  Hobart Paperback 16 173pp, ISBN: 0255364105

  December 1997 (pb) £12.00

- **Choice, Contract, Consent: A Restatement of Liberalism**

  Anthony de Jasay

  In restating liberalism, the author finds its rock-bottom foundations in six 'first principles' that are either self-evident, or readily acceptable to bona fide reason. These simple, relatively undemanding principles dictate the outline of a stable political doctrine which confines the state to mandatory tasks.

  Hobart Paperback 30 124pp, ISBN: 0255362463

  June 1991 (pb) £8.95

- **US and UK Unemployment Between the Wars: A Doleful Story**
Dan Benjamin and Kent Matthews

In this stimulating analysis of inter-war economic policy, the authors explore why positive government action failed so miserably in reversing industrial depression and was completely unable to tackle the high unemployment of the period.

Hobart Paperback 31 174pp, ISBN: 0255363052

May 1992 (pb) £12.95

- **Should Developing Countries Have Central Banks?**
Currency Quality and Monetary Systems in 155 Countries
Kurt Schuler

In this radical study Dr Schuler challenges the view that developing countries with central banks out perform those without such banks. Using comprehensive data on economic performance, he compares the success of developed countries with central banks, developing countries with central banks and developing countries without central banks to reach some startling conclusions.

Research Monograph 52 128pp, ISBN: 0255363826

July 1996 (pb) £10.00

- **Taking the Measure of Poverty**
A Critique of Low Income Statistics: Alternative Estimates & Policy Implications
Richard Pryke

In this critique of the DSS's HBAI poverty statistics Dr Richard Pryke suggests six major weaknesses which, once taken into account, give a radically different picture of poverty in the UK.

Research Monograph 51 98pp, ISBN 0255363710

October 1995 (pb) £ 9.00

- **Taxes, Benefits and Family Life: The Seven Deadly Traps**
Hermione Parker

This pioneering piece of research analyses the interactions of the tax and benefit systems. The author explains the 'seven deadly traps' which produce disincentives to work and affect family life.

Research Monograph 50 149pp, ISBN: 0255363702

September 1995 (pb) £12.00

- **Testing the Market: Competitive Tendering for Government Services in Britain and Abroad**
Robert Carnaghan and Barry Bracewell-Milnes

The authors provide an account of the growth of competitive tendering in Britain and make comparisons with experiences abroad. They review the extensive literature on the subject and show that, in general, expectations of cost savings and service improvements have been justified.

Research Monograph 49 164pp, ISBN: 0255363176

February 1993 (pb) £14.95

- **Overseas Investments, Capital Gains and the Balance of Payments**
Cliff Pratten

The author argues that the contribution of services such as banking, insurance and shipping has ensured that the balance of payments is in much better shape than is generally contended.

Research Monograph 48 121pp, ISBN: 0255363036

February 1992 (pb) £7.95

- **The Case for Earmarked Taxes: Government Spending and Public Choice**
  Ranjit S Teja and Barry Bracewell-Milnes
  The authors argue that identifying taxes with defined parts of public spending can assist in achieving a closer alignment of individual preferences with spending priorities.
  Research Monograph No 46 103pp, ISBN: 0255362412
  First published February 1991 (pb) £7.95

- **British Economic Opinion: A Survey of a Thousand Economists**
  Martin Ricketts and Edward Shoesmith
  In this fascinating paper the authors have use empirical evidence to disentangle some of the lines of disagreement between economists.
  Research Monograph 45 100pp, ISBN: 0255362331
  May 1990 (pb) £7.95

- **Money, Credit and Inflation: An Historical Indictment of UK Monetary Policy and a Proposal for Change**
  Gordon Pepper
  In this incisive paper Professor Pepper describes and explains the institutional failings in the development of British monetary policy that have lead to the recurring inflation in the UK over recent years.
  Research Monograph 44 80pp, ISBN: 0255362285
  First Published April 1990
  Second Impression February 1991 (pb) £6.95

- **Regulating Utilities: A New Era**
  Various
  1999 volume of this popular series on the latest developments in utility regulation
  Readings 49 248pp, ISBN: 025536427X
  October 1999 (pb) £17.00

- **Regulating Utilities: Understanding the Issues**
  Various
  Readings 48 259pp, ISBN: 0255364180
  September 1998 (pb) £17.00

- **Does the Past Have a Future? The Political Economy of Heritage**
  Various
  Examines the economic and political issues raised by the burgeoning heritage sector.
  Readings 47 154pp, ISBN: 0255364148
  June 1998 (pb) £15.00

- **Regulating Utilities: Broadening the Debate**
  Professor David Currie, Professor Martin Cave, Thomas Sharpe QC, et al
  Introduced and Edited by M E Beesley
  The 1997 edition of the IEA's annual volume of utility regulation essays is the most comprehensive and up-to-date guide available with the unique feature of commentaries by the regulators themselves. Highlights this year include: The New Zealand Solution: An Appraisal, Competition Law in the EC and UK, and Regulating Utilities: The Labour View.
  Readings 46 330pp, ISBN: 0255364067
  September 1997 (pb) £17.00

- **Re-Privatising Welfare: After the Lost Century**

Arthur Seldon, P M Jackson, E G West, David G Green, Martin Ricketts, Michael Beenstock, Charles Hanson, George Yarrow, Dennis O'Keefe, Nigel Ashford

Edited by Arthur Seldon

There is now widespread recognition of the difficulties of continuing with state monopolies of 'welfare provision'. In this volume, 10 authors use counterfactual analysis to explore the development of welfare before the state take-over in the late 19th Century and draw lessons for the future.

Readings 45 128pp, ISBN: 0255363842

November 1996 (pb) £11.00

- **Regulating Utilities: A Time For Change?**

Stephen Sayer, Dr Stephen Glaister, George Yarrow, Professor John Vickers, et al

Edited and introduced by Professor M E Beesley

This title assesses the state of regulation in 1995-96, considers what problems have arisen, and discusses how they might be solved. To stimulate debate the authors adopt no common political or ideological stance. The inclusion of the utility regulators and the heads of the general competition authorities is a unique feature of the Readings which present a comprehensive and up to date review of utility regulation in Britain with some lessons from the United States.

Readings 44 225pp, ISBN: 0255363818

June 1996 (pb) £17.00

- **Markets and the Media: Competition, Regulation and the Interests of Consumers**

Edited by by M E Beesley

The 'media' industries in all their forms are favoured candidates for regulation. Governments seem unwilling to let markets in media work, claiming 'imperfections' and 'failures' which require regulation. This volume explores the substance of these claims.

Readings 43 146pp, ISBN: 0255363788

March 1996 (pb) £15.00

- **Utility Regulation: Challenge and Response. The State of Britain's Regulatory Regime**

M E Beesley, Alan Bell, Ian Byatt, Sir Bryan Carsberg, Christopher Chataway, et al

Edited and introduced by M E Beesley

The regulators themselves discuss the problems they face and leading commentators assess the regulators' contributions. The result is a wealth of detail about utility regulation in Britain – where it is now and where it may be going.

Readings 42 139pp, ISBN: 0255363494

May 1995 (pb) £15.00

- **Regulating Utilities: The Way Forward**

M E Beesley, Martin Cave, Stephen Glaister, Dieter Helm et al

Edited and Introduced by M E Beesley

The state of regulation is examined both by leading commentators and by the regulators themselves. Fundamental principles are analysed as well as the practical issues involved in regulating each of the six major utilities. Two papers examine general issues – regulating networks and abuse of monopoly power.

Readings 41 160pp, ISBN: 0255363370

July 1994 (pb) £15.00

- **Major Issues in Regulation**

Sir Gordon Borrie, Sir James McKinnon, Sir Sydney Lipworth, Alan Booker, et al

Edited and introduced by M E Beesley

This collection presents a dialogue between the regulators, allies and critics on the fundamental issues and questions arising out of the regulation of public utilities.

Readings 40 155pp, ISBN: 0255363249

July 1993 (pb) £14.95

- **The State of the Economy 1993**

Tim Congdon, Bill Martin, Neil MacKinnon, Patrick Minford, Wynne Godley, et al

Introduced by Colin Robinson

Every year the IEA convenes a number of eminent economic analysts to express their views about economic prospects and policy at its 'State of the Economy' conference. In 1993 topics included; 'Moving to EMU', 'The Housing Market and the Economy' and 'British Economic Prospects in the mid 1990s.'

IEA Readings 39 120pp, ISBN: 0255363184

March 1993 (pb) £12.95

- **A Discredited Tax: The Capital Gains Tax Problem and its Solution**

Bruce Sutherland, Adrian Beecroft, Cedric Sandford, Ronald Utt, et al

Introduction by John Chown and edited by Barry Bracewell-Milnes

The authors argue that the UK system of capital gains tax is flawed both at the theoretical and practical level, creating substantial anomalies and compliance costs. They advocate reform through abolition.

IEA Readings 38 90pp, ISBN: 0255363095

September 1992 (pb) £7.95

- **The State of the Economy 1992**

Giles Keating, Peter Warburton, Walter Eltis, Douglas Fraser, John Ip, Mark Boleat, et al

Introduced by Colin Robinson

Chapters include: 'The British Economy: Sustained Recovery Depends Upon Low Interest Rates', 'Float Sterling, Cut Interest Rates', 'The Engineering Challenge', 'The Housing Market', 'Town Planning and the Supply of Housing' and 'EMU: Economic Reflections'.

IEA Readings 37 160pp, ISBN: 0255363044

March 1992 (pb) £10.95

- **Britain's Constitutional Future**

Stephen Haseler, Richard Holme, Lord Hunt of Tanworth, David King, Graham Mather, Gerard Radnitzky, Richard Rose and Frank Vibert

Edited and Introduced by Frank Vibert

This volume brings together a series of essays on the subject of institutional and constitutional change. Topics include: 'The Social Market and the Constitution of Liberty', 'Constitutional Reform in the UK', 'Britain's Feudal Constitution', 'The Political Economy of Cabinet Change', 'Government by Contract', 'The Cabinet and Next Steps', 'Local Government Taxation', 'Electoral Reform- What are the Consequences?'

IEA Readings 36 147pp, ISBN: 025536301X

November 1991 (pb) £ 9.95

- **Regulators and the Market**

  An Assessment of the Growth of Regulation in the UK

  Cento Veljanovski, M E Beesley, S C Littlechild, Irwin M Stelzer, Sir Alan Peacock, Sir Gordon Borrie, James McKinnon, Sir Bryan Carsberg, I C R Byatt, Sir Christopher Tugendhat, David Glencross, Bruce L Benson, W S Siebert and Antony W Dnes

  Edited by Cento Veljanovski

  Bringing together academic commentators and the industry regulators themselves, this book provides a comprehensive overview of the nature of the regulatory environment in the UK.

  IEA Readings 35 243pp, ISBN: 0255362498 (hd), 025536248X (pb)

  September 1991 (pb) £10.95 (hb) £20.00

- **The State of the Economy 1991**

  Mark Boleat, Roger Bootle, John Chown, Walter Eltis, Patrick Foley, et al

  Contributions include: 'UK Investment and Finance', 'The Conduct of UK Monetary Policy', 'Competition Policy', 'The Vital UK Role in Europe', 'Britain's Labour Market Prospects in an Integrated Europe' and 'The Housing Market'.

  IEA Readings 34 158pp, ISBN: 0255362439

  March 1991 (pb) £9.95

- **Europe's Constitutional Future**

  James M. Buchanan, Graham Mather, Karl Otto Pohl, Victoria Curzon Price, Frank Vibert

  A symposium of papers on the future of Europe. Chapters include: 'Europe's Constitutional Opportunity', 'Towards Monetary Union', 'The Threat of Fortress Europe', 'Europe's Constitutional Deficit', 'The Powers of the European Parliament'.

  IEA Readings 33 146pp, ISBN: 0255362374

  December 1990 (pb) £8.95

- **Which Road to Fiscal Neutrality?**

  Philip Chappell, John Kay, Bill Robinson

  Introduction by Barry Bracewell-Milnes

  This set of four papers discusses the taxation of investment income and of saving more generally. The authors argue that the present system is far from neutral, with some forms of saving taxed more heavily than others. They argue why this is unsatisfactory and advocate a number of policy changes.

  IEA Readings 32 56pp, ISBN: 0255362366

  September 1990 (pb) £6.95

- **The State of the Economy**

  An Assessment of Britain's Economy by Leading Economists at the Start of the 1990s

  Tim Congdon, Walter Eltis, Jonathan Haskel, John Kay, Giles Keating, David Lomax, et al

  Introduction by Graham Mather

  Chapters include: 'What Went .Wrong with UK Demand and Trade Performance? How to Put it Right?, 'British Industrial Policy for the 1990s', 'Productivity in British Industry Under Mrs Thatcher', 'Monetary Control, Past, Present, and Future', 'European Monetary Integration in the 1990s', 'The Keys to Success: Consuming Less and Producing More'.

  IEA Readings 31 140pp, ISBN: 0255362307

  February 1990 (hb) £14.95

- **Do We Need the IMF and the World Bank?**
  Sir Alan Walters
  Lady Thatcher's former economic adviser considers the performance of these two international institutions on their fiftieth anniversaries, and considers them in need of abolition or at least major reform
  Current Controversies 10 22pp, ISBN: 0255363397
  September 1994 (pb) £3.00

- **Britain's Student Loan System in World Perspective: A Critique**
  Edwin G West
  E G West examines the student loan system in this country and finds it deficient in several ways. Professor West shows that better loans systems exist elsewhere, especially in New Zealand.
  Current Controversies 9 41pp, ISBN: 0255363354
  June 1994 (pb) £4.00

- **The Road to Monetary Union Revisited**
  John Chown, Geoffrey E Wood and Massimo Beber
  The authors explain why monetary union is desirable, but can only be achieved by a 'parallel currency', which would avoid the political and economic costs associated with a more centralised approach.
  Current Controversies 8 33pp, ISBN: 025536332X
  April 1994 (pb) £3.50

- **Should the Taxpayer Support the Arts?**
  David Sawers
  The author examines the arguments for state support of the arts and finds them unconvincing. The development of artistic talent should be left to individuals and the Department of National Heritage and the Arts Council should be abolished.
  Current Controversies 7 44pp, ISBN: 0255363257
  September 1993 (pb) £3.95

- **Social Engineering in the European Community: The Social Charter, Maastricht and Beyond**
  John T Addison and W Stanley Siebert
  An analysis of the effects of the social chapter of the Maastricht Treaty which shows that such intervention is likely to increase unemployment and harm the competitive position of European economies.
  Current Controversies 6 42pp, ISBN: 0255363230
  July 1993 (pb) £3.95

- **New Directions for British Railways? The Political Economy of Privatisation and Regulation**
  Stephen Glaister and Tony Travers
  The authors discuss proposals to privatise the railway industry and provide a detailed critique of this complex privatisation.
  Current Controversies 5 66pp, ISBN: 0255363214
  June 1993 (pb) £4.95

- **Central Bank Independence: What Is It and What Will It Do For Us?**
  Geoffrey E Wood, Terence C Mills and Forrest H Capie
  Three distinguished economists discuss what central bank independence means, and its effects on monetary policy.
  Current Controversies 4 32pp, ISBN: 025536315X
  January 1993 (pb) £2.95

- **Making a Market in Energy**
  Colin Robinson
  A detailed examination of the UK energy market and recommendations of a number of bold free-market reforms.
  Current Controversies 3 33pp, ISBN: 0255363141
  December 1992 (pb) £2.95

- **Trade Wars: A Repetition of the Inter-War Years?**
  Forrest Capie
  Analyses the world's last lapse into protectionism in the 1930s and draws worrying conclusions for the present.
  Current Controversies 2 17pp, ISBN: 0255363133
  December 1992 (pb) £2.00

- **Restoring Credibility: Monetary Policy Now**
  Gordon Pepper
  Explores and analyses Government monetary policy in the late eighties, and explains why the last recession differed from earlier ones.
  Current Controversies 1 20pp, ISBN: 0255363117
  October 1992 (pb) £2.50

- **Private Money: The Path to Monetary Stability**
  Kevin Dowd
  Professor Kevin Dowd presents a compelling case for 'free-banking'. Monetary stability can be achieved through a competitive banking system. This requires complete financial deregulation, the abolition of the Bank of England, and a re-definition of the monetary standards in terms of a general commodity index.
  Hobart Paper 112 71pp, ISBN: 0255362161
  First Edition 1988
  Second Impression June 1996 (pb) £7.00

- **The Myth of Social Cost**
  A Critique of Welfare Economics and the Implications for Public Policy
  Steven N S Cheung
  Prologue by Charles K Rowley, Epilogue by John Burton
  A critique of 'welfare economics', arguing that the costs of government intervention to alleviate social costs often outweigh the perceived social benefits.
  Hobart Paper 82 93pp, ISBN: 0255361122
  First published September 1978, Second Impression May 1981
  Third Impression February 1992 (pb) £5.95

- **Denationalisation of Money: The Argument Refined**
  F A Hayek
  In the third edition of his classic, Professor Hayek argues that the problem of recurrent inflation is due to government monopoly provision of money, competition being the solution.
  Hobart Paper 70 93pp, ISBN: 0255362390
  First published October 1976, Second Edition February 1978
  Third Edition October 1990 (pb) £8.95

- **Pricing for Pollution: Market Pricing, Government Regulation, Environmental Policy**
  Wilfred Beckerman

  Dr Beckerman makes a case for pollution control through taxation. In skilfully scotching many of the fallacies which plague discussions of pricing systems, Dr Beckerman shows that if pollution charges were adopted, they would help poor countries as well as rich ones.

  Hobart Paper 66 80pp, ISBN: 0255362293

  First published December 1975

  Second Edition January 1990 (pb) £4.95

- **Privatisation and Competition: A Market Prospectus**
  Edited by Cento Veljanovski

  There is a growing concern in the utility industries that monopolies have been transferred from the public to the private sector. The contributors to this book examine the interplay between privatisation, competition and regulation in these emerging private industries.

  Hobart Paperback 28 239pp, ISBN 0255362110²

  First published January 1989

  Second Impression May 1992 (pb) £9.50

- **Farming for Farmers? A Critique of Agricultural Support Policy**
  Richard W Howarth

  Argues that in the post-war period agriculture has been run principally for the benefit of farmers through an inefficient system of price support. The numerous costs of the system are examined in detail as are the supposed justifications.

  Hobart Paperback 20 206pp, ISBN: 025536234X

  First published January 1985

  Second Edition August 1990 (pb) £10.95

- **Beyond Left and Right: The New Politics of Britain**
  John Blundell and Brian Gosschalk

  Challenging traditional notions of the political spectrum, this piece of research presents new evidence about the nature of political alignment in Britain. Based on data compiled by Mori, the report shows that discussions about a simple 'left-right' political axis in Britain are simplistic and ignore the subtleties of public opinion and ideology.

  IEA Working Paper 1 77pp, ISBN: 0255364113

  December 1997 (pb) £25.00

- **Inside Thatcher's Monetarist Revolution**
  Gordon Pepper

  Published in conjunction with Macmillan, this book is a unique 'fly-on-the-wall' insight into Margaret Thatcher's revolution in British monetary and economic policy. Gordon Pepper is credited with teaching monetarism to the City of London and had 'insider' status in the early 1980s. He has written a masterly critical account of a fascinating and revealing period in British post-war economic history.

  Published in association with Macmillan

  pp214, ISBN: 0333720121

  First Published March 1998 (pb) £15.99

- **Free Banking in Britain:Theory, Experience and Debate 1800–1845**
  Lawrence H White

  Since the first (1984) edition of Lawrence H White's pioneering work, Free Banking in Britain, the literature on free banking has expanded considerably. In this second edition, the author has not only revised the text (especially Chapter 2), he has added a new chapter which incorporates a revised version of a reply to his critics first published in 1991. The result is a significantly revised and updated edition of a book about privately issued currency.

  First published 1984 176pp, ISBN: 025363753
  Second Revised Edition 1995 (pb) £12.00

- **The Supply Side Revolution in Britain**
  Patrick Minford

  Patrick Minford made an important contribution to the ideas of Thatcherism and Britain's monetarist/supply side programme in the 1980s. This book brings together essays written for a wide audience as a contribution to the supply side revolution in Britain.

  Published in association with Edward Elgar
  346pp, ISBN: 1852784261
  First published 1991 (pb) £15.95

- **Economic Freedom of the World: 1997 Annual Report**
  James Gwartney and Robert Lawson

  In this thoroughly revised and updated study 115 countries are rated for their degree of economic freedom. It is the product of 60 researchers in 11 countries, and quantifies the extent to which individuals are free to engage in economic activities. Major changes in the new 1997 edition include: more country profiles and in particular the addition of profiles of China and Russia.

  We presume that economic freedom contributes to economic prosperity and growth by encouraging creative entrepreneurship and a more productive workforce. Yet research on this subject has been hampered by incomplete and inadequate measures of freedom in economic life. This book helps fill the void with detailed measures for over one hundred nations . . .' – Gary S Becker, Nobel Laureate

  Published in Association with the Fraser Institute et al
  ISBN: 0889751757, 300pp
  April 1997 (pb) £35.00

- **Recent Controversies in Political Economy**
  Edited by Russell Lewis

  This volume is made up of a collection of articles on political economy and economic policy taken from Economic Affairs, the Institute's journal, in areas as diverse as taxation, education, housing, and the environment.

  Published in association with Routledge
  346pp, ISBN: 0415079799
  1992 (pb) £14.99

- **Reclaiming Education**

  James Tooley

  Drawn on global research, this offers an alternative to poor quality and wasteful inefficiency in education and that education can be radically transformed to guarantee freedom and higher standards.

  Published by Cassell

  258pp, ISBN: 03040705675

  2000 (pb) £12.99

- **The Triumph of Liberty: A 2000 Year History, Told Through the Lives of Freedom's Greatest Champion.**

  Jim Powell, with a foreword by Paul Johnson

  Chronicles the story of liberty through sixty-five biographical portraits.

  Published by Free Press

  574pp, ISBN: 068485967X

  2000 (hb) £25.00

- **Earth Report 2000: Revisiting the True State of the Planet**

  Edited by Ronald Bailey

  A Number of high-profile authors comprehensively refute many of the more fanciful ideas proposed by the environmental movement.

  Published by The Competitive Enterprise Institute

  362pp, ISBN: 0071342605

  2000 (pb) £15.00

- **Overfishing: The Icelandic Solution**

  Hannes H Gissurarson

  A historical chronology of the development of individual transferable quotas (ITQs) in Icelandic fisheries.

  Studies on the Environment 17, 68pp, ISBN: 025536489x

  March 2000 (pb) £8.00

- **Fur and Freedom: In Defence of the Fur Trade**

  Richard D North with a Foreward by Roger Scruton

  Refuting every claim put forward by the animal rights lobby, arguing that the fur trade is neither cruel or immoral and that a ban is based on flawed logic and sentimentality.

  Studies on the Environment 16, 100pp, ISBN: 0255364865

  March 2000 (pb) £8.00

- **Tropical Rain Forest**

  Philip Stott

  Subtitled 'A Political Ecology of Hegemonic Mythmaking'. Stott challenges the conventional wisdom about rain forests.

  Studies on the Environment 15, 44pp, ISBN: 0255364857

  November 1999 (pb) £8.00

- **Wild in Woods: The Myth of the Noble Eco Savage**
  Robert Whelan

  Argues that the noble eco savage is a white Western artifact with native peoples equally as destructive of their environments as Western man.

  Studies on the Environment 14, 69pp, ISBN: 0255364474

  May 1999 (pb) £8.00

- **Property Rights and the Environment**
  Various

  Shows the practical solutions obtainable by property rights approaches to environmental problems.

  Studies on the Environment 13, 56pp, ISBN: 0255364717

  March 1999 (pb) £6.00

- **Reforming Land Use Planning**
  Various

  Outlines the flaws in Britain's land use planning system and provides an alternative.

  Studies on the Environment 12, 88pp, ISBN: 0255364466

  August 1998 (pb) £8.00

- **Fishing for Solutions**
  Michael de Alessi

  Argues that the primary cause of fish stock depletion is a lack of ownership. The author proposes a clearly defined, enforceable and tradeable property rights in fish.

  Studies on the Environment 11, 88pp, ISBN 025536444X

  February 1988 (pb) £8.00

- **Climate Change: Challenging the Conventional Wisdom**
  Ed. by Julian Morris

  Contributions from Robert Balling, Roger Bate, Sonja Boehmer-Christiansen, Deepak Lal and Thomas Gale Moore

  With politicians and opinion formers across the world issuing apocalyptic predictions about the effects of man-made climate change, this controversial new book examines the substance to the claims that 'there is a discernible human influence on the global climate' at all.

  Studies on the Environment 10 109pp, ISBN: 0255364431

  December 1997 (pb) £12.00

- **Environmental Education**
  Benjamin Aldrich-Moodie and Jo Kwong

  This original piece of research examines the teaching of environmental issues in the UK and US. Looking at a variety of textbooks and how specific issues are taught, they find that the teaching of the environment is characterised by bad science, sloppy thinking and indoctrination.

  Studies in Education 3 & Studies on the Environment 9 126pp, ISBN: 0255364423

  October 1997 (pb) £10.00

- **Green Goods: Consumers, Product Labels and the Environment**

Julian Morris

In the late 1980s governments and private sector companies developed seal of approval 'ecolabels' purporting to denote the most environment-friendly products available. In this major new study the numerous practical difficulties with both voluntary and compulsory 'ecolabel' schemes are examined.

Studies on the Environment 8 102pp, ISBN: 0255363441S

March 1997 (pb) £10.00

- **Down to Earth II: Combating Environmental Myths**

Matt Ridley

A second collection of essays by Matt Ridley, this book represents the best of the author's columns in the Sunday Telegraph, Daily Telegraph and others. Ridley challenges the views of the vested interests of environmental lobbyists and politicians. Witty and often humorous, his essays comment on recurring environmental themes and problems.

Studies on the Environment 7 102pp, ISBN: 0255363834

August 1996 (pb) £8.00

- **Conservation and the Countryside: By Quango or Market?**

Mark Pennington

The author explains why government and bureaucratic attempts at environmental protection have failed and argues that to safeguard the countryside we need to restore private property rights.

Studies on the Environment 6 68pp, ISBN: 0255363796

April 1996 (pb) £6.00

- **The Political Economy of Land Degradation: Pressure Groups, Foreign Aid and the Myth of Man-Made Deserts**

Julian Morris

The root causes of land degradation are the actions of political entrepreneurs, aid agencies, and governments of developing countries who misuse 'aid' money. Only when individuals are permitted to own property, especially land and water, to engage in free trade, and to resolve disputes through customary law, will the problems of land degradation, poverty, and hunger be reduced to acceptable levels.

Studies on the Environment 5 107pp, ISBN: 0255363486

May 1995 (pb) £9.00

- **Rhinos: Conservation, Economics and Trade-Offs**

Michael 't Sas-Rolfes

In this paper Michael 't Sas-Rolfes carefully examines the benefits and costs of reopening the trade in rhino products. He suggests a strategy for managing the opening of this trade to increase the probability that rhinos as a wild species will survive.

Studies on the Environment 4 69pp, ISBN: 0255363478

April 1995 (pb) £ 6.00

- **Down to Earth: A Contrarian View of Environmental Problems**

Matt Ridley

Dr Ridley is one of a number of environmentalists who are seeking to counter the inaccurate and misleading opinions of 'mainstream environmentalism'. This volume brings together a selection of 30 of Dr Ridley's 'Down to Earth' columns which appeared in The Sunday Telegraph.

Studies on the Environment 3 80pp, ISBN: 0255363451

February 1995 (pb) £ 8.00

- **Elephants and Ivory: Lessons from the Trade Ban**
  Ike C Sugg and Urs P Kreuter
  The authors examine the example of elephants in this exposition of the arguments favouring 'sustainable utilization'. This approach ensures species survival by employing a framework based upon property rights, enforcement of those rights and local community involvement.
  Studies on the Environment 2 74pp, ISBN: 0255363427
  November 1994 (pb) £ 7.00

- **Global Warming: Apocalypse or Hot Air?**
  Roger Bate and Julian Morris
  Foreword by Wilfred Beckerman
  In this study the authors examine the so-called scientific 'consensus' about global warming. They argue climate change is a problem of great complexity, and such analysis as has been made by no means supports the view that climate change would place intolerable burdens on future generations.
  Studies on the Environment 1 53pp, ISBN: 0255363311
  First published February 1994
  Second Impression August 1994 (pb) £ 5.00

- **Does CITES work? Four Case Studies**
  Michael 't Sas-Rolfes
  Michael 't Sas-Rolfes presents four case studies to show the ineffectiveness of CITES in protecting endangered species. Examining the cases of rhinos, elephants, tigers and bears, he demonstrates that state-driven regulatory regimes have failed to protect wildlife.
  Environment Briefing Paper 4 11pp, ISBN: 0255364423
  June 1997 (pb) £3.00

- **Learning From The Past, Freeing Up The Future: The Political Economy of Regulatory Change**
  Fred L Smith Jr
  In this third IEA Environment Briefing Paper, Fred Smith, President of the Competitive Enterprise Institute (CEI) in Washington D.C. describes the recent history of environmental protection in the US.
  Environmental Unit Briefing 3 32pp, ISBN: 0255364407
  November 1996 (pb) £3.00

- **Establishing a Market in Emissions Credits: A Business Perspective**
  John Palmisano
  As scientists continue to debate the existence and implications of global warming, policy makers are advocating drastic cuts in emissions of greenhouse gases. In this paper, John Palmisano presents an alternative to the conventional solution to the problems of air pollution; a system of tradeable emission permits.
  Environment Unit Briefing 2 68pp, ISBN: 0255363869
  July 1996 (pb) £5.00

- **The Political Economy of Climate Change Science: A Discernible Human Influence on Climate Documents?**
  Roger Bate
  The director of the IEA's Environment Unit explains how science has been subverted in the debate surrounding climate change. He argues that powerful interests have manipulated the political process to seek policy decisions that reflect their own narrow ideological agenda.
  Environment Unit Briefing 1 26pp, ISBN: 0255363877
  July 1996 (pb) £3.00

- **Emerging Technologies and the Private Stewardship of Marine Resources**
  Michael De Alessi

  De Alessi examines the new technologies that enable for the first time property rights to be established over marine resources – the crucial means in ensuring the survival of depleted stocks.

  Environment Unit Working Paper 1 32pp, ISBN: 0255363850

  October 1996 (pb) £4.00

- **Benefit Dependency: How Welfare Undermines Independence**
  David G Green

  In this controversial new paper, Dr David Green suggests that poverty statistics are misleading and that contrary to the claims of those in the 'poverty industry', the poor have not been getting poorer.

  Choice in Welfare 41 48pp, ISBN: 0255364334

  January 1998 (pb) £6.00

- **Should Pharmaceutical Prices be Regulated?**
  David G Green (editor), Philip Brown, M L Burstall, Elias Mossialos, Heinz Redwood and W Duncan Reekie

  In this stimulating new title a critique is presented of the Pharmaceutical Price Regulation Scheme (PPRS). The scheme, which seeks to control the prices of drugs, is one of a range of measures which interferes with one of Britain's most successful high-tech industries and the book is effectively a case-study of the effects of government over regulation of industry.

  Choice in Welfare 40 133pp, ISBN: 025536430X

  October 1997 (pb) £12.00

- **From Welfare to Work: Lessons from America**
  Lawrence M Mead

  Commentaries by Alan Deacon (editor), Dee Cook, Alistair Grimes, Eithne McLaughlin, Melanie Phillips, John Philpott and Frank Field MP

  In this timely collection of essays, the issue of 'welfare to work' is examined in detail. Professor Lawrence Mead of New York University summaries his extensive research on the merits of 'workfare', which is then critiqued by a number of UK experts from across the political spectrum.

  Choice in Welfare 39 154pp, ISBN: 0255363990

  November 1997 (pb) £8.00

- **Does Prison Work?**
  Charles Murray

  Commentaries by Malcolm Davies, Andrew Rutherford and Jock Young

  In this topical new collection four commentators make important contributions to the contemporary debate on crime and punishment and the relationship between the two. Coming from a variety of standpoints this is a succinct and accessible introduction to the issues.

  Choice in Welfare 38 54pp, ISBN: 0255363982

  July 1997 (pb) £6.00

- **How to Pay for Health Care: Public and Private Alternatives**
  David Gladstone (editor), Judith Allsop, Michael Goldsmith, David G Green, Chris Ham

  In this collection of essays the authors investigate different ways in which health care could be funded. Representing a wide diversity of viewpoints, this book is a timely contribution to the debate surrounding the future of the NHS.

  Choice in Welfare 37 60pp, ISBN: 0255363974

  June 1997 (pb) £6.00

- **Stakeholding and its Critics**
  Will Hutton
  Commentaries by Tim Congdon, David G Green, Stanley Kalms, Martin Ricketts and Elaine Sternberg
  A comprehensive symposium bringing a rigorous and forthright analysis of the 'stakeholding' phenomenon.
  Choice in Welfare 36 102pp, ISBN: 0255363966
  June 1997 (pb) £7.00

- **Zero Tolerance: Policing a Free Society**
  William J Bratton, Norman Dennis, Ray Mallon, John Orr, Charles Pollard
  This book brings together police officers from both sides of the Atlantic to describe their efforts to deal effectively with rising crime. Commenting on the controversial 'zero tolerance' strategy they reach a number of different conclusions.
  Choice in Welfare 35 138pp, ISBN: 0255363958
  April 1997 (pb) £8.00

- **The Invention of Permanent Poverty**
  Norman Dennis
  Dennis attacks the so called 'no-fault' theory of human conduct which holds that crime and societal breakdown are caused, not by individual conduct, but by poverty and unemployment. He shows this position to be based on distorted statistics and a lack of historical perspective.
  Choice in Welfare 34 212pp, ISBN: 0255363923
  January 1997 (pb) £10.00

- **Charles Murray and the Underclass: The Developing Debate**
  Charles Murray
  Commentaries by Ruth Lister (Editor), Frank Field MP, Joan C Brown, Alan Walker, Nicholas Deakin, Pete Alcock, Miriam David, Melanie Phillips, Sue Slipman. Statistical Update by Alan Buckingham
  This book brings together Murray's previous two works for the IEA. Published with a new introduction, the book provides a comprehensive overview of the entire 'underclass' debate and is therefore invaluable as a teaching aid.
  Choice in Welfare 33 180pp, ISBN: 0255363915
  November 1996 (pb) £8.00

- **Stakeholder Welfare**
  Frank Field
  With commentaries by Alan Deacon (editor), Pete Alcock, David G Green, Melanie Phillips
  In this book four thinkers who stretch across the political divide 'think the unthinkable' about the welfare state. The lead article is by Frank Field MP who advocates a radical overhaul of the present system to harness self-interest by extending the scope of contributory benefits.
  Choice in Welfare 32 115pp, ISBN: 0255363907
  November 1996 (pb) £7.00

- **Who Needs Parents?**
  The Effects of Childcare and Early Education on Children in Britain & USA
  Patricia Morgan
  In this timely book Morgan reveals that a considerable amount of evidence has been accumulating which calls into question the idea that third-party childcare is good for children.
  Choice in Welfare 31 164pp, ISBN: 0255363680
  October 1996 (pb) £9.00

- **Medicine Prices and Innovations: An International Survey**

  W. Duncan Reekie

  Professor Duncan Reekie examines the economic and clinical benefits that would arise from competition in pharmaceuticals. He finds the sector to highly over-regulated much to detriment of consumers and the industry alike.

  Choice in Welfare 30 66pp, ISBN: 0255363699

  September 1996 (pb) £12.00

- **The Corrosion of Charity: From Moral Renewal to Contract Culture**

  Robert Whelan

  Throughout the Twentieth Century the welfare state has progressively widened its embrace so much that many find it hard to imagine a private alternative. In this book the author explores the history of charitable institutions, and the extent to which they have been compromised by their increasing involvement with the state.

  Choice in Welfare 29 116pp, ISBN: 0255363672

  July 1996 (pb) £7.00

- **Unequal But Fair? A Study of Class Barriers in Britain**

  Peter Saunders

  There is a widespread belief that British society is unfair. Drawing on authoritative new evidence Professor Peter Saunders demonstrates that Britain is much more open than most people have realised – rebutting claims that 'life chances' are determined by background.

  Choice in Welfare 28 100pp, ISBN: 0255363664

  July 1996 (pb) £7.00

- **Community Without Politics: A Market Approach to Welfare Reform**

  David G Green

  It is now almost a truism that the welfare state creates dependency amongst some benefit recipients, but in a new study by Dr David G. Green it is also shown that the nationalisation of welfare has undermined the tradition of non-political action for the public good.

  Choice in Welfare 27 184pp, ISBN: 0255363648

  December 1995 (pb) £8.00

- **Prescribing the Price of Pharmaceuticals**

  W Duncan Reekie

  The author examines the claims made by some government officials that the pharmaceutical industry is uncompetitive and finds, on the contrary, that on all the usual measures there is considerable competition.

  Choice in Welfare 26 120pp, ISBN: 025536363X

  November 1995 (pb) £12.00

- **Making a Lottery of Good Causes: The National Lottery and the Politicisation of Charity**

  Roger Cummins and Robert Whelan

  The authors comment that the National Lottery has led to a politicisation of charity with various 'good causes' pitted against each other in the political process. The solution is to disband the state-run National Lottery and open the lottery market up to competing private lotteries.

  Choice in Welfare 25 28pp, ISBN: 0255363621

  September 1995 (pb) £3.00

- **Just a Piece of Paper? Divorce Reform and the Undermining of Marriage**
James Q Wilson, Melanie Phillips, Patricia Morgan, Norman Barry, Bryce Christensen
Edited by Robert Whelan
In this report authors from the US and Britain argue that a series of recent divorce reforms have led to the 'casualisation' of marriage with wide ramifications.
Choice in Welfare 24 94pp, ISBN: 0255363613
July 1995 (pb) £6.00

- **Patients or Customers: Are the NHS Reforms Working?**
J I L Bayley, Gillian and Ben FitzGerald, Geoffrey Glazer, Robert Kennedy, Hamish Laing, and John C Nicholls. Commentaries by Peter Collison, Arthur Seldon and Sir Richard Storey. Edited by Sir Reginald Murley
A panel of medical professionals, surgeons, consultants and GPs, write of their experiences of the day-to-day working of the reforms.
Choice in Welfare 23 87pp, ISBN: 0255363605
June 1995 (pb) £6.00

- **The De-moralization of Society: From Victorian Virtues to Modern Values**
Gertrude Himmelfarb
From one of America's leading historians comes a piece of historical research which corrects misconceptions about the values of Victorian England and offers a provocative critique of modern society, calling for a return to the eternal moral 'virtues'.
Choice in Welfare 22 314pp, ISBN: 0255363591
March 1995 (pb) £12.50

- **Farewell to the Family? Public Policy and Family Breakdown in Britain and the USA**
Patricia Morgan
In this wide ranging study Patricia Morgan shows how successive governments have implemented policies which have been to the detriment of the family unit and explores the destructive consequences for society.
Choice in Welfare 21 194pp, ISBN: 0255363567
January 1995 (pb) £9.00

- **Underclass: The Crisis Deepens**
Charles Murray
Commentaries by Peter Alcock, Miriam David, Melanie Phillips and Sue Slipman
Murray presents evidence that the 'emerging underclass' he described in 1990 is growing with potentially cat-astrophic results. To add to the value for those in education who wish to see both sides of the argument, the book contains four commentaries by critics.
Choice in Welfare No.20 69pp, ISBN: 0255363559
September 1994 (pb) £5.99

- **Liberating Women . . . From Modern Feminism**
Norman Barry, Mary Kenny, Michael Levin, Patricia Morgan, Joan Kennedy Taylor, Glenn Wilson. Edited by Caroline Quest
A collection of essays by leading commentators assessing to what extent the 'feminist movement' is compat-ible with liberty and a free society.
Choice in Welfare 19 101pp, ISBN: 0255363532
March 1994 (pb) £6.95

- **Rising Crime and the Dismembered Family: How Conformist Intellectual Have Campaigned Against Common Sense**
  Norman Dennis
  Norman Dennis demolishes the claims of 'conformist intellectuals', who subscribe to the politically correct doctrines of the day, by carefully drawing attention to the facts about rising crime and family breakdown.
  Choice in Welfare 18 92pp, ISBN: 0255363508
  October 1993 (pb) £5.95

- **Reinventing Civil Society: The Rediscovery of Welfare Without Politics**
  David G Green
  David G Green criticises the hard-boiled economic rationalism of the Thatcher years. Thatcherite emphasis on the 'vigorous virtues' was necessary to halt economic decline, but ignored the 'civic virtues' of duty, service and self-sacrifice.
  Choice in Welfare 17 166pp, ISBN: 025536279X
  September 1993 (pb) £7.95

- **Medicard: A Better Way To Pay for Medicines?**
  David G Green and David A Lucas
  In the face of expanding costs and the changing nature of the doctor patient relationship, the NHS system for paying for medicine is in need of review. The authors make proposals for change.
  Choice in Welfare 16 33pp, ISBN: 0255362781
  July 1993 (pb) £4.95

- **The Family: Is it Just Another Lifestyle Choice?**
  Brigitte Berger and Allan Carlson
  Edited by Jon Davies
  Is every moral value just another lifestyle option? Or is there a minimum stock of values which we ignore at our peril? This authors examine the proper social value of the family and conclude that it is vital to the underpinning of our society; the weakening of it is the cause of the malaise and degradation affecting society.
  Choice in Welfare 15 109pp, ISBN: 0255362765
  April 1993 (pb) £6.95

- **God and the Marketplace: Essays on the Morality of Wealth Creation**
  Michael Novak, Bishop John Jukes, Rev Dr Simon Robinson, Richard Roberts, Rev John Kennedy, Geoff Moore, Rev Dr James Francis, and Vin Arthey
  Edited by Jon Davies
  Catholic, Anglican and Methodist theologians ask whether capitalism is morally acceptable.
  Choice in Welfare 14 145pp, ISBN: 0255362757
  March 1993 (pb) £4.90

- **Undermining Innovation: Parallel Trade in Prescription Medicines**
  M L Burstall and Ian S T Senior
  Introduction by Patrick Minford
  Examines the unintended side effects of EC regulation of the pharmaceutical industry which, through controlling prices, has deterred research.
  Choice in Welfare 13 76pp, ISBN: 0255362749
  First published October 1992 (pb) £12.95

- **Families Without Fatherhood**

  Norman Dennis and George Erdos

  Introduction by A H Halsey

  The authors argue that the traditional family system developed as a coherent strategy for the ordering of relations in such a way as to equip children for their own eventual adult responsibilities, but they present evidence that since the 1960s there has been a weakening of these norms with dangerous consequences.

  Choice in Welfare 12 127pp, ISBN: 025536230

  First published September 1992 (pb) £7.95

- **Equal Opportunities: A Feminist Fallacy**

  Michael Levin, Ellen Frankel Paul, David Conway, Ivy Papps, Joan Kennedy Taylor, Wendy McElroy and edited by Caroline Quest

  Throughout public life, there seems to be an uncritical acceptance of the feminist message about work. This book attacks this most modern of sacred cows on a range of fronts.

  Choice in Welfare 11 114pp, ISBN: 0255362722

  July 1992 (pb) £6.95

- **The Moral Foundations of Market Institutions**

  John Gray

  Commentaries by Chandran Kukathas, Patrick Minford and Raymond Plant

  Distinguished Oxford philosopher John Gray, examines the moral legitimacy of the market economy. While upholding the value of the market economy he insists on the importance of an enabling welfare state.

  Choice in Welfare 10 142pp, ISBN: 0255362714

  May 1992 (pb) £7.95

- **Morality, Capitalism and Democracy**

  Michael Novak

  Distinguished commentator Michael Novak attacks the notion that capitalism promotes selfishness and provides an authoritative re-statement of the ideal of liberty based upon a pluralist, open and tolerant society, with a vital, dynamic ethos.

  Choice in Welfare 5 39pp, ISBN: 0255362668

  September 1990 (pb) £3.95

- **Citizenship and Rights in Thatcher's Britain: Two Views**

  Raymond Plant and Norman Barry

  Two leading political theorists discuss the rights and obligations of citizenship, Prof Plant arguing from a socialist standpoint and Prof Barry from a classical-liberal perspective.

  Choice in Welfare 3 77pp, ISBN: 0255362617

  June 1990 (pb) £3.95

- **The Emerging British Underclass**

  Charles Murray

  Commentaries by Frank Field, Joan C. Brown, Alan Walker and Nicholas Deakin

  Murray examines Britain's social problems and provides convincing evidence for the emergence of a British underclass, defined not only by its poverty but also by its behaviour. Murray's paper is published with commentaries by four distinguished British social policy analysts, all critical of his thesis.

  Now available in a revised format, see Charles Murray and The Underclass

  Choice in Welfare 2 82pp, ISBN: 025536263 May 1990 (pb) £5.95

- **Perestroika in the Universities**

  Elie Kedourie

  Kedourie's study reveals the dangers of over reliance on state funding. The Education Reform Act enforces tight control over all aspects of university life which runs counter to the Government's aim of greater autonomy. Councils and committees proliferate and the Committee of Vice-Chancellors and Principals works in unholy harmony with the DES.

  Choice in Welfare 1 53pp, ISBN: 0255362579

  November 1989 (pb) £5.00

- **Death by Regulation: The Butchery of the British Meat Industry**

  Richard North

  Introduction by Colin Robinson

  The Fresh Meat (Hygiene and Inspection) Regulations 1992, introduced by the Ministry of Agriculture, Fisheries and Food, go far beyond the requirements of the EC directive on which they claim to be based. They are not only highly damaging to the British meat industry but will fail to achieve any real improvement to standards of meat hygiene.

  Health Series 12 30pp, ISBN: 0255362773

  May 1993 (pb) £4.95

- **Chickengate: An Independent Analysis of the Salmonella in Eggs Scare**

  Richard North and Teresa Gorman, MP

  Introduced by J P Duguid

  The authors argue that while government has a role in raising standards of food safety, the process is prone to over-regulation which has devastating consequences.

  Health Series 10 117pp, ISBN: 0255362609

  April 1990 (pb) £4.95

- **1992 and the Regulation of the Pharmaceutical Industry**

  M L Burstall

  The book presents a detailed analysis of the structure of the European drug market and explores the potential for deregulation.

  Health Series 9 88pp, ISBN: 0255362595

  April 1990 (pb) £6.95

- **Awakening from Nihilism: Why Truth Matters**

  Michael Novak

  In 1994 Michael Novak was awarded the Templeton Prize for Progress in Religion. This is his acceptance speech in which he spoke of the difference between truth and falsehood and the consequences of blurring it, and of the triumph of the market economy and democracy.

  Religion and Liberty 4 28pp, ISBN: 0255363583

  February 1995 (pb) £3.00

- **Teaching Right and Wrong: Have the Churches Failed?**

  Rt Rev Michael Adie, Jon Davies, Rabbi Dr Julian Jacobs, Revd John Kennedy,

  Rt Rev David Konstant and Rev William F Wallace

  Edited by Robert Whelan

  In this collection of essays the representatives of the leading churches discuss the extent to which churches can be blamed for problems which occur in a largely secular society. No one doubts that moral values should be taught: these essays indicate a range of views within the churches about the best methods to adopt.

Religion and Liberty 3 44pp, ISBN: 0255363575

November 1994 (pb) £5.00

- **A Moral Basis for Liberty**

Revd Robert A Sirico, CSP

Commentaries by Rt Hon The Lord Lawson of Blaby and William Oddie

Father Robert Sirico argues that the market has its own moral foundation based on respect for private property and voluntary activity, and that economic progress itself is threatened if market apologists are unwilling or unable to engage in moral debate.

Religion and Liberty 2 38pp, ISBN: 0252363540

August 1994 (pb) £4.95

- **Christian Capitalism or Christian Socialism?**

Michael Novak and Ronald Preston

In this volume Michael Novak and Ronald Preston address the competing claims of capitalism and socialism upon the Christian conscience. Writing from different political standpoints and Christian traditions, both authors confront the shortcomings of their preferred systems.

Religion and Liberty 1 38pp, ISBN: 0255363524

April 1994 (pb) £4.95

- **Octavia Hill and the Social Housing Debate: Essays and Letters by Octavia Hill**

Edited by Robert Whelan

Octavia Hill (1838-1912) was one of the most remarkable women of the late Victorian era, being famous for her pioneering work among the poor and in particular her work in the field of housing. In this new book a selection of her writings and speeches are reproduced for the benefit of modern audiences with a 39 page editor's introduction.

Rediscovered Riches 3 134pp, ISBN: 0255364318

February 1998 (pb) £7.00

- **Memoir on Pauperism**

Alexis de Tocqueville

Translated by Seymour Drescher with an introduction by Gertrude Himmelfarb

Written in 1835 after a visit to England, Tocqueville explores the paradox that while England was the wealthiest country of the time, it also had the largest number of paupers. Ascribing this to the dependency inducing effects of state welfare, this book has important lessons for our current age.

Rediscovered Riches 2 40pp, ISBN: 025536394X

May 1997 (pb) £5.00

- **Self-Help, with illustrations of Conduct and Perseverance**

Samuel Smiles

With a Foreword by Lord Harris of High Cross

Self-Help was one of the great success stories of Victorian publishing, selling over a quarter of million copies by the turn of the century. Smiles uses inspiring stories of hundreds of individuals to convey the timeless message that success owes little to birth or fortune, but depends entirely on an individual's capacity for hard work and perseverance in the face of difficulty.

Rediscovered Riches 1 250pp, ISBN: 0255363656

June 1996 (hb) £12.00, (pb) £9.00

- **Education For Citizenship**

  Anthony Flew

  Cricism of the report of the 'Advisory Group on Citizenship' on which the government is basing its curriculum for citizenship education.

  Studies in Education 10 36 pp, ISBN: 0255364792

  2000 (pb) £10.00

- **Political Correctness and Public Finance**

  Dennis O'Keefe

  Political correctnes flourishes because of state-financing of education, which leads to a lack of competition and the dominance of producer interests over those of educational consumers.

  Studies in Education 9 113pp, ISBN: 0255364784

  2000 (pb) £10.00

- **Teacher Education in England and Wales**

  Geoffrey Partington

  Nature and history of teacher education, theories of teaching and ideologies and policies implemented by governments in the post-war period. Concludes with a plea to the government to free-up the education system as a whole and teacher education in particular.

  Studies in Education 8 163pp, ISBN: 0255364768

  1999 (pb) £10.00

- **The Global Education Industry**

  James Tooley

  A snapshot of private education across a range of countries in the devloping world. Argues that the private sector is not the exclusive domain of the wealthy and that it is having a positive effect upon the lives of millions.

  Studies in Education 7 89pp, ISBN: 025536475x

  1999 (pb) £10.00

- **Rethinking Higher Education: On the Future of Higher Education in Britain**

  Thomas Lange

  It is suggested that the government may have sacrificed the quality of higher education for its concern to raise numbers, and that there is no convincing economic argument to back this expansion. Additionally, the current funding mechanisms undermine equity.

  Studies in Education 6 60pp, ISBN: 0255364200

  1998 (pb) £10.00

- **The Debate on Higher Education: Challenging the Assumptions**

  Adrian Seville and James Tooley

  With higher education in the UK at a critical juncture in its history, two leading commentators offer new perspectives on the fundamentals of this on-going debate. Seville examines the implications of 'modularity', while Tooley presents a comprehensive critique of government intervention in the university system, questioning whether the state has to be involved at all.

  Studies in Education 5 120pp, ISBN: 0255364091

  November 1997 (pb) £10.00

- **Towards Self-Governing Schools**

Dick Atkinson

In this challenging paper Dr Dick Atkinson asks why local education authorities are needed. Finding reasons lacking, he puts forward a proposal for all schools to be self-governing and thereby removed from the debilitating effects of politicised education.

Studies in Education 4 86pp, ISBN: 0255364083

November 1997 (pb) £10.00

- **Environmental Education**

Benjamin Aldrich-Moodie and Jo Kwong

This original piece of research examines the teaching of environmental issues in the UK and US. Looking at a variety of textbooks and how specific issues are taught, they find that the teaching of the environment is characterised by bad science, sloppy thinking and indoctrination.

Studies in Education 3 & Studies on the Environment 9 126pp, ISBN: 025536442

October 1997 (pb) £10.00

- **Why Schoolchildren Can't Read**

Bonnie Macmillan

Dr Bonnie Macmillan describes the findings of the most up-to-date experimental research on beginning reading instruction. Research points decisively to the need for direct teaching of certain key skills in order to produce maximum reading success.

Studies in Education 2 205pp, ISBN: 0255364032

March 1997 (pb) £12.00

- **Education Without the State**

James Tooley

Functional illiteracy, youth delinquency and lack of technical innovation all point to the failures of state schooling, raising the question of why government should be involved in education at all. In this radical study Dr James Tooley provides a damning critique of the justifications for state schooling and proposes practical policies to increase market provision of education.

Studies in Education 1 120pp, ISBN: 025536380X

April 1996 (pb) £12.00

The IEA also publishes the *Journal of Economic Affairs*.

John Stuart Mill Institute

Address	1 Whitehall Place
	London
	SW1A 2HE
Tel	01582 615067
Fax	01582 896452
Email	J.Wates@ntlworld.com
Website	www.jsmillinstitute.org.uk
Secretary	Julian Wates
Number of Employees	1
Year of Foundation	1992
Cost of Membership	£10 per annum, £15 for publications

History

The Institute was established in October 1992 to stimulate debate on public policy issues through a consistent and telling challenge to current thinking based on the concepts of the freedom of the individual and responsible democratic participation. It develops an established and respected tradition of thought on political, economic and social questions particularly associated with John Stuart Mill and makes it relevant to the 1990s – and beyond. Its primary objective is to put issues and policy options which might otherwise be ignored on to the public and political agenda.

Objectives

The principal aim of the Institute is to advance the education of the general public in social, economic and international affairs, in particular as they relate to the rights of the individual, the environment and communities.

These concerns give primacy to liberty so that all should have equal opportunities to develop their potential. This approach sees the freedom of each as being dependent on respect for the freedom of all others and the full expression of liberty as requiring responsible participation in the affairs of the communities to which we all belong. The Institute is thus founded on firm principles. It considers the implications of them for analysing, and finding solutions to, present-day problems.

The Institute publishes pamphlets and reports and organises seminars, discussions and fringe meetings at party conferences. Each year it arranges a John Stuart Mill Lecture, the edited text of which is subsequently printed, and holds a John Stuart Mill Dinner, with an informal presentation from a guest speaker. Occasional conferences are planned.

The John Stuart Mill Institute has charitable status. It does not receive any public funds and obtains grants and donations for specific projects and publications.

Publications

- **John Stuart Mill, the Free Market and the State,**
  Conrad Russell, 1999
  ISBN: 1871952050
  24 page pamphlet with stiff cover, stapled, A5 size.
  The text of the inaugural John Stuart Mill Lecture, considering the relationship of economic and political freedom and stressing that the market is a mechanism which should serve society.

- **Human Rights and International Intervention,**
  Anthony Parsons, 1994
  ISBN: 1871952069
  £3.00
  24 page pamphlet with stiff cover, stapled, A5 size.
  The United Nations was created to regulate relations between nations, not conflicts within them. The end of the Cold War has emphasised the need for the international community to protect human rights in such disputes.

- **Long To Reign Over Us?: The Future of the Monarchy,**
  R L Borthwick, 1994
  ISBN: 1871952077
  £6.00
  51 page pamphlet with stiff cover, stapled, A5 size.
  A consideration of whether the monarchy should continue as it is, be reformed or be replaced by a republic, looking at why this has become the subject of public debate

- **Liberty and Sustainability: Where One Person's Freedom is Another's Nuisance,**
  Jonathon Porritt, 1995
  ISBN: 1871952085
  £3.50
  24 page pamphlet with stiff cover, stapled, A5 size.
  Green politics must be based on liberty; sustainability could not be achieved through coercion, as population policy experiments show. Greens should articulate new values based on freedom to replace current materialism.

- **A Few Words on Intervention: John Stuart Mill's Principles of International Action applied to the post Cold War World,**
  Edward Mortimer, 1995
  ISBN: 1871952107
  £6.00
  48 page pamphlet with stiff cover, stapled, A5 size.
  The problems experienced in Somalia, the former Yugoslavia, Rwanda and elsewhere indicate that we need a new understanding of the role of the international community and new mechanisms for peace-keeping and intervention.

- **Identity Cards: A response to the Home Office's Consultation Paper, 1995**
  £1.00
  12 page paper with heavy cover, spiral bound, A4 size.
  A review of the case for identity cards, concluding that, without proper defences for the individual, their introduction would create unacceptable risks for personal liberty.

- **Controlling Executive Power: Papers from a seminar,**
  1995
  ISBN: 1871952093
  £2.00
  18 page paper with heavy cover, spiral bound, A4 size.
  Power is becoming increasingly diffuse and unaccountable and a new constitutional settlement is urgently needed to address the problem.

- **Disinterested Bystanders: Reconciling Media Freedom and Responsibility**
  Anthony Smith, 1996
  ISBN: 1871952115
  £3.50
  26 page pamphlet with stiff cover, stapled, A5 size.
  Journalists must scrutinise government and others but the media also has great power to define issues and there are problems of concentration of control. How is the right balance to be struck?

- **Accountability in the European Union**
  Dr Alan Butt Philip, 1996
  ISBN: 1871952123
  £6.00
  48 page pamphlet with stiff cover, stapled, A5 size.
  The institutions of the European Union lack democratic legitimacy and popular support. The problem is analysed and recommendations put forward to create a Europe with which its citizens will identify.

- **The Erosion of Judicial Independence**
  Lord Ackner, 1997
  ISBN: 1871952131
  £3.50
  20 page pamphlet with stiff cover, stapled, A5 size.
  The Conservative Government failed to understand and properly protect judicial independence, which is essential for safeguarding civil liberties.

- **A Conservative Economist? The Political Liberalism of Adam Smith Revisited**
  Robert Falkner, 1997
  ISBN: 187195214X
  £7.50
  53 page pamphlet with stiff cover, stapled, A5 size.
  A re-evaluation of Adam Smith's writing, challenging the common misperception of him as simply an economic liberal, asserting the political element of his thinking and indicating its contemporary relevance.

- **Towards a Humane Individualism**
  Samuel Brittan, 1998
  ISBN: 1871952158
  £7.50
  57 page pamphlet with stiff cover, stapled, A5 size.
  Three essays which in turn
  • consider and reject communitarian critiques of individual liberalism
  • examine different currents of liberalism and asserts common liberal values
  • offer liberal approaches to current policy issues.

- **Freedom in the Electronic Age**
  Baroness Nicholson
  ISBN: 1871952174
  31pp, A5, £4.50
  An examination of the effect of the electronic media on individual freedom in a society without a written constitution.

- **British European Policy: Options & Opportunities**
  Professor Helen Wallace
  ISBN: 1871952174
  12pp, £3.00

New Europe

Address	52 Walnut Tree Walk
	London
	SE11 6DN
Tel	020 7582 1001
Fax	020 7582 5852
Email	info@new-europe.co.uk
Website	www.new-europe.co.uk
Chairman	David Owen
Director	Janet Bush
Researcher	Austin Todd
Campaign Manager	John Grimley
Number of Employees	3
Year of Formation	1999
Advisory Council	Lord Ashburton KG KCVO DL
	Roger Bootle
	Sir Ewen Fergusson GCMG GCVO
	Rt Hon the Lord Healey CH MBE
	Rt Hon the Lord Owen CH
	Rt Hon the Lord Prior PC
	Lord Sainsbury of Preston Candover KG
	Mary Ann Sieghart
	Christopher Smallwood
	Martin Taylor
	Janet Bush
	Sir Malcolm Rifkind
	Frank Field MP
	Dr Caroline Lucas
	Sir Antony Acland
	Sir John Coles
	Neil Mendoza
	John Wakefield
	Christopher Leaver

Objectives

New Europe is a group of people who have always been pro-European and in favour of Britain's constructive membership of the European Union. We are internationalists and come from all political backgrounds.

We want to see:

- a European Union of 26 or more independent countries.

- Euroland within but not controlling the Union.

- an EU that is market oriented, socially concerned and lightly regulated.

We believe that Britain is better off outside the single currency. Staying out now would not preclude us from joining later. For now, however, we are in the enviable position of being able to wait and watch others take part in an experiment which may or may not be a success

What is needed in the UK is the self confidence to wait patiently as events develop over economic and monetary union rather than looking apprehensively at whether we should or should not have joined the 'euro' at the start. Instead we should be championing the new enlarged EU: an EU where all its members are safe-guarded as well as inhibited by the Treaties; where they can develop their European identity at different speeds and in different ways; where there is no inevitability about the UK ever joining the 'euro' because the British people feel comforatable following a different path within the EU to joining Euroland.

Publications

- **The Euro and 'regional' divergence in Europe**
  Professor Tony Thirlwall
  Argues that the euro could become a threat to European integration and stability if it exacerbated regional differences within the EU.
  ISBN: 0953576000
  30pp, £5.00

- **The Good European's Dilemma**
  Robin Guthrie
  ISBN: 0953663020210
  £5.00
  The EU is described as one of the great political achievements, but one that is increasingly moving away from its core values of unity, democracy and inclusiveness to become the most divisive force in Europe.

- **Head to Head on the Euro: the constitutional and economic questions**
  Editor Janet Bush
  ISBN: 0953636038
  £5.00
  The Rt Hon Kenneth Clarke QC MP and the Rt Hon Sir Malcolm Rifkind KCMG QC debate the euro and discuss whether there are constitutional and economic implications to UK membership.

- **The 'Straight Banana' Republic or What's Wrong with The European Ideal?**
  Aidan Rankin
  ISBN: 095357606X
  £5.00
  Aiden Rankin argues that the greatest threat to the European project emanates not from scepticism but from what he calls pan-European ideology. He argues that the EU must encourage democratic participation and not attempt to limit political self-expression among member-state citizenry.

- **The Euro – a loss of faith**
  Bridget Rosewell
  ISBN 0953576051
  £5.00
  Bridget Rosewell argues that Britain has the muscle to exert considerable influence on the future develop-ment of Europe. Furthermore, Britain must maintain its independence of thought and action to exert the maximum influence within the EU.

- **The Euro or a Sustainable Future for Britain? A Green Critique of the single Currency**
Dr Caroline Lucas MEP and Dr Mike Woodin
ISBN: 0953576078
Price £5.00
It is argued that because the progressive internationalists in the British Greens have a wider vision about the role of Europe they are critical of the narrowly defined economic objectives of the EU. They oppose EMU and the single currency because they belive that the economic logic of this dubious experiment is flawed.

- **The Constitutional Implications of the Euro**
David Owen
Free

- **Everything you always wanted to know about the euro but were afraid to ask a Tory**
Janet Bush
ISBN: 0953576027
£6.99
Lord Healey, Frank Field and Alan Simpson are joined by voices from the Trade Union movement, the Liberal Democrats, the Green Party and the German Social Democratic Party in a collection of essays which reveal that opposition to UK membership of the euro cuts across all political parties and goes right to the heart of the new Labour government.

- **British Influence and the Euro**
Sir John Coles
0953576035
£5.00
The former Head of the Diplomatic Service and Permanent Secretary at the Foreign Office argues that to avoid losing influence it is better for Britain to stay out of the single currency. Warning against a major surrender of national decision making powers, he believes that in the world at large we shall be much more influential if we keep our distinctive currency, assets and policies.

- **The Euro and Regional Divergence in Europe**
Tony Thirlwall
0953636011
£5.00
Thirlwall argues that within the EMU straitjacket regional economies will diverge, causing insupportable social and political tensions.

- **The Single European Currency: A Bad Idea**
Professor Sir James Ball
ISBN: 0953576000
18pp, Pamphlet, £5.00
Professor Ball, Emeritus Professor at the London Business School, argues that the economic arguments for the Euro simply do not add up and that the Single Currency, with its 'one size fits all' monetary policy can only be regarded with alarm. He rejects the case for UK membership and launches an attack on the British government for misleading the electorate about the true, political implications of the Euro.

- **Confidence in the City outside the Euro**
  David Lascelles
  ISBN: 0953576019
  26pp, Pamphlet, £5.00

  The former Banking Editor of the Financial Times argues that, far from being damaged if Britain remains outside the European single currency, the City of London and, indeed, Britain's highly successful financial services industry, will become even more competitive.

- **Head to Head on the Euro**
  Adair Turner versus Martin Taylor
  ISBN: 0953636003
  26pp, Pamphlet, £5.00

  Transcipt of Beneath the Rhetoric: the real issues surrounding the Euro, a Seminar hosted by the Confederation of British Industry on May 26, 1999. Speaking for Britain's membership of the European single currency was Adair Turner, Director General of the CBI. Against him was Martin Taylor, previous CEO of Barclays. Forward by Janet Bush

New Policy Institute

Address	109 Coppergate House
	16 Brune Street
	London
	E1 7NJ
Tel	020 7721 8421
Fax	020 7721 8422
Email	info@npi.org.uk
Website	www.npi.org.uk
Executive Director	Dr Peter Kenway
Non Executive Director	Guy Palmer
Research Officer	Dr Marie C Lall
Research Officer	Catherine Howarth
Research Officer	Dr Cathy Street
Research Officer	Mohibur Rahman
Research Officer	Andy Harrop
Quality Assessor	Doug Edmonds
Number of Employees	7
Year of Formation	1996
Cost of Subscription	N/A
How to Order	Via Politico's Bookstore
Credit Cards	None

History

The New Policy Institute is a progressive think tank founded in 1996. Wholly independent, it has neither financial backing nor political patrons. Its funding is project based, from charitable foundations, private and public companies, and trade unions. Over the last three years, it has developed a public profile from scratch, and following the publication at the end of 1998 of its Key Indicators of Poverty and Social Exclusion, it now has a national standing and a reputation for high quality work on important and usually complicated subjects where clear thinking is at a premium.

Objectives

The focus of the Institute's work is policy, by which is meant the practical action that can be taken in order to achieve certain ends. Drawing on, and complementing, good quality academic research into the nature and characteristics of particular problems, the Institute's work is forward looking, examining what can be done and considering what the consequences might be. It is especially interested in how government can indirectly influence the behaviour of non-governmental organisations, whether large private companies or local community bodies, by altering the environment in which they make their decisions.

The scope of the work is modern society's major services, from health to finance, whether provided by the public, voluntary, private or privatised sectors.

Publications

- **Responsibility for All. A National Strategy for Social Inclusion**
  Catherine Howarth et al
  £17.00

- **Indicators of Poverty and Social Exclusion in Rural England**
  A Countryside Agency Report by Andrew Harrop et al
  Free

- **Sidelined. Young Adult's Access to Service**
  Catherine Howarth and Cathy Street
  £30.00/£10.00

- **Water Charging and Social Justice. Why Politicians Must Act**
  Guy Palmer
  £15.00/£10.00

- **Key Indicators of Poverty in Scotland. A report for the Joseph Rowntree Foundation**
  Peter Kenway and Mohibur Rahman
  Website only

- **Gateways. Routes to Financial Services**
  ed by Mohibur Rahman
  £30.00/£10.00

- **Changing Views of Rural Britain – Why Services Matter**
  ed Andy Harrop
  1902080394
  £7.50

- **Monitoring Poverty & Social Exclusion 1999**
  Catherine Howarth et al
  1859350534
  £30.00

- **Council Tax – The Case for Reform**
  Peter Kenway & Guy Palmer
  1902080386
  £40.00

- **Food for Thought – Breakfast Clubs & their Challenges**
  Cathy Street & Peter Kenway
  1902080351
  £12.50

- **Meaningful Choices – The Policy Options for Financial Exclusion**
  Nick Donovan & Guy Palmer
  1902080351
  £40.00

- **A Real Commitment to Partnership? Building a New Relationship between the Council & Voluntary Sector in Islington**
  Guy Palmer & Peter Kenway
  1902080343
  £30.00

- **Fit for School – How Breakfast Clubs Meet Health, Education & Child Care Needs**
  ed Nick Donovan & Cathy Street
  1902080335
  £7.50

- **Monitoring Poverty & Social Exclusion: Labour's Inheritance**
  Catherine Howarth et al
  1859350496
  £16.95

- **Financial Exclusion: Can Mutuality Fill the Gap?**
  ed Jenny Rossiter
  1902080289
  £5.00

- **Quality Assurance or Benchmarking? Presenting Information about Pensions**
  ed Guy Palmer
  1902080319
  £30.00

- **Beyond Privatisation: Government Strategies for Influencing Outcomes**
  Peter Kenway et al
  1902080327
  £5.00

- **Second Chances: Exclusion From School & Equality of Opportunity**
  ed Nick Donovan
  1902080300
  £7.50

- **Fair & Sustainable: Paying for Water**
  Bob Hills et al
  1902080270
  £20.00

- **Housing Risks & Opportunities: Reforming Mortgage Finance**
  Michael Ball et al

- **Monitoring Poverty & Social Exclusion: Why Britain Needs a Key Indicators Report**
  1902080297

Politeia

Address	22 Charing Cross Road
	London
	WC2H 0HR
Tel	020 7240 5070
Fax	020 7240 5095
Email	info@politeia.co.uk
Website	www.politeia.co.uk
Director	Sheila Lawlor
Patron	Viscount Cranbourne
Hon President	Rt Hon the Lord Parkinson
Advisory Council	Professor Tim Congdon
	Maurice Cowling
	Professor David Dilks
	Professor Harold James
	Sir Paul Judge
	Professor Deepak Lal
	Sir Geoffrey Leigh
	Dr Oliver Letwin MP
	Rt Hon Francis Maude MP
	The Lord Pilkington
	David Willetts MP
Number of Staff	3
Cost of Membership	Corporate £100, Academic £50, Individual £25
How to Order	Telephone, Fax, Post
Credit Cards	None

History

Politeia, a forum for social and economic thinking, opened in November 1996 as a focus for thinking on social and economic policy. Its aim is to encourage reflection, dsicussion and debate about the place of the State in the daily lives of men and women across the range of issues which affect them, from employment and tax to education, health and pensions.

Politeia seeks to question the proper role and cost of government and the levels of taxation for good government. Areas for work in the future include the future range of benefits and provision for pensions and long-term care; primary and hospital healthcare; strategies for high employment; labour regulation and law; the respective roles of the State and of parents in educating children; and the debate over constituional change.

The forum is distinguished from existing institutions by concentrating its attention on this range of policy, which will be central to the political debate in the coming decades. It is independently funded and it welcomes contributions and discussion from specialists in their field of expertise from a range of perspectives.

Publications

- **Liberal Conservatism: the tradition of small government**
  Sheila Lawlor
  ISBN: 1900525143
  26pp, Pamphlet
  November 1995, £5.00
  Community and values are favoured themes of political discourse today, especially for the exponents of 'New Labour'. But do they disguise a return to the statism which the liberal economics practised since 1979 had begun to unravel? In this pamphlet Sheila Lawlor sets out the tradition of liberal conservatism, based on a scepticism of big government and a respect for individual freedom. She argues that from this tradition there can be found a coherent and practical answer to the problems of the immediate future in every area of the welfare state.

- **A Question of Standards: finding the balance**
  Chris Woodhead
  ISBN: 1900525011
  21pp, Pamphlet
  December 1995, £5.00
  Chris Woodhead, Her Majesty's Chief Inspector of Schools, opens Politeia's education debate, 'A Question of Standards'. What do we mean by 'standards' in education, and how can they be raised? Do we need more, or less government intervention, or is the balance roughly right? The author argues that fundamental con-flicts about the nature of education militate against any real rise in standards. He discusses how the provision of more information to parents will improve quality and reflects on the future role of local education author-ities. He also argues the need to take definite action to improve standards of teaching and the importance of maintaining the distinction between academic and vocational education. The debate will continue early next year, with two further pamphlets from opposing perspectives, asking whether the state needs a greater or smaller role.

- **Unfinished business: the economic case for a more liberal labour market**
  Warwick Lightfoot
  ISBN: 190052502X
  27pp, Pamphlet
  January 1996, £6.00
  Since 1979, government reforms have made the British labour market the most liberal in the European Union. But it is still over-regulated. Unnecessary restrictions continue to distort employers' decisions, reduce economic activity and raise unemployment. The framework of employment legislation on redundancy com-pensation and unfair dismissal remains, and the courts have already shown their readiness to apply it in novel and unexpected circumstances. Without a radical move to further deregulation, the most recent gains in eco-nomic freedom are in danger. Warwick Lightfoot gives the economic arguments for the freeing of the labour market, and he shows why further liberalisation is now both desirable and practicable.

- **Providing for Pensions**
  Peter Lilley
  ISBN: 1900525038
  13pp, Pamphlet
  February 1996, £3.00
  In his inaugural lecture for Politeia the Rt Hon Peter Lilley MP explains why Britain is uniquely well placed amongst major European countries to meet the challenge of providing for the elderly. He warns against pro-

posals to take pension funds into government control and advocates continuing development along the present lines: financial encouragement for people to supplement state provision by private schemes. Prosperity in retirement is, Mr Lilley concludes, part of the wider strategy for a flourishing economy with scope for lower taxes and more job creation.

• **Answering the challenge of Communitarianism**
John Marenbon
ISBN: 1900525062
38pp, Pamphlet
May 1996, £7.50

Communitarianism is a powerful creed which has been adopted by those intent on reconstructing politics in Britain today, especially the leaders of New Labour. John Marenbon explains the recent origins of the movement in the critique of liberalism. He warns that its language and doctrine of moral reconstruction is intellectually incoherent and politically dangerous. Communitarianism will prompt an extension of state powers, so that government and its appointed experts will seek to determine how people live large parts of their lives. The author answers the communitarian challenge by providing an alternative model of a 'medial' state, where considerations of freedom and choice are complemented by transparent redistribution.

• **A Moral Maze: government values in education.**
John Marenbon
ISBN: 1900525105
18pp, Pamphlet
December 1996, £5.00

There has been a wide welcome for the recent decision by the School Curriculum and Assessment Authority (SCAA) to issue a statement of moral and spiritual values to be taught in all schools. John Marenbon argues that it is misplaced. SCAA's attempt to impose uniformity will harm good moral and religious education and also detract from academic teaching. In this area above all parental responsibility and individual choice should prevail; intervention by government bureaucracies is counter-productive and disturbingly authoritarian.

• **A Question of Standards: raising standards through choice**
Robert Skidelsky
ISBN: 1900525082
20pp, Pamphlet
September 1996, £5.00

Education, argues Robert Skidelsky, should be privatised if standards are to be raised. He considers and rejects the case for greater state intervention through centrally imposed curricular reform or the organisation of schooling on selective principles. Instead of the government's attempt at top-down reform, all existing state schools should become legally independent non-profit-making bodies. The role of the state would be restricted to the following functions: laying down a period of compulsory schooling; enforcing regulations for health, safety and civilised standards (the National Curriculum and associated assessment would become voluntary and the examination boards freed to offer syllabuses other than those leading to GCSE – for instance, 'O' levels); setting up a statistical service, with powers to carry out national and other tests on schools and publish results, and an information office to provide information about schools in different localities; providing all parents of school-age children with a means-tested voucher for education at an approved (i.e. charitable) establishment.

- **What Future Local Authority Social Services?**

Stephen Dorrell

ISBN: 1900525070

18pp, Pamphlet

November 1996, £3.00

In his address to Politeia, the Rt Hon Stephen Dorrell, MP, Secretary of State for Health, reviews the role of modern Social Service Departments and their costs – which have grown explosively over the last 25 years. This high level of expenditure cannot be sustained, and Mr Dorrell explores alternative ways in which social care can be provided – through families, insurance and voluntary organisations. The implications of change for social service departments will be serious. They will need to reconsider the mix of responsibilities undertaken in recent years.

- **The Individual, the Constitution and the Tory Party**

Robert Cranborne

ISBN: 1900525097

18pp, Pamphlet

December 1996, £5.00

How can Tories build on their tradition to ensure the prosperity and success of British society in an age of rapid technological change? Viscount Cranborne, Lord Privy Seal and Leader of the House of Lords, argues that expansive bureaucratic government, which advocates of a European super-state wish to entrench, is not the answer, but small government, free trade, lack of regulation, competition and low taxes. Britain's unwritten constitution provides both the flexibility and the sense of continuity for the nation to resist dirigisme and flourish in the next century. But, Cranborne adds, we must recognise that our present arrangements (like every set of human arrangements) are imperfect, and so we should not be against all change in them. For instance, Cranborne suggests that reform of the House of Lords might be contemplated, though it would need to be in the context of reforming both Houses of Parliament

- **Global Opportunities: liberalising world trade and labour markets**

Harold James

ISBN: 1900525119

34pp, Pamphlet

January 1997, £7.00

Globalisation – a global economy with worldwide competition – is often seen as a threat to high employment, living standards and good wages, and has led to calls for protectionism and increased state management of the economy. By contrast, Professor Harold James sees 'globalisation' as a second industrial revolution with new opportunities, new ideas, new civilisation and new wealth. He addresses the fallacies which have led to unfounded fears; proposes a reduced role for the state; and explains that a high wage economy, international deregulation of the labour market and international free trade, offer the path to high employment and a prosperous future.

- **Mounting Debts: the coming European pension crisis**

Gabriel Stein

ISBN: 1900525127

43pp, Pamphlet

March 1997, £7.00

Few problems offer so great a challenge to western governments as that of paying for future pensions. In this pamphlet, Gabriel Stein, an international economist with Lombard Street Research, examines the position and implications of pension costs in four major European economies, Britain, France, Germany and Italy. His analysis reveals the disparity between the continental economies, where unfunded pension liabilities range from 70 per cent GDP in Italy to 110 per cent of GDP in Germany and that of Britain where the figure is far better at just 7 per cent. The author proposes a policy for reform without which the continental pension systems will eventually become insolvent. He also warns that EU moves to harmonise fiscal and social security systems might eventually mean higher taxes in Britain to pay for unfunded pensions in continental Europe.

- **Working for Benefit**
  Hugh Sykes
  ISBN: 19005250135
  31pp, Pamphlet
  May 1997, £5.00

Although it continues to fall, unemployment remains a serious problem both economically and socially. Does it not make better sense, asks Hugh Sykes, to pay people to work than, as the present benefits system does, to remain idle? The workfare scheme he proposes here would achieve a reduction of at least 200,000 in unemployment over three years. Developing from and extending the government's own schemes, it is – unlike other schemes suggested by left and right – both straightforward and detailed enough to be put into practice immediately. It gives incentives to employers to create, and to the unemployed to take, real productive jobs, whilst also providing opportunity to work where such jobs are not available. NERA, the leading experts on the economies of workfare, have provided technical advice and data for the scheme.

- **The Dominance of Centrism and the Politics of Certainty**
  Leader Series
  ISBN: 1900525151
  22pp, Pamphlet

This pamphlet is the first of Politeia's Leaders, a new series which will identify and consider the themes and issues central to political discussion. The Dominance of Centrism analyses centrism which, particularly with New Labour, now dominates British politics. It shows that centrism is a distinct doctrine based on self-conscious seeking of the middle ground and appeal to experts. It has strong links with centralisation and communitarianism. Whereas centrism may have some appeal to socialists and to some brands of conservatives, it is irreconcilable with the liberal tradition especially that which has been a powerful strand in conservative thinking.

- **Banking on Change: independence, regulation and the Bank of England**
  David Gowland
  ISBN: 190052516X
  42pp, Pamphlet
  June 1997, £7.00

When, within days of Labour's election victory, Gordon Brown announced that he would give the Bank of England independence, his move was widely accepted as an example of sensible, decisive economic management. In fact, Professor David Gowland argues, the matter is far less straightforward. Brown's announcement contained a number of elements. One of them gave the Bank of England not complete, but contract-limited independence. Whether this limited independence will lead to lower inflation is doubtful: the economic arguments certainly are not clear. Another element was supposed to bring all financial regulation under the control of a single body. But, as Gowland shows, Brown's policy here is inchoate. The third element deprives the Bank, for no good reason, of the role in debt management it has performed so well for centuries. Brown has acted over-hastily, Gowland suggests, imposing changes which will be distracting and time-consuming to implement and in themselves promise few obvious benefits.

- **A Conservative Future**

Maurice Cowling

ISBN: 1900525178

15pp, Pamphlet

July 1997, £3.00

In this address, Maurice Cowling, the distinguished historian, considers the Conservative party, its past, its present, and above all its future – against the reconstruction by Mr Blair of the Labour party and the particular Conservative themes which developed since the 1960's. While the functions of the Conservative party are clear, the challenge is subtle: to expose, as the author explains, the politics of 'virtue' and to show why 'virtue', Blairite or otherwise, is a threat to freedom and needs to be taken with a very large pinch of salt. It is not Socialism, but the dismantling of 'virtue' and exposure of the emptiness which lurks not very far below its surface that is the problem of the 1990's.

- **The Many and the Few: rhetoric and reality in the universities after Dearing**

Reader Series

ISBN: 1900525186

28pp, Pamphlet

September 1997, £4.00

British higher education has very quickly changed from an elite to a mass system. This transformation has produced many problems, which Sir Ron Dearing was asked to tackle in his recently published Report. One problem, which has received less publicity than questions of funding and participation, is how the academic excellence of the best universities can be maintained in a mass system. Dearing claims to be a supporter of academic excellence, but his proposals will undermine it by reducing institutional independence and scholarly and scientific freedom, and by subjecting all universities to common regulations on courses, examining and teacher training, all of them inimical to academic teaching and good research. Only proper differentiation between the best institutions and the others, this pamphlet argues, can save the qualities which have made British universities the envy of the world. An appendix looks in detail at the much discussed question of Oxford and Cambridge college fees.

- **The Chain of Authority**

Robert Cranborne

ISBN: 1900525194

17pp, Pamphlet

November 1997, £3.00

Mr Blair is in the process of making radical changes to Britain's Constitution. Already assemblies for Scotland and Wales are being set up. Proportional Representation is promised for the European elections and the House of Lords is to be reformed. In this Address, Viscount Cranborne, Shadow Leader of the Lords, points out the danger of such precipitate and ill-considered change. Whereas present arrangements provide a clear chain of authority, the changes will make it far more difficult to know where power really lies and who can be held to account. They threaten to undermine the position of parliament which has been the bulwark of Britain's democracy.

- **A Little Local Difficulty: mayors and managers – American models for Britain.**

Tim Hames

ISBN: 1900525208

24pp, Pamphlet, £3.00

Local government, which has long been the Cinderella of British Politics, is now becoming a supermodel. All parties are rushing to advocate new forms of local democracy, and the idea of elected mayors, in the US model, is proving especially popular. But what is the US model? Dr Timothy Hames, formerly lecturer in Politics at Christ Church, Oxford and now political writer at The Times, shows that the examples which can be drawn from the US are more diverse than is usually acknowledged and argues that a more sophisticated approach to local government reform is needed.

- **Welfare to Work – The New Deal: Maximising the Benefits**
Hugh Sykes
ISBN: 1900525216
37pp, Pamphlet, £5.00

The New Deal – the government's welfare to work scheme – aims to increase employment in the long term by helping some of the unemployed to become more employable, thereby increasing the pool of effective labour and so facilitating sustainable economic expansion. Sir Hugh Sykes, until recently Chairman of the Sheffield Development Corporation, welcomes the scheme and its aims. But, he argues, there are serious problems in implementing the scheme which should be urgently addressed. The fact that the scheme does not aim to create new jobs in the short term will cause widespread disappointment, unless the public is given a better understanding of the scheme's aims. Sir Hugh also contends that the scheme should aim at short-term job creation- something which will be possible if it can be flexibly implemented in the regions, rather than rigidly run from the centre, and if it takes proper account of regional and local priorities.

- **Funding the Future? Problems in Pension Reform**
Christopher Daykin
ISBN: 1900525224
48pp, Pamphlet
March 1998, £7.50

Countries all over the world are redefining their pensions schemes to meet the challenges of ageing popula-tions and higher expectations of a diminishing workforce. Chris Daykin, Government Actuary of the UK, provides a masterly survey of these international developments and the principles behind them, comparing them with the position in Britain which is far less problematic than in other European countries and else-where in the OECD. He argues in particular that we should be careful to preserve our valuable heritage of defined benefit schemes. We should not destroy parts of our inherited system which work well but concen-trate on reforming those parts which are less effective.

- **Playing at Politics: First-time Voting in the 1997 UK General Election**
Una McCormack
ISBN: 1900525240
35pp, Pamphlet
June 1998, £6.00

Conventional analysis of young people and their policies seeks to pigeon-hole them. Research is carried out in ways which restrict the multiple potential responses. The young are thus expected to espouse certain well-defined causes and to eschew conventional political processes. Young people can play at politics, but they can-not be political players. Using a more sophisticated methodology, Una McCormack, research associate at the Judge Institute, University of Cambridge, shatters this stereotyping of the young, which reduces them to minor-ity status. She challenges the assumption that young people form a single group with common goals and a shared agenda. They are like everyone else, various in their beliefs and aspirations – not one group, but many.

- **Beveridge of Brown**
Sheila Lawlor
ISBN: 1900525259
72pp, Book
July 1998, £10.00

The basis of British social security has been benefit in return for contributions. But over the last 50 years the contributory principle has been whittled away and now, with Gordon Brown's drive to integrate tax and benefits, it looks set for extinction. Lawloe shows that the abandonment of the contributory principle has come about through short term political expediency and through confusion between the different roles of tax and benefit. She argues that restoration of this principle is central to successful social security reform. Treasury dicated integration should not be allowed to destroy the principles which Beveridge saw as essential to incentive, self-reliance and small government.

- **The Future of Welfare Reform**
  Frank Field
  ISBN: 1900525367
  July 1998, £3.00
  What is the future for universal benefits after Thatcherism, the skills revolution, labour market change and the recasting of gender relations?

- **The Coming Constitutional Crisis**
  Tim Hames
  ISBN: 1900525305
  30pp, Pamphlet
  September 1998, £5.00
  A set of referenda has left Britain facing profound constitutional change and probably constitutional crisis. The present piecemeal settlement is unsustainable.

- **The End of an Era of Representative Democracy**
  Robert Cranborne
  ISBN: 1900525313
  12pp, Pamphlet
  October 1998, Price £3.00
  What will be the effect of Labour's programme of constitutional reform? Cranborne says they will remove power from parliament to the Executive.

- **The Cost of Sharing**
  Shane Kavanagh & Louis Opit
  ISBN: 1900525321
  82pp, Pamphlet
  December 1998, £10.00
  Intellectual disability has a profound and enduring impact on the quality of life of this eaffcted by it and their families. A range of care services are available yet information about their cost is insufficient. Are we getting value for money

- **From Beggars to Choosers: University Funding**
  Graham Hills
  ISBN: 190052533X
  22pp, Pamphlet
  February 1999, £5.00

- **Dilemmas of Decommissioning**
  Kirsten Schulze
  ISBN: 1900525348
  38pp, Pamphlet
  March 1999, £5.00

Decommissioning paramilitary arms has been one of the most contentious issues in the Northern Ireland peace process. This pamphlets sets it in an historical context and draws from the example of other conflict situations.

- **European Tax Harmonisation & British Taxes**
  Tim Congdon
  ISBN: 1900525356
  28pp, Pamphlet
  May 1999, £7.00

- **What will be the impact of the euro on taxes in Britain? Is European Integration Really the Friend of Free Trade?**
  James Forder
  ISBN: 1900525364
  28pp, Pamphlet
  June 1999, £7.00
  The practical importance of the arguments for free trade and the removal of tariffs has been an instrument in advancing European integration. Forder argues that it should not be assumed that the case for protection holds no attraction for European policy makers.

- **Conservative Debates**
  Oliver Letwin
  ISBN: 1900525372
  48pp, Pamphlet
  June 1999, £7.00
  Civilised Conservatism and little platoons or a free society

- **Allegiance: the Nation State, Parliament & Prosperity**
  Robert Cranborne
  ISBN: 1900525381
  16pp, Pamphlet
  September 1999, £3.00
  The nation state commands an allegiance lacking for supra national federations. Central to the British nation state is its directly electable and accountable parliament argues Robert Cranbrone.

- **Holding our Judges to Account**
  Liam Fox
  ISBN: 1900525399
  16pp, Pamphlet
  September 1999, £3.00
  Fox says the appointment of judges should be subject to parliamentary scrutiny.

- **Reforming Local Government: accounability, finance & function**
  Gillian Shephard
  ISBN: 1900525429
  20pp, Pamphlet
  December 1999
  Local Government is under threat of execution: ignored by the majority of voters, top heavy with a number of responsibilities for which it is no longer suited, and so often regarded as simply the outer tier of a centralised reg-

ulatory system. Shephard argues that local government should concentrate only on its essential functions concerned with the local environment and planning. Finance from central government would be drastically cut and the local authorities of the future would raise their own finance so as to fulfil their essential role.

- **Comparing Standards: The Report of the Politeia Education Commission**
  Sig Prais, Caroline, St. John Brooks, Chris Woodhead and others
  Edited by Sheila Lawlor
  ISBN 19005254437
  January 2000, £7.50

- **Browned-Off: what's wrong with Gordon Brown's social policy?**
  David Willetts MP
  ISBN: 1900525402
  March 2000, £6.00

- **What Tories Want**
  Simon Heffer
  ISBN: 1900525410
  April 2000, £5.00

- **Caring for the Long Term: financing provision for the elderly**
  Philip Booth
  ISBN: 190052550X
  May 2000, £6.00

- **Answer the Question: Prime Ministerial Accountability and the Rule of Parliament**
  John Hayes
  ISBN: 1900525518
  July 2000, £5.00

- **Incapacity and Disability: paying for the consequences**
  Chris Daykin
  ISBN: 1900525526
  October 2000, £5.00

- **A Free Schools Future**
  William Hague
  ISBN: 1900525526
  December 2000, £5.00

Out of print publications: *The Long View: Financing Care for the Elderly* by Philip Booth; *A Question of Standards: The Need for a Local Democratic Voice* by Tim Brighouse

Social Affairs Unit

Address	314–322 Regent Street
	London
	W1B 3BB
Tel	020 7637 4356
Fax	020 7436 8530
Email	mosbacher@socialaffairsunit.org.uk
Website	www.socialaffairsunit.org.uk
Director	Dr Digby Anderson
Adminsitrator	Judi Brown
Deputy Director	Michael Mosbacher
Number of Staff	3
Year of Foundation	1980
Cost of Membership	N/A
Cost of Subscription	N/A
How to Order	By post
Credit Cards	None

Objectives

The Social Affairs Unit 'is famous for driving its coach and horses through the liberal consensus [The SAU would say any unjustified or premature consensus] scattering intellectual picket lines as it goes [and] for raising questions which strike most people most of the time as too dangerous or too difficult to think about' (The Times).

The Unit translates research with a potential to inform public policy from academe into public debate. Unusually, the ideas it promotes come largely from non-economists; from historians, sociologists and philosophers but also medical doctors and hard scientists. Its books and reports are widely and prominently covered in the media.

History

The Unit was founded in 1980. Though always an independent institute, it was started with active encouragement from the Institute of Economic Affairs. Founder Chairman was Professor Julius Gould, founder Director Dr Digby Anderson. The Unit is funded by sale of publications and donations from foundations and a highly diverse array of companies. Donations have come from over a hundred sources. Authors published now number well over 200.

In its early years the Unit was concerned with the critical evaluation of the welfare state. Many of its authors' ideas, then very controversial, especially on schools and higher education – local autonomy, parental accountability, curricular rigour – have now found their way into the policy mainstream; so too has early work on adoption and social security.

In the mid eighties the Unit added a concern with values and started a series about virtue and social policy, including books on manners, and sanctions for deviant behaviour. These too have been reflected in the return of moral language in current crime policy. This more 'cultural' work continues with a recent study of women's magazines, and with Faking It – The Sentimentalisation of Modern Society which entered the Best Sellers Top Ten within a month of publication.

The Unit also pioneered discussion of hazard regulation with books such as The Death of Humane Medicine and the Rise of Coercive Healthism, A Diet of Reason and Drinking to Your Health – The allegations and the evidence. These study both the use and abuse of science in making allegations about products and lifestyles and the consequences of regulation. Currently this is being linked with analyses of calls for change in company governance. New titles include: The Corporation under Siege – Exposing the devices used by activists and regulators in the non-risk society; No Man Can Serve Two Masters – Shareholders versus Stakeholders in the Governance of Companies; and What has Ethical Investment to do with Ethics?

Publications

Virtue and personal responsibility

• **The Reform of Criminal Legal Aid: When more accountability means less justice**
Jan Davies
ISBN: 0907631894
28pp, 2000, £6
Recent reforms undermine the independence of the legal profession and could lead to the 'de facto' nationalisation of criminal law. Criticisms of elitism and unaccountability illustrate a failure to understand the nature of the profession and mistake accountability for bureaucratic box ticking.

• **Not Fit to Fight: The Cultural Subversion of the Armed Forces in Britain & America**
edited Gerald Frost
ISBN: 0907631819
80pp, 1999, £11.95

• **Come Back Miss Nightingale: Trends in Professions Today**
edited Digby Anderson
ISBN: 0907631797
110pp, 1998, £11.95

• **Faking It – The Sentimentalisation of Modern Society**
edited by Digby Anderson & Peter Mullen
ISBN: 0907631754
217pp, 1998, £15.95
'The more people who read this book the better' *Sunday Telegraph*

• **Gentility Recalled – 'mere' manners and the making of social order**
edited by Digby Anderson
ISBN: 0907631665,
206pp, 1996, £15.95
'Addresses some real problems' *Guardian*

• **This Will Hurt – the restoration of virtue and civic order**
edited by Digby Anderson
ISBN: 0907631630
183 pp, 1995, £15.95
'Reflects a strong trend in public debate, a move away from the economic preoccupations of the 1980s to concern for the social fabric . . . It is a merit of This Will Hurt that the authors confront the difficulties involved.' *Sunday Telegraph*

- **The Loss of Virtue – moral confusion and social disorder in Britain and America**
  edited by Digby Anderson
  ISBN: 0907631509
  258pp, 1992, £15.95
  'cogent, brave and timely' *Catholic Herald*

- **Loyalty Misplaced – misdirected virtue and social disintegration**
  edited by Gerald Frost
  ISBN: 0907631703,
  125 pp, 1997, £12.95
  A discussion of the fissiparous tendencies in modern society, suggesting a range of contributory factors.

Health, lifestyle and the environment

- **Green Imperialism: a prescription for misery and war in the world's poorest countries**
  Deepak Lal
  ISBN: 0907631878
  28pp, 2000, £6
  Western activist groups not the multinationals are the real threat to the Third World and its developement.

- **Overspending in the NHS – an analysis by 5 doctors**
  edited by Digby Anderson
  ISBN: 0907631908
  64pp, 2000, £7.50
  Areas of spending in the NHS, other than bureaucracy, are wasteful or of limited medical efficacy.

- **Another Country**
  edited by Michael Mosbacher & Digby Anderson
  ISBN: 0907631835
  200pp, £20.00
  'Another country is a collection of 31 essays on subjects of concern to country people – the threat to jobs, livelihoods, culture and traditional leisure pursuits. It is a stimulating and sitrubing volume and should be read by all policy wonks, marchers and armchair members of the resistance.' *The Spectator*

- **Green Imperialism: A Prescription for Misery and War in the World's Poorest Countries**
  Deepak Lal
  ISBN: 0907631878
  24pp, 1999, £6.00

- **NonSense about Nature**
  Anthony O'Hear
  ISBN: 090763172X
  30 pp, 1997, £5.00
  'The definitive work debunking the myths associated with "natural"' *Farming News*

- **Biotechnology Regulation – The unacceptable costs of excessive caution**
  Henry Miller
  ISBN: 090763169X
  38 pp, 1997, £5.00

- **Environmental Alarms: A Medical Audit of Environmental Damage to Human Health**
  James Le Fanu
  ISBN: 0907631576
  38pp, 1997, £5.00

- **The Death of Humane Medicine and the Rise of Coercive Healthism**
  Petr Skrabanek
  ISBN: 0907631592
  212 pp, 1994, £12.95
  "This excellent book" *Independent.* "An astute critic of modern medical humbug . . . devastatingly accurate" *The Times*

- **Magic in the Surgery – Counselling & the NHS: A Licensed State Friendship Service**
  Myles Harris
  ISBN: 0907631568
  38pp, 1994, £5.00

- **A Phantom Carnage: The Myth that Low Incomes Kill**
  James Le Fanu
  ISBN: 0907631517
  33pp, 1993, £5.00

- **Health, Lifestyle and Environment: Countering the Panic**
  Published in co-operation with the Manhattan Institute
  ISBN: 0907631444
  152 pp, 1991, £9.95
  'Suggests that the nation is gripped by a "health panic" generated by often contradictory advice from researchers' *The Times*

- **Preventionitis: the exaggerated claims of health promotion**
  edited by James Le Fanu
  ISBN: 0907631584
  133 pp, 1994, £9.95

- **Take a Little Wine – or Beer or Whisky – for Your Stomach's Sake**
  Digby Anderson
  ISBN: 0907631606
  32 pp, 1995, £5.00

- **Drinking to Your Health: The allegations and the evidence**
  edited by Digby Anderson
  ISBN: 0907631371
  229 pp, £14.95

- **A New Diet of Reason: healthy eating and government policy 1985–1995**
  David Conning
  ISBN: 0907631649
  24 pp, 1995, £5.00

- **A Code of Ethics for Health Promotion**
  Michael Kelly
  ISBN: 0907631681
  28 pp, 1996, £5.00
  'This very important issue' *Daily Telegraph*

- **Risk, Health & the Consumer**
  James McCormick & Digby Anderson
  ISBN: 0907631479
  20pp, 1992, £4.00

- **Do Animals Have Rights?**
  Tibor Machan
  ISBN: 0907631401
  34pp, 1990, £4.00

Consumer affairs

- **Keeping Cures from Patients: the perverse effects of pharmaceutical regulations**
  Mark Neal
  ISBN: 0907631622
  34 pp, 1995, £5.00

- **False Economies: the true cost of 'cheap drugs'**
  Diane B Fairweather & Ian Hindmarch
  ISBN: 0907631614
  23 pp, 1995, £5.00

- **Advertising Bans: administrative decisions or matters of principle**
  John Gray
  ISBN: 0907631436
  37pp, 1991, £5.00

- **Advertising Bans: consequences for consumers**
  Mark Bentley & Mai Fyfield
  ISBN: 0907631452
  51 pp, 1991, £5.00

- **Reaching for the Counter. The new child consumers: regulation or education?**
  Adrian Furnham
  ISBN: 0907631541
  55 pp, 1993, £7.50

Corporate & Economic Affairs

- **American Lessons for European Company Directors: the emerging consensus in corporate governance**
Joseph F Johnston
ISBN: 0907631894
44pp, 2000, £6
The Anglo-American model of corporate governance is making inroads into Europe. The imposition of stakeholder nostrums, either by Brussels or by national governments, would reverse this trend.

- **Good Companies Don't Have Missions**
Digby Anderson
ISBN: 0907631908
28pp, 2000, £6
Failings of many company mission statements by ignoring shareholders and using vacuous and grandiloquent language.

- **Stakeholding: Betraying the Corporation's Objectives**
Elaine Sternberg
ISBN: 0907631827
18pp, 1999, £5.00

- **When is a Cat Fat? A Critical Look at Executive Remuneration**
Elaine Sterberg
ISBN: 0907631827
18pp, 1999, £5.00

- **The Many Ways of Governance: Perpectives on Control of the Firm**
Martin Ricketts
ISBN: 0907631843
57pp, 1999, £7.50

- **The Corporation under Siege – exposing the devices used by activists and regulators in the non-risk society**
Mark Neal & Christie Davies
ISBN: 0907631770
123 pp, 1998, £9.95
'Knowledge and scepticism are found in abundance in this publication' *Daily Telegraph*

- **Corporate Irresponsibility – Is Business Appeasing Anti-Business Activists?**
Robert Halfon
ISBN: 0907631789
25pp, 1998, £5.00

- **No Man Can Serve Two Masters – shareholders versus stakeholders in the governance of companies**
Joseph F Johnston
ISBN: 0907631762
31 pp, 1998, £5.00

- **A Balloon Waiting to be Burst? – Pseudomanagement training**
Stephen Williams
ISBN: 0907631673
37 pp, 1996, £5.00

- **What has 'Ethical Investment' to do with Ethics?**
Digby Anderson et al
ISBN: 0907631657
35 pp, 1996, £5.00

- **The Secret of the Miracle Economy: Different Attitudes to Competitiveness & Money**
Richard Lynn
ISBN: 090763141X
110pp, 1991, £8.95

- **Consumer Debt: Whose Responsibility?**
K Alec Chrystal
ISBN: 0907631533
27pp, 1993, £5.00

United Nations

- **Chattering International: How UNICEF Fails the World's Poorest Children**
James Le Fanu
ISBN: 0907631533
23pp, 1993, £5.00

- **Who Benefits from WHO? The Decline of the World Health Organisation**
Robert Tollison & Richard Wagner
ISBN: 090763155X
33pp, 1993, £5.00

- **Who Needs WHO? Three Views on the World Health Organisation's Dietary Guidelines**
Petr Skrabanek, Mike Gibney & James Le Fanu
ISBN: 090763149X
39pp, 1992, £5.00

General

- **Children and Advertising: The allegations and the evidence**
Adrian Furnham
ISBN: 0907631924
64pp, 2000, £7.50
A survey of over 20 studies published between 1967 and 1999 on children as consumers, finding that notions which are still popular in the press have lost any academic credence.

- **The Dictionary of Dangerous Words**
  Digby Anderson
  ISBN: 0907631932
  150pp, 2000, £5.50
  Assesses recent cultural change through the change in use of some 200 words including inclusiveness, fortitude and precautionary.

- **Scot-Free: How England would Fare Without Scotland**
  Simon Green, Robert Davies & Michael Mosbacher
  ISBN: 090763186X
  40pp, 1999, £6.00

- **The Case as Yet Unheard: Hereditary Peers & the Hereditary Principle**
  Richard North & Dogby Anderson
  ISBN: 0907631851
  41pp, 1999, £6.00

- **The British Woman Today: A qualitative survey of images in women's magazines**
  edited by Digby Anderson & Michael Mosbacher
  ISBN: 0907631746
  88 pp, 1997, £7.50

- **The Silencing of Society – The true cost of the lust for news**
  Kenneth Minogue
  ISBN: 0907631718
  73 pp, 1997, £7.50

- **Unwelcome Truths: Edmund Burke on today's political conceits**
  Ian Crowe
  ISBN: 0907631711
  26 pp, 1997, £5.00

- **A Future for Anti-Racism**
  Antony Flew
  ISBN: 0907631460
  37pp, 1992, £5.00

- **The Unmentionable Face of Poverty in the 1990s – Domestic Incompetence, Improvidence & Male Irresponsibility in Low Income Families**
  Digby Anderson
  29pp, 1991, £5.00

- **Families in Dreamland: Challenging the New Consensus for State Childcare**
  Patricia Morgan
  ISBN: 0907631487
  21pp, 1992, £5.00

Social Market Foundation

Address	11 Tufton Street
	London
	SW1P 3QB
Tel	020 7 222 7060
Fax	020 7 222 0310
Email	info@smf.co.uk
Website	www.smf.co.uk
Chairman	Lord Skidelsky
Director	Philip Collins
Company Secretary	Evan Davis
Head of Research	Selina Chen
Office Manager	Joanne Wilson
Research Officers	Sarah Fitzpatrick
	Don McCarthy
	Gillian Pennington
	Nick O'Shea
	David Leam
Business and Events Manager	Valerie Johnson
Economist	Donald McCarthy
Number of Employees	10
Cost of Membership	Corporate £500 plus VAT, Individual £50 plus VAT

Objectives

The Social Market Foundation's main activity is to commission and publish original papers by independent academic and other experts on key topics in the economic and social fields, to stimulate public debate on the performance of markets and the social framework within which they operate. The Foundation is a registered charity and a company limited by guarantee. It is independent of any political party or group and is financed by the sales of publications and by voluntary donations from individuals, organisations and companies.

History

The Social Market Foundation was established in 1989 as an in-house research unit for David Owen's continuing SDP. After the demise of that party, the SMF was re-launched in 1992 as a politically independent think-tank and registered charity with an Advisory Council drawn from both major parties and from those with no political affiliation.

Since that time the Social Market Foundation has established itself as one of Britain's most influential think tanks and one of its most respected sources of original analysis and ideas.

Under the Chairmanship of the eminent historian and political economist Robert Skidelsky, the SMF undertakes and commissions original research and writing on a range of public policy issues where understanding both the vitality of markets and the need for social consent can advance debate and help to shape new ideas. It specialises in publishing academics, journalists and policy practitioners, with the aim of bringing their work to the attention of a wider public policy audience.

In 1997 the Centre for Post-Collectivist Studies was established as an autonomous body within the SMF. The premise of the Centre is that we live in a post-collectivist age. The most dramatic evidence for this is the collapse of communism. The Centre's aim is to focus on the requirements of a durable post-collectivist order. To this end it brings together scholars and policy makers from around the world to examine the transition from communism to capitalism and to study the social and economic implications of this change of system.

Publications

SMF Papers

- **A State of Dependency**
  Frank Field
  £10.00, 2000

- **Universities and Innovation**
  Ian Pearson
  £6.00, 2000

- **Annuities: The Case for Change**
  Donald McCarthy
  £6.00, 2000

- Consuming Affairs
  Sarah Fitzpatrick (ed.)
  £8.00, 2000

- **Small Business and its Discontents**
  Philip Collins and Anthony Noun
  £5.00, 2000

- **The Social Market & the State**
  Various
  Collection of papers to mark the 10th anniversary of the SMF. Academics, politicians and journalists examine what is meant by the Social Market today
  ISBN: 1874097496
  308pp, £12.99

- **The Purpose of Politics**
  Oliver Letwin
  Letwin re-examines the history of political thought and action and devises a philosophy for the future of politics. The true purpose of politics, he claims, is the unceasing debate and revision of arguments and, without them, the future looks bleak.
  ISBN: 1874097496
  308pp, £8.00

- **Wanted: A New Consumer Affairs Strategy**
  Mark Boleat
  Examines the reforms necessary to improve the efficiency of the current regulatory system and to empower the consumer.
  £10.00

- **Will Europe Work?**

  David Smith

  Is the Anglo Saxon economic model the answer for the rest of Europe? Smith examines the popular myths about labour markets and unemployment, and asks whether you can have it all – low unemployment, low inequality and job security.

  ISBN 1861971028

  262pp, £8.99

- **Capital Regulation: For & Against**

  Robert Skidlesky, Nigel Lawson, John Flemming and Meghnad Desai

  Four perspectives on the desirability of controlling cross border financial flows as well as looking at the reasons behind the recent currency crises and their relation to capital regulation.

  ISBN: 1874097372

  69pp, £5.00

- **Millennium Doom: Fallacies about the End of Work**

  Mauricio Rojas

  Explodes the myth that the growth of a global market economy will exclude most of the world's population from the labour market. Argues that man's potential is greater than ever before.

  ISBN: 1874097291

  61pp, £10.00

- **State of the Future**

  Robert Skidlesky, Norman Gemmell, Walter Eltis, Evan Davis & Meghnad Desai

  Examines the role of the British State and its impact on incentives to work, the productivity of capital, the quality of public service provision and income equality.

  ISBN: 1874097275

  134pp, £10.00

- **Russia: The 1998 Crisis and Beyond**

  Kalin Nikolov

  Offers an account of the fits and starts of economic reform during the last 7 years.

  ISBN: 1874097429

  50pp, £5.00

- **Rise & Fall of the Swedish Model**

  Mauricio Rojas

  Charts the rise of the 'People's Home', from its origin in Sweden's rapid industrial development to its collapse under the difficulties of transforming the nation into a post-industrial society.

  ISBN: 1874097232

  186pp, £10.00

- **Politics of Economic Reform**

  Various

  Why is economic reform often driven by periodic crises than by rational calculation?

  ISBN: 1874097240

  286pp, £12.00

- **Universities & Innovation: Meeting the Challenge**

  Ian Pearson

  Britain's universities, once a source of national pride, are at a crossroads, if not in crisis. Our ability to exploit the innovative capaicity locked up in academia now falls far short of the success achieved by comparable nations. How can we marshal untapped talent and turn Britain into a centre for innovation?

  ISBN: 187409747X

  £6.00

- **A European Harmony?**

  Various

  Collection of essays looking at the political and economic impact of tax harminisation in the EU.

  ISBN: 187409733X

  £6.00

- **The Social Market Economy**

  Robert Skidelsky

  In this, The Social Market Foundation's first paper, Skidelsky defines the term 'Social Market Economy' and discusses both its historical value and its role in the future of society.

  ISBN: 095145660

  23pp, £3.50

- **Responses to Robert Skidelsky on the Social Market Economy**

  Sarah Benton, Kurt Biedenkopf, Frank Field, Danny Finkelstein, et al

  Commentators with diverse approaches give their reactions to Robert Skidelsky's inaugural statement on The Social Market Economy. Variously attacked and supported by left and right, Skidelsky draws the debate together in his afterword with a development of his ideas about liberty, social reform and the market.

  ISBN: 095145661

  32pp, £3.50

- **Europe Without Currency Barriers**

  Samuel Brittan & Michael Artis

  Brittan and Artis look at the reasons for and the repercussions of a single European Monetary Unit. They examine the prospects of a 'United States of Europe' by evaluating the success of the European Monetary System.

  ISBN: 0951456628

  35pp, £5.00

- **Greening The White Paper: A Strategy for NHS Reform**

  Gwyn Bevan & Marshall Marinker

  Using their combined experience as health practitioner and academic, the authors consider the contemporary debate at the time of the late 1980s health reforms. They call for experimentation in a radical approach to NHS reform focusing on what they see as the 'pivotal function' of general practice.

  ISBN: 0951456636

  47pp, £5.00

- **Education and the Labour Market: An English Disaster**

Adrian Wooldridge

Wooldridge claims that the performance of a sophisticated economy is increasingly dependent not on its fund of physical capital but on its capacity to mobilise the brain-power of its citizens. He goes on to discuss how the shortage of properly trained brain-power will prevent economic growth in the next century just as did raw materials in the last.

ISBN: 09514566444

30pp, £5.00

- **Crisis in Eastern Europe: Roots and Prospects**

Robin Okey

Okey traces the history of Eastern Europe and presents a more sympathetic general picture of their experience as he outlines the gradual decay of the communist system.

ISBN: 0951456652

23pp, £4.00

- **Fighting Fiscal Privilege: Towards a Fiscal Constitution**

Deepak Lal

Lal concentrates on the principals at play in the debate over British tax reform and examines why the system as it stands came about. His analysis leads to an outline for tax reform which takes a more realistic and sceptical view of the State, and considers the implications for reform for a modern Western democracy.

ISBN: 0951456660

17pp, £4.00

- **Eastern Europe in Transition**

Clive Crook & Daniel Franklin

Crook and Franklin recap the events that followed the end of communism in Eastern Europe. Franklin discusses the three stages used to cope with the deterioration of the Berlin wall, while Crook discusses the causes, results, and solutions of the transition to follow.

ISBN: 0951456679

28pp, £5.00

- **The Open Network and its Enemies**

Danny Finkelstein & Craig Arnall

Danny Finkelstein and Craig Arnall consider the central issues in the opening up of the market in telecommunications. A response to the government consultative document of November 1990, the authors argue that the future of telecommunications competition lies in the theory of contestable markets to ensure both an effective market and a satisfied customer.

ISBN: 0951456687

26pp, £5.00

- **Restatement of Economic Liberalism**

Samuel Brittan

In a paper that serves as an introduction to his book of the same title, Brittan here develops his own perceptions of the social market, the nature of liberalism and the essential importance of personal freedom. He urges the upholders of market orthodoxy to take account of liberalism and not to rely wholly on competitive capitalism as a 'painless cure-all'.

ISBN 095145669

24pp, £5.00

- **Standards in Schools: Assessment, Accountability and the Purposes of Education**

  John Marks

  Within his general theme of standards in schools, John Marks' paper ranges over the history of educational reform, the importance of public accountability and the difficulties in finding a practical way forward. His use of historical example reveals how reform has affected standards in the past, while discussion of contemporary issues focuses on improvement of standards and the dangers inherent in overburdening schools.

  ISBN: 1874097003

  47pp, £6.00

- **Deeper Share Ownership**

  Matthew Gaved & Anthony Goodman

  Gaved and Goodman show that the value of private direct shareholdings has declined to the point that it accounts for less than 20% of the total capitalisation of the stock exchange. The authors also propose measures aimed at helping those wishing to own shares directly to do so more easily.

  ISBN: 187409702

  70pp, £6.00

- **Fighting Leviathan: Building Social Markets that Work**

  Howard Davies

  Davies, then Director-General at the CBI, starts from the premise that the aim in public service provision should be to imitate as far as possible the conditions which obtain in competitive markets. The paper identifies ten common features of properly functioning public services and looks at each in turn, making observations about their prevalence in current service provision. It culminates in a call for institutional change to provide more pressure for public sector reform.

  ISBN: 1874097038

  59pp, £6.00

- **The Age of Entitlement**

  David Willetts

  Willetts argues that the real problem isn't that too many people live too long, it is that too many people stop working too soon. This is accompanied by a series of suggestions about how to start putting the problem right.

  ISBN: 1874097046

  43pp, £6.00

- **Schools and the State**

  Evan Davis

  The author argues that schools should be allowed to expand and contract in response to demand, pay teachers according to local conditions, and teach a slimmed down national curriculum. Education is both a private and public good, which should be funded out of general taxation. The state should act as facilitator and guarantor, not as a provider and a manager.

  ISBN: 1874097070

  46pp, £6.00

- **Public Sector Pay: In Search of Sanity**

  Ron Beadle

  Beadle criticises the rigidities of a national system of pay determination, which has largely exempted public employees from having reward linked to performance. This is the result, he says, of Government using pay in the public sector as an instrument of macro-economic policy.

  ISBN: 1874097208

  54pp, £8.00

- **Beyond Next Steps: a Civil Service for the 1990s**
  Sir Peter Kemp
  A guide to the civil service's 'next steps' programme. £8.00

- **Post-Communist Societies in Transition: A Social Market Perspective**
  John Gray
  Gray rejects the notion that Western exemplars of market institutions can be transplanted to the historical circumstances of most post-communist countries, and he argues that the expectation for Russia to converge smoothly and peacefully onto any Western model is 'politically frivolous and dangerous to the highest degree'.
  ISBN: 1874097305
  45pp, £8.00

- **Two Cheers for the Institutions**
  Stanley Wright
  The benefits of companies' accountability to shareholders are espoused in Stanley Wright's paper. Shareholders should be encouraged to exercise greater responsibility while British capitalism would operate more effectively were legal reform applied to the relationship between owners and managers.
  ISBN: 1874097356
  69pp, £10.00

- **Civic Conservatism**
  David Willets
  Willetts' paper sets out to rescue limited government and market institutions from the rationalism of the Neo-Liberals while at the same time promoting free independent institutions as better instruments of social policy than an all-embracing state. He develops his ideas and produces a paper that provides an elegant defence of free markets and a fresh approach to social policy.
  ISBN: 1874097402
  55pp, £10.00

- **The Undoing of Conservatism**
  John Gray
  This paper argues that unfettered global markets undermine the traditions and institutions on which they depend. Therefore they rely on the uncertain promise of continuous growth for their legitimacy. The author believes that the domination of Conservative thought by market liberalism has left it unable to retreat to a moral fundamentalism that progress has rendered obsolete.
  ISBN: 1874097453
  53pp, £10.00

- **Meritocracy and the 'Classless Society'**
  Adrian Wooldridge
  Wooldridge attacks the social and welfare policies of the last 30 years, saying they have undermined meritocracy and substituted group entitlements over individual achievement. These policies have resulted in greater inequalities and a society that is more polarised than ever. The paper argues that it is time to reinvent meritocracy and to recreate the consensus for which it existed across the political spectrum before the 1960s.
  ISBN: 1874097704
  48pp, £12.00

- **Public Spending into the Millennium**

  Nick Bosanquet

  The author argues that the reform of the public sector over the last decade has succeeded only in increasing pressure for more public spending. Bosanquet suggests that the only way the state will be able to provide for people who can ill-afford to pay for themselves is by reducing public spending and searching for new ways to finance services.

  ISBN: 1874097801

  46pp, £10.00

- **Communities in the Countryside**

  Damian Green

  To explore what common identity is, and how it can be fostered, Damian Green looks at the communities of rural life. He argues that the continued existence of a sense of community in the countryside can be preserved and enhanced by a programme of decentralisation and deregulation. This would promote the voluntary spirit and initiative which is typical of so much of rural Britain.

  ISBN: 1874097119

  35pp, £10.00

- **The Ties that Bind Us**

  Matthew D'Ancona

  In a companion volume to Communities in the Countryside, Matthew D'Ancona considers the nature of identity in towns, taking Swindon as his example. Once a thriving industrial centre built around the railways, it has since experienced boom and bust in the hi-tech business that took over. He examines Swindon's civic identity, its strength and adaptability, and the impact it has had on the town's ability to regenerate itself so successfully.

  ISBN: 187409716

  38pp, £10.00

- **The Prospects for Public Spending**

  Andrew Tyrie

  Tyrie describes the ways in which levels of public expenditure are determined, and considers ways in which they could be improved. In particular he calls for greater transparency in the costing of public spending proposals and in the policing of our national accounts. He goes on to suggest that an annual taxpayers statement would heighten awareness of how much money we pay to the state and what we receive in return.

  ISBN: 1874097461

  103pp, £15.00

- **Taxing and Spending Dilemmas**

  Norman Gemmell

  Norman Gemmell argues that the lack of accurate measurements for state spending has impeded sensible discussion about the future role and size of the state. He claims that the demand for public services is set to grow faster than the economy as a whole while at the same time it is becoming increasingly difficult for governments to raise more revenue through taxation.

  ISBN: 1874097569

  71pp, £10.00

- **Making Shoplifters Pay**

  Joshua Bamfield

  Every year there are 1.7 million incidents of retail theft in the UK. However only 1 in 12 offenders receive a police caution and only 1 in 400 are imprisoned. Bamfield looks at the use of a system of Civil Recovery in the United States and Canada which offers retailers easy access to a system of civil prosecution which increases the likelihood of punishment without overburdening the police or the criminal courts.

  1997 ISBN: 1874097712

  66pp, £12.00

- **Britain's Relative Economic Decline 1870-1995**

  Nicholas Crafts

  Professor Nicholas Crafts offers a quantitative analysis of the country's relative economic performance since the industrial revolution. He argues that although policy errors and institutional failings caused Britain to fall further behind its main European competitors between 1950's and 1970's, the reforms of the last twenty years have arrested that decline.

  ISBN: 1874097763

  68pp, £12.00

- **Beyond the Welfare State**

  Robert Skidelsky

  Skidelsky claims that the Welfare State has become a tax on efficiency, liberty and morality. He claims that it impedes economic growth by creating unsustainable budget deficits, removes incentives from self-reliance and puts behaving rationally in conflict with behaving well. Skidelsky calls for dramatic reform aimed at making those who can, take greater personal responsibility for the provision of their health education and social insurance. Otherwise, the future of those that the Welfare State was intended to help looks bleak.

  ISBN: 1874097135

  104pp, £12.00

- **Lessons from the Republicans**

  Tim Hames & Alan Grant

  Lessons from the Republicans, looks at what happened in the United States when the Republican Party found itself in opposition and needed to renew itself politically and ideologically. They claim that the Republican Revolution may offer lessons for the UK in the areas of economic policy, crime and welfare reform.

  ISBN: 187409781

  56pp, £12.00

- **Reforming Welfare**

  Frank Field

  A series of lectures and essays delivered by Frank Field in which he addresses issues such as the deterrent effect of means-testing on honesty and concludes that attempts to dispense social assistance which do not go with the grain of human nature are bound to end
  in failure.

  ISBN: 1874097917

  129pp, £10.00

- **Dilemmas in Modern Health Care**

  Edited by John Spiers

  A collaborative work reflecting the thoughts of practitioners, managers, consumers, and the private sector as they seek to come to terms with the pressures of delivering better quality care to a more demanding public in a climate of financial restraint.

  ISBN: 1874097070

  161pp, £10.00

- **Ready for Treatment**

  Nick Bosanquet & Stephen Pollard

  Bosanquet and Pollard look at how the evolution of the NHS has shaped the pattern of health care delivery in the past and its likely role in the future. The authors use a new survey of public opinion to find out what our attitudes are to the contemporary health care. The results are startling.

  ISBN: 187409702

  149pp, £10.00

- **The Future of Welfare**

  Various authors (Edited by Roderick Nye)

  A collection of essays by commentators, academics, politicians, and policy practitioners looking at the progress of welfare reform in Britain and the United States. They offer a link between the theory and the practice of welfare reform.

  ISBN: 1874097127

  151pp, £10.00

- **Reflections on Welfare Reform**

  Frank Field

  Former Minister for Welfare Reform revisits the main issues at the heart of the debate on the future of social security and pension provision in light of his experiences in government.

  ISBN: 1874097321

  195pp, £10.00

- **The State of Dependency: Welfare Under Labour**

  Frank Field

  Field shows how to protect and promote the interests of the poor in an age when Labour can win elections without them. Field outlines what he wanted to do as a Minister but was prevented from doing so.

  ISBN: 1874097526

  £10.00

- **Welfare to Work**

  David Willetts

  David Willetts examines the claims of the 'New Deal' and offers a dispassionate account of active employment measures, the current state of the UK labour market and the factors which prevent more people from joining it.

  ISBN: 1874097186

  83pp, £10.00

- **A Question of Choice**

  Stephen Pollard & Katharine Raymond

  Examines the public's attitude to to public health and their future expectations and priorities for change

  ISBN: 1874097593

  60pp, £10.00

- **A Cue for Change**

  Oliver Morgan

  Looks at the founding principles of the NHS and examines how relevant they are today. Also asks if lessons can be learnt from Europe.

  ISBN: 1874097445

  332pp, £12.00

- **Back on Target**

  Nick Bosenquet & Tony Hockley

  Gives insights into new directions in health policy – limitations of the state, responsibilities of the individual and independent organisations.

  ISBN: 1874097194

  69pp, £10.00

- **A Better State of Health**

  John Willman

  Shows how the NHS must be reformed if we are to get the services we need and deserve.

  ISBN: 1861971897

  297pp, £8.99

Reports

- **Environment, Economics and Development after the 'Earth Summit'**

  Andrew Cooper

  Cooper reviews the 'Earth Summit' in Rio and summarises some of the scientific evidence and economic ideas which may be useful in the environment debate after Rio.

  26pp, £3.00

- **Another Great Depression? Historical lessons for the 1990s**

  Robert Skidelsky & Liam Halligan

  Skidelsky and Halligan compare the current economic downturn with the slump of the 1930s and attempt to provide a framework of analysis for economic policy makers.

  28pp, £5.00

- **Exiting the Underclass: Policy towards America's urban poor**

  Andrew Cooper & Catherine Moylan

  Cooper and Moylan discuss the history of America's underclass and the problems that have occurred. They outline the causes and effects of the ever widening gap between poverty and mainstream America.

  27pp, £5.00

- **Britain's Borrowing Problem**

  Bill Robinson

  Robinson examines the underlying causes of Britain's deteriorating public finances. He explains why the public sector deficit matters and how declining tax revenues and increased public spending fuelled by popular expectations has led us to our current position. Finally he sets out a new set of principles to govern public spending in the long term.

  35pp, £5.00

Occasional Papers

- **Deregulation**

  David Willetts

  Willetts sets out to explore why the burden of regulation has increased in Britain since the 1980s. He describes how calls for more equality, subsidiarity and safety have fuelled a growing bureaucracy, and goes on to offer an alternative path.

  ISBN: 1874097054

  27pp, £3.00

- **'There is no such thing as society'**

  Samuel Brittan

  Brittan examines the meaning of the phrase 'there is no such thing as society' by saying that 'it is the individuals, not collectives, who feel, exult, triumph or despair'. He argues against the idea that the good of the nation can be advanced if it is not good for the individuals who make it up.

  ISBN: 1874097062

  37pp, £3.00

- **The Opportunities for Private Funding in the NHS**

  David Willetts

  This paper by David Willetts focuses on six different types of project in which private finance could be involved. He argues that each of his six categories show there is considerable scope for the NHS to benefit from the Autumn Statement initiative on private finance.

  ISBN: 1874097089

  15pp, £3.00

- **A Social Market for Training**

  Howard Davies

  Davies argues for portable financial credits, a range of providers, better information for consumers and better inspection and audit procedures. He also urges private enterprise to use wage differentials as a price signal to encourage future entrants into labour market to improve their qualifications.

  ISBN: 1874097003

  20pp, £3.00

- **Beyond Unemployment**

  Robert Skidelsky & Liam Halligan

  Skidelsky and Halligan assert that persistent joblessness and a large national deficit require the reinstatement of full employment as a primary economic goal. They identify failures in the markets for training and set out a series of measures designed to address these.

  ISBN: 1874097054

  30pp, £6.00

- **Brighter Schools**

  Michael Fallon

  Fallon offers a range of policies that he believes will lead to an increase in the quantity of capital available for our schools and an improvement in the way it is allocated.

  ISBN: 1874097151

  22pp, £6.00

- **Understanding Shock Therapy**

  Jeffrey Sachs

  Sachs argues that the Western model remains the most powerful and appropriate source of inspiration for economic reform throughout the world and shock therapy the most successful approach to integrating transition economies into the global system

  ISBN: 187409750

  44pp, £8.00

- **Recruiting to the Little Platoons**

  William Waldegrave

  In this collection of speeches and lectures delivered as Chancellor of the Duchy of Lancaster, Waldegrave examines some of the most pressing problems of our age with the theme that these problems can best be resolved by applying the central principles of Conservatism.

  ISBN: 1874097550

  28pp, £6.00

- **The Culture of Anxiety: The Middle Class in Crisis**

  Matthew Symonds

  Symonds examines how the once self-confident and prosperous middle classes of the 1980s have come to be affected by unprecedented anxiety in the 1990s. Here he looks at how mistaken policies have made matters worse and suggests the issues that all governments must tackle to prevent anxiety giving way to something more deliberating.

  ISBN: 1874097607

  28pp, £8.00

- **What is left of Keynes?**

  Samuel Brittan, Meghnad Desai, Deepak Lal, Robert Skidelsky and Tom Wilson

  This paper is an assessment of the legacy of Keynes and Keynesianism by five of Britain's most eminent economic commentators. The contributions provide a study of whether Keynesianism was in fact responsible for the post-War golden age of economic prosperity, and ask what, if anything, should replace it.

  ISBN: 1874097658

  34pp, £8.00

- **Winning the Welfare Debate**

  Peter Lilley, (Introduction by Frank Field)

  This paper is a collection of lectures given by Peter Lilley, as Secretary of State for Social Security. It constitutes a clear and well made argument for a programme of gradual reform of the welfare state and set out the strategy Lilley used successfully to curb the growth in social security spending.

  ISBN: 1874097755

  50pp, £10.00

- **Financing the Future of the Welfare State**

Robert Skidelsky & Will Hutton

Hutton and Skidelsky debate how future public services will be paid for. Hutton argues that the current Welfare State is largely affordable, while Skidelsky counters that nations are reaching the limit of their taxable capacity and should contain the costs of the Welfare State.

ISBN: 1874097909

17pp, £8.00

- **Picking Winners: The East Asian Experience**

Ian Little

The 'Tiger' economies of East Asia and the myths surrounding the reason for their extraordinary growth are Ian Little's subject. Not only does he conclude that their higher growth rates were not the miracle they appear to be, but also argues that government intervention, far from being the linchpin of success, had marginal, or even harmful effects.

ISBN: 187409795

34pp, £8.00

- **Over-The-Counter Medicines**

Alan Maynard & Gerald Richardson

The authors examine the major changes in the supply of pharmaceutical products in recent years. They consider the impact of liberalisation on the cost and efficiency of delivering health care, what savings will be made, if any, and what else needs to be changed if they are to be achieved.

ISBN: 1874097216

36pp, £10.00

- **Pressure Group Politics in Modern Britain**

William Waldegrave, Charles Secrett, et al (Introduction by Peter Riddell)

The authors examine the roles of pressure groups in the modern political process. They look at the relationship with government, the press, and with their own members where they have them.

ISBN: 1874097267

36pp, £10.00

- **Design Decisions: Improving the Effectiveness of Public Purchasing**

Mark Fisher MP, John Sorrell, Nick Stephenson, et al (Introduction by Stephen Taylor MP)

The authors look at the role of effective purchasing in reducing 'whole life' costs of products and at how new methods of public accounting could encourage the public sector to factor in the returns from investing in good design practice.

ISBN: 1874097313

46pp, £10.00

- **Stakeholding Society vs. Enterprise Centre of Europe**

Robert Skidelsky & Will Hutton

Hutton and Skidelsky debate whether we should become a 'stakeholding' society in which employees have a greater say in the way that the companies they work for are run. Hutton argues that there is no contradiction between a competitive market economy and co-operation between owners and employees. Skidelsky believes that stakeholding is at best platitudinous and at worst a recipe for dangerous interventionist policies.

ISBN: 1874097518

20pp, £10.00

- **Setting Enterprise Free**
Ian Lang

In this collection of speeches, Ian Lang outlines what he sees as the prerequisites of a more competitive Britain. He argues the need for: contestability in the privatised utilities; the promotion of freer trade in Europe and the rest of the world; and business involvement in regional regeneration. He also talks about the role of government in promoting scientific research
ISBN: 18740973644
46pp, £10.00

- **Community Values and the Market Economy**
John Kay

John Kay explores the social dimensions of market economics. In particular he looks at the relationship between trust, co-operation and mutual support and the successful operation of an enterprise economy. He attempts to reconcile current economic theory with modern strands of moral philosophy, such as communitarianism, which go beyond traditional liberal individualism.
ISBN: 1874097666
67pp, £10.00

Other Papers

- **Local Government and the Social Market**
George Jones
ISBN: 1874097011
23pp, £3.00

- **Full Employment without Inflation**
James Meade
ISBN: 094843428
19pp, £6.00

Memoranda

- **Provider Choice: Opting In through the Private Finance Initiative**
Michael Fallon

Fallon, the former schools minister, calls for a radical extension of the PFI that would allow the private sector to opt in to the private provision of services as well as capital projects.
7pp, £5.00

- **The Importance of Resource Accounting**
Evan Davis

Davis argues that the adoption of new accounting practices in the public sector could transpire to be one of the budget's more enduring and important measures, having a powerful effect on the way public services are financed and operated.
8pp, £3.50

- **Why there is no time to teach: What is wrong with the National Curriculum 10 Level Scale**
  John Marks

  Marks describes how teachers misplaced their trust in the 10-level scale and explains what is wrong with Sir Ron Dearing's proposals for assessment. He also suggests some simpler and more constructive alternatives.

  18pp, £5.00

- **All free health care must be effective**
  Brendan Devlin, Gwyn Bevan

  Bevan and Devlin argue that reducing variations will do more to address the excess of demand over supply in health care than limiting the types of operation performed under the NHS or excluding patients whose illnesses result from irresponsible behaviour.

  11pp, £5.00

- **Recruiting to the Little Platoons**
  William Waldegrave

  Waldegrave discusses an approach to public services, which draws on the traditions of Burke and Disraeli and attempts to meet the contemporary demands for a more cost-effective, efficient and customer-facing public sector.

  7pp, £5.00

- **Labour and the Public Services**
  John Willman

  Willman argues that the failure of Labour to make the public sector reform agenda its own reflects serious shortcomings in the party's political thinking.

  18pp, £8.00

- **Organising Cost Effective Access to Justice**
  Gwyn Bevan, Tony Holland and Michael Partington

  Bevan, Holland, and Partington attempt to make sense of legal aid by offering an economic analysis of the present system. They argue that its current problems are similar to those faced by other publicly funded services such as health care.

  Pages: 27pp, £5.00

- **A Memo to Modernisers**
  Ron Beadle, Andrew Cooper, Evan Davis, Alex de Mont, Stephen Pollard, et al

  A Memo to Modernisers is a collection of policy initiatives designed to show how imaginative, market-led ideas can be used to address some of Britain's most pressing social and economic problems.

  34pp, £8.00

- **Conservatives in Opposition: Republicans in the US**
  Daniel Finkelstein

  Finkelstein examines the experience of the Republican Party after almost two years in opposition and reports that it has brought them no intellectual dividend.

  18pp, £5.00

- **Housing Benefit: Incentives for Reform**
  Greg Clark
  Using an extensive survey with Rent Officers around Britain backed up by economic analysis, Clark concludes that the present system of Housing Benefit is flawed because it gives tenants no incentive to bargain with landlords over rent levels.
  29pp, £8.00

- **The Market and Clause IV**
  Stephen Pollard
  Pollard agues not only that Labour's commitment to public ownership is outdated as a means but that the end to which it has been directed, the equitable allocation of resources, is best achieved through the market.
  20pp, £5.00

- **Yeltsin's Choice: Background to the Chechnya Crisis**
  Vladimir Mau
  Dr Vladimir Mau offers an analysis of the economic and political events of 1994 that led to the Chechnya Crisis. He considers this process and shows the real picture of Russian politics and follows trends that determine the process of their decision making.
  11pp, £8.00

- **Teachers Practices: A New Model for State Schools**
  Tony Meredith
  Meredith argues that the creation of a performance culture in state schools relies on giving teachers a long-term stake in the education system, one which offers tangible rewards for success and the scope to innovate.
  10pp, £8.00

- **The Right to Earn: Learning to Live with Top People's Pay**
  Ron Beadle
  As public concern over the remuneration of senior executives continue to grow, Ron Beadle explains why recent pay increases are justifiable both in political terms and in the way markets operate.
  23pp, £8.00

- **A Memo to Modernisers II**
  John Abbott, Peter Boone, Tom Chandos, Evan Davis, Alex de Mont, et al
  A collection of policy initiatives designed to show how market-led ideas can address some of the most pressing issues on Britain's public policy agenda.
  34pp, £8.00

- **Schools, Selection and the Left**
  Stephen Pollard
  Pollard says that the key to raising standards and broadening opportunities in education lies not in promoting rigid uniformity, but in creating a more diverse state sector.
  23pp, £8.00

- **The Future of Long-Term Care**
  Andrew Cooper & Roderick Nye
  Cooper and Nye examine the role of the state in funding long term care and argue that future provision of a decent standard will require people to set aside income during their working lifetime so that the costs of their own social care needs in old age are provided for.
  17pp, £8.00

- **Better Job Options for Disabled People: Re-employ and Beyond**

  Peter Thurnham

  Peter Thurnham argues that much of the support given by the taxpayers to assist disabled people into work is being misdirected.

  20pp, £8.00

- **Negative Equity and the Housing Market**

  Andrew Cooper & Roderick Nye

  Cooper and Nye challenge some of the popular misconceptions surrounding negative equity and the current state of the housing market.

  14pp, £6.00

- **Industrial Injuries Compensation: Incentives to Change**

  Dr Greg Clark & Iain Smedley

  Clark and Smedley argue that the Government's Industrial Injuries Scheme is ripe for reform. They describe two anomalies that developed from the current arrangements for paying no-fault compensation to people who sustain injury or contract a disease at work.

  15pp, £8.00

- **Better Government by Design: Improving the Effectiveness of Public Purchasing**

  Katharine Raymond & Marc Shaw

  Raymond and Shaw argue that it is time the public sector woke up to the potential cost savings involved in good design. If properly implemented, better design practice could end up improving public service delivery while cutting costs.

  10pp, £8.00

- **A Memo to Modernisers III**

  Evan Davis, John Kay, Alex de Mont, Stephen Pollard, et al

  The notion of a 'stakeholder society' has excited much comment and speculation, particularly about what it might mean in policy terms. This memo attempts to flesh out the idea of stakeholding by suggesting a range of ideas.

  24pp, £8.00

- **The Citizen's Charter Five Years On**

  Roderick Nye

  Nye examines how effective the Charter has been in making public services more responsive to customers, and looks at how the Charter initiative might keep pace with rising public expectations in a time when the ability of governments to meet these is hampered by expenditure constraints.

  8pp, £8.00

- **Standards of English and Maths for Primary Schools in 1995**

  John Marks

  Using DfEE data covering nearly half a million pupils and some 90% of all English primary schools, John Marks has built up the first national picture showing the disturbing results of England's 11-year-olds in the key subjects of Maths and English.

  25pp, £10.00

- **Standards of Reading, Spelling & Maths for 7 year olds in Primary Schools for 1995**
  John Marks

  In this study of 1995 National Curriculum test results for 7-year-olds, Marks shows that the chances of achieving a good grounding in the basics of education vary dramatically from school to school even with the same LEA.

  37pp, £10.00

- **An Expensive Lunch: The Political Economy of Britain's New Monetary Framework**
  Robert Chote

  Far from being a panacea for inflation, Chote points to evidence that suggests independent central banks have to inflict more damage than governments in order to deliver a given reduction in inflation.

  19pp, £10.00

- **A Memo to Martin Taylor**
  David Willetts

  Drawing on his time at the No 10 Policy Unit and from the failed attempts by the Wilson and Heath governments to integrate the tax and benefit systems, Willetts raises ten points which the government will have to address if it is to implement its plans for welfare reform.

  13pp, £10.00

- **Why Fundholding Should Stay**
  David Colin-Thome

  At a time when the future of the Health Service is once again under review, Colin-Thome argues that the great strides which have been made in terms of clinical resource management, referral pattern and provider responsiveness, should make politicians reconsider their opposition to GP fundholding.

  13pp, £10.00

- **Lessons from Wisconsin's Welfare Reform**
  J Jean Rogers

  Rogers, director of Governor Thompson's welfare programmes, describes the philosophies behind the Wisconsin reforms and the lessons learned in implementing them over the last decade which could be applied to the UK.

  19pp, £5.00

- **The Sex Change State**
  Melanie Phillips

  Phillips argues that in their effort to realise quick savings to the social security budget, policymakers are ignoring the underlying problems of single parenthood because they are opposed to being judgmental about the type of family unit.

  21pp, £8.00

- **Freedom & the Family**
  William Hague

  Hague outlines an approach which combines openness and tolerance towards those living outside the bounds of what are considered normal families with a recognition that the nuclear family remains the bedrock of society, and one which ought to be supported

  11pp, £5.00

- **Practical Road Pricing**

  Stephen Glaister

  Dr Glaister of the LSE outlines the nature of the problems caused by traffic congestion and how measures such as fuel taxation fail to address these adequately. He then talks about the features of road pricing and what he sees as the essential elements of a successful scheme.

  11pp, £5.00

- **New Dynamics in Public Health Policy**

  Nick Bosanquet and Tony Hockley

  Bosanquet and Hockley argue that the shift towards a public health strategy based less on aspirations and more on evidence of effectiveness, is a positive one and in step with the rethinking of public health policy being undertaken by the European Union and the World Health Organisation.

  24pp

- **Education Action Zones: The Conditions of Success**

  Robert Skidelsky and Katharine Raymond

  Skidelsky and Raymond examine the background of Education Action Zones, what they set out to achieve, and how the Department for Education and Employment has begun to put the policy into effect.

  12pp, £8.00

Hard Data

- **The Rowntree Inquiry and 'Trickle Down'**

  Andrew Cooper & Roderick Nye

  Cooper and Nye discuss the recent Joseph Rowntree Foundation Inquiry into Income and Wealth found that income inequality in the UK has grown rapidly since 1977, with the gap between the earnings of the rich and poor wider than at any time since World War II.

  3pp, £5.00

- **Costing the Public Policy Agenda: A week of the Today Programme**

  Andrew Cooper

  Cooper attempts to identify the magnitude of cost implied by the public policy agenda of the day by looking at BBC Radio Four's Today Programme.

  7pp, £5.00

- **Universal Nursery Education & Playgroups**

  Andrew Cooper & Roderick Nye

  Cooper and Nye compare Britain's current nursery education system with that of America's Head Start Programme. They review the programme's success in giving underprivileged children the opportunity to excel and therefore break the underclass cycle.

  4pp, £5.00

- **Social Security Costs of the Social Chapter**

  Andrew Cooper & Marc Shaw

  Cooper and Shaw discuss the controversy of Britain's opt-out of The Maastricht Treaty. They review the terms of the Social Chapter and how it would affect the UK with the æharmonisation of the European Social Systems.

  6pp, £5.00

- **What Price a Life?**

  Andrew Cooper & Roderick Nye

  Cooper and Nye argue that the on-going review of risk assessment methodologies and life values across government should lead to the necessary removal of anomalies.

  5pp, £5.00

Trident Trust/SMF Contributions to Policy

- **Welfare to Work: The America Works Experience**

  Roderick Nye, (Introduction by John Spiers)

  In this, the first of a series of papers, Nye looks at the problem of re-integrating the long-term unemployed back into the active labour market and at the lessons which Britain can draw from the United States.

  ISBN: 1874097410

  26pp, £10.00

- **Job Insecurity vs. Labour Market Flexibility**

  David Smith (Introduction by John Spiers)

  Smith examines what, if any, relationship exists between job insecurity and labour market flexibility. He finds that the average job tenure in the UK hardly changed between 1975 and 1995 and most part time work is taken on out of preference. He also claims that even if job insecurity is a state of mind rather than an economic reality, it threatens to divert the attention of policy makers away from those who have genuinely become more marginal in the labour market.

  ISBN: 1874097615

  38pp, £10.00

- **How Effective is Work Experience?**

  Greg Clark & Katharine Raymond

  Clark and Raymond examine the effectiveness of work experience in preparing people for employment. They look at its impact on young people with low educational attainment and poorly developed social abilities who have the least chance of finding and keeping a job even at a time of relatively low unemployment.

  ISBN: 1874097968

  77pp, £8.00

Centre for Post Collectivist Studies

- **Welfare After Communism**

  Janos Kornai

  1999 ISBN: 1874097380

  £6.00

  The end of communism bequeathed would be reformers inefficient and unresponsive productive sectors dominated by bloated state monopolies and welfare sectors in a similar state of disarray. While great, though often not wholly successful, efforts have been made to reform the great command economies of the transition countries, no such efforts have been afforded the command welfare states of these same nations. Kornai blieves this disparity will soon be redressed and that the long awaited reform process may be about to start in earnest.

- **Financial Crises**

  Various

  1999 ISBN: 1874097437,

  £9.50

  Analyses the past and proposed solutions for the future in order to avert financial crises in the world economy.

- **Killing Development: Money Laundering in the Global Economy**

  Various

  1999 ISBN: 1874097488

  £6.00

  The authors examine the criminal practices and methods of money laundering, the implications of current legilsation and its effect on developing nations, socially and economically.

- **Russia's Stormy Path to Reform**

  Edited by Robert Skidelsky

  An edited version of a conference on held in Moscow in April 1995 which offers a unique insight into what Russia's own leaders were thinking and arguing about in the run-up to the critical parliamentary elections held in December 1995

  ISBN: 1874097852

  Pages: 145pp, £20.00

- **Macroeconomic Stabilisation in Russia: Lessons of Reform, 1992–1995**

  Robert Skidelsky and Liam Halligan

  Skidelsky and Halligan examine the theories behind Russia's persistently high inflation rate and chart the attempts of successive governments at macroeconomic stabilisation since the end of communism.

  ISBN: 1874097062

  41pp, £10.00

- **The End of Order**

  Francis Fukuyama

  The author of The End of History examines the reasons for the decline of marriage and observes its consequences as an increasing number of children grow up without fathers and go on to lead lives of educational under-achievement, violence and crime.

  ISBN: 1874097860

  148pp, £9.50

- **Russia on Russia I: Russia in the World**

- **Russia on Russia II: The Fate of Post-Soviet Man**

- **Russia on Russia III: Russia under Putin**

- **A Guide to Russia's Parliamentary Elections**

  Liam Halligan & Boris Mozdoukhov

  Halligan and Mozdoukhov offer a comprehensive guide to Russia's elections. They consider the impact of the first two years of Russia's Parliamentary system and explain the major implications both of the constitution itself and of other legislation introduced since the 1993 Parliamentary elections.

  41pp, £10.00